Table of Contents

Acknowledgments

In Gratitude

I never exactly made a book. It's rather like taking dictation. I was given things to say.

–C. S. Lewis quoted in Hall, *Seldom as They Seem*

If I were asked ... to what the singular prosperity and growing strength of [the Americans] ought mainly to be attributed, I should reply: to the superiority of [the] women.

–Alexis de Tocqueville, *Democracy in America*, 1835

We would like to thank Susan and Jan, without whose tireless support, patience, and re-re-re-reading of chapters, this book never would have happened.

Nor would it have happened if Ruby K. Payne had not written *A Framework for Understanding Poverty*. Payne brought on writers and trainers, many of whom wrote other books and introduced key innovations. There are countless wonderful consultants and people on the staff of the company Payne founded, aha! Process, who have built this work to national and international prominence. Many thanks to them. Terie Dreussi Smith and Jodi Pfarr also must be thanked specifically for helping to build the Bridges model described in this book from the ground up.

Further, we would like to recognize Count Alexis de Tocqueville, whose book written almost 200 years ago still gives pertinent insight into the functioning of our nation's grand experiment in democracy. Quotations from *Democracy in America* are scattered throughout our book, as you already have found above.

Democracy is based on the Frenchman's travels in the young United States of America in the 1830s, which was, like now, a time of rising anti-elite sentiment among the working classes. It is a book people love to quote, but seldom actually read. Still relevant to modern America and still insightful regarding how and why we make our decisions, *Democracy in America* has been very helpful to us. We encourage you to read it also.

Tocqueville, however, never said that as long as America is good, it will be great.[1] That is why you won't see that quotation listed. We had to raise it here in order to dismiss the concern later as to why you'll never see the famous non-quotation in the book.

In addition to Tocqueville, the following individuals gave helpful insights and pointed the authors in many correct directions:

Ron Amstutz, Quinton Askew, Teresa Ballinger, Karen Barber, Bonnie Bazata, John Begala, Janine Boyd, John Brower, Toni Brown, Jennifer Brunner, Heidi Calendar, Jamie Calendar, Randy Cole, John Corlett, Greg Dennis, Tim Derickson, Chris Hytry Derringer, Christina Fulsom, Sheila Gilbert, Mary Hicks, Ned Hill, Chuck Holt, Ines Jindra, Michael Jindra, Susan Kempf, Melissa Knopp, Karla Krodel, Brie Lusheck, Bill Lybrook, Ted Lybrook, Stephen MacDonald, Steve Marks, Tom Martindale, Debora McDermed, Erin O'Donnell, Jim Ott, Dominic Paretti, Bruce Perry, Deborah Price, Carol Robb, Mike Saccocio, Andy Shifflette, Mike Simon, Elizabeth Wahler, and Laura Newberry Yokley.

Thanks also to the aha! Process publishing team who worked so well with us: Peggy Conrad, vice president of publications, and Dan Shenk and Jesse Conrad, editors.

We extend our heartfelt gratitude to all—and we thank *you,* the reader, for embarking on this journey with us as together we seek to bridge the divides.

Philip DeVol and Gene Krebs

Foreword

by Judge Jennifer Brunner

The focus of *Bridges Across Every Divide* is on solving generational poverty by bridging the current and historic American political divide with shared concepts that do not require a political outlook. While the book's emphasis is on generational poverty and how Americans can and will need to come together to change it, the "Bridges" concepts apply to myriad contemporary and future problems that seem for now to be stuck in the mud of partisan rancor and intractability.

Phil DeVol and Gene Krebs, both experienced public servants and social entrepreneurs from opposite ends of the experiential and political spectrums, have collaborated to describe how we can reach agreement and undertake real solutions regarding poverty. They bring an understanding of how poverty harms not just those who bear its brunt, but also the many (perhaps like you or me) who see it but don't know what to do about it—or maybe say, "Never me," or proclaim it's "their" fault, or who evince pity or just prefer to ignore it.

Poverty can be *eliminated.* Yes, I actually said eliminated. And this book sounds the bell for *why* it should be, especially in the foreboding shadow of the technological extinction of what many now know as "work." *Bridges Across Every Divide* offers ways to develop collaborative community- and citizen-based leadership to work at this task.

Overcoming the political divide and coalescing the cacophony involves settling on and promoting tested ways to use limited public funding for individual empowerment, so that individuals can reach goals they want, and our democracy can thrive in raising each life for individual betterment. This book proposes ways to do that. Its authors firmly and directly challenge the "elite" to reverse the ever-growing class divides between the extreme haves and the extreme have-nots—and in the process throw a life preserver to a thinning middle class that tends to be sliding more toward the "have-nots" than the "haves."

I first encountered the *Bridges Out of Poverty* curriculum in 2001 when a Republican Chief Justice of the Ohio Supreme Court, Thomas Moyer, offered to the judges of the State of Ohio a chance to take a three-hour class taught by Phil DeVol. Being a new trial judge, elected as a nominee of the Democratic Party, I found myself faced with a seemingly endless stream of criminal defendants accused of committing felonies. Many of "my defendants" were not in court for the first time.

The dynamics of how so many of them came to be standing in front of me in short-sleeved orange jail suits, in handcuffs, and in the shadow of sheriff's deputies with guns packed neatly in holsters at their waists were many:

- At least half of "these people" were black.

- At least half of them had not finished high school.

- At least 80% of them were involved in some way with drugs or alcohol or were affected by mental illness or both.

- Most of them had no one sitting in the court gallery for them.

- The vast majority of them were jobless and poor—and still are.

Phil DeVol's curriculum gave me strategies and was a key factor in building a verifiable relapse-prevention component into the felony drug court program I started working on the next year.

Later, I got to know Gene Krebs when I was elected Ohio's first woman Secretary of State. My job was to supervise elections in this perennial swing state. But as the state's record keeper, my team and I developed—with Phil's help and later with Gene's support (they had not yet met)—a social-health index, rich in data about the quality of people's lives in Ohio, called "Better Lives, Better Ohio."

After I finished my term, having lost a primary for the U.S. Senate in lieu of re-election, Gene and I continued our new-found friendship across our political divide (Gene is a Republican). At Gene's suggestion, we purposely scheduled meetings in public places so that the political class in Ohio's "Capital Square" could see well-known members of opposite political parties breaking bread together and actually having cordial conversations.

One afternoon at a lunch table at the Statehouse café, surrounded by legislators and lobbyists, Gene asked me about poverty. I said, "Do I have the guy for you!" Of course, I meant Phil DeVol.

The Bridges curriculum and its progeny had given me answers and made me a better judge and Secretary of State. I had witnessed how it helped people at every level.

My successor in state office, a former Speaker of the Ohio House of Representatives, declined to continue with Better Lives, Better Ohio. With his blessing, however, I tried several times to work with other institutions to keep it going. It's ironic that it wasn't a government program that mainly moved the concept forward in state government in Ohio. It was people from different backgrounds and political approaches coming together, Gene and Phil, who helped turn the Bridges concepts into a viable political-empowerment tool in a Republican legislature.

Bridges demonstrates what I think most of us instinctively know: when there are no easy solutions, the best ones are holistic, using tested theories and integrating people helping people.

A new and constructive dialogue begins with this book. It's a springboard melded of the collaborative and cooperative efforts of two vastly different people whom I had the privilege to introduce to one another. Phil DeVol developed Bridges. Gene Krebs has embraced it, and together they have worked to make it a reality for the people of Ohio. Since the presidential election of 2016, Gene has identified emerging types of Democrats and Republicans within each party and their roles in our political future. Phil and Gene, working together, describe to their leaders and everyday citizens how to chart the course in a changing landscape, beginning with reducing, then eliminating, poverty.

I'm grateful I was in the right place at the right time to connect Phil and Gene. I think you will enjoy this book and appreciate their approach. As you settle in, I suggest you relax your long-held beliefs, allow your mind to stretch, and most of all let your imagination out of its confines to see what really can be.

For in the end, democracy always has been about and for people, so that they can continue to do as Alexis de Tocqueville observed, "imagine that their whole destiny is in their hands."

Chapter 1

The Song That Is America: Rhythms of History

Gene Krebs

The history of the world affords no instance of a great nation retaining the form of republican government for a long series of years.

–Alexis de Tocqueville, *Democracy in America*

In the opening chapter we investigate why our system of government is struggling to meet the needs and aspirations of so many Americans. We outline the dangers of self-separation into polarized camps, and we present a historical case in which similar separation led to war.

In the United States, many people are losing the ability to understand how other Americans think and why they think that way. We're also losing our ability to reconcile our differences and move public policies to address our common problems, especially in the social services. This has happened before, and it's part of the history of a free people. What do we do?

Here's a possible answer—or at least a good start: *Bridges Out of Poverty* and *Getting Ahead in a Just-Gettin'-By World.* These two books, which we will describe further, have spawned significant strategies for addressing the question raised above, as well as others, particularly around the problem of poverty in the United States. Added now is this book, *Bridges Across Every Divide*, which focuses on policy implications of the Bridges and Getting Ahead philosophy and practice.

Questions range from *How do we begin to understand what subtle influences have driven us apart?* to *Why do reforms often fail?* and, using an adaptation of the Bridges/Getting Ahead methodology, *How do we restore interconnectedness in our country, state, and community again?*

1

Walt Whitman wrote, "I hear America singing, the varied carols I hear" in his *Leaves of Grass* back in 1867.[2] The tune is still being sung by a chorus; this country is like a song that for more than 240 years has inspired successive generations around the world.

But now there are lyrics in our song that are harshly critical of others with unfamiliar visages and thoughts. We are better than this, and we can rise above our differences as we have in the past. We can achieve a better understanding of how those who are not like us think and act. We can motivate our leaders and citizens to tune in to their better natures, and we can work together on breaking down divisions in order for America to live up to its ideals.

Our country has problems, but we have a self-correcting system, and we can influence the system to a faster pace if we know how. This book will help you elevate your capacity for effecting change in both the political and policy spheres based on an understanding of how others come to their decisions.

The increasing virulence of the epithets tossed around in the public arena is approaching that of previous eras of civil distress and unrest. Our country could unravel like a knitted scarf. As Tocqueville notes: "I know of no countries in which revolutions are more dangerous than in democratic countries."[3]

A practical effort to move public policies

Against this fragmented national backdrop, Phil and I hope to show how, in practical, distinct steps, it's possible to move public policies in the human-service arena that can break the artificial class divisions and multigenerational poverty cycle by bringing the Bridges model into the political and community discussion. We also hope to help people in those communities understand those who are not like themselves, and thereby create a better country. This is not without certain risks. If you like life to be safe, return this book to the shelf or to Amazon.

From jailing people for being poor to throwing money at their poverty, as a society we seem to have tried everything—and anything in between. Yet chronic poverty has an enduring presence in communities spanning the nation. The Bridges strategy is different from these largely failed methods because it takes a holistic approach to working with individuals, institutions (or organizations), and communities in developing new policies.

The Bridges model is organic and adaptive where most federal and state social policies are universal and linear. As James Gleick notes in *Chaos: Making a New Science,* slight differences at the beginning of each situation lead to radically different outcomes. And where can you find more differences than among people?

Yet massive governmental programs try to approach poverty in a linear fashion where solutions, like spikes in a railroad bed, are driven home with steam-powered sledgehammers.

In fact, public policy is more like quantum mechanics: It's more difficult to understand, and each particle (or person) has its own unique spin. Rabbi Dov Baer puts it this way: "Each person consists of a certain song of existence, the one by which our innermost being was created and is defined."[4]

Equally important, the Bridges model appeals to both conservatives and progressives and gives some of us hope that the usual partisan, public-policy gulf might itself be bridged.

This creeping division has bled into our social lives as we view with suspicion if not disdain a family member marrying outside our partisan affiliation. One-third of conservatives say they would be unhappy if an immediate family member married a Democrat, and about a quarter of progressives feel that way about a Republican blending into their gene pool.[5]

How you are aligned politically tends to influence strongly how you marry. Nowadays we seldom have "mixed marriages" of couples with differing political perspectives, raising children who hear all sides at the dinner table. Now our dinner discussions tend to be dichromatic, either red or blue, with no purple.[6]

Research also indicates that in Congress (a group that is supposed to represent the people), the Republicans and Democrats no longer even speak the same language. They often use completely different words to describe public-policy problems and solutions.[7]

In *The Big Sort,* Bill Bishop (a progressive) outlines how this economic demographic segregation has affected the U.S. in a practical manner. In our churches and politics, we rarely rub elbows with those not like ourselves.

In the 1976 presidential election, just one-quarter of America's counties were "landslide counties" where Carter or Ford won by a large margin. In the presidential elections of 2004, and again in 2012, that gap rose to *half* of U.S. counties; landslide counties are becoming the new normal. In 2016, three-fifths of the counties were landslide counties.[8]

We are now more than twice as likely as we were just a few years ago to live near people who share our views, who parrot the same political groupthink, and who drink the same Kool-Aid we do.

This theme also is repeated on the libertarian right in Charles Murray's book, *Coming Apart*. He lays out how the America of olden times, where the bank president and bank janitor lived in the same town and worshiped at the same church, has now largely disappeared, with educational attainment being a major sorting mechanism.

Both Bishop's and Murray's cases are to a degree being driven by how we now build our houses: in developments where the houses usually fall into a narrow price range. The price you can afford is determined by your annual income. Your income is largely driven by your educational level. You end up living next to people who have very similar backgrounds, and most of your social activities, school events, and worship experiences take place in a narrow milieu. In fact, just living next to people of a given political persuasion can influence how you view public policy. Gradually you become more like your neighbors; groupthink tends to bend you toward the neighborhood norms.[9]

Compare this with the small towns from our idealized golden age where the school superintendent lived three blocks away from the school cook. The ruling elite now know no poor, except their domestic staff, and tend to stand aloof, offering aloof solutions. They "helicopter" into low-income communities, spout bromides urging hard work, then "helicopter" back to their gated communities.

Let's take a moment to define what we mean by "ruling elite" (this term also will be explored in Chapter 18 in particular):

The "ruling elite" is a very flexible term that encompasses the people locally who have the most leverage, and the more leverage you have, the broader your definition of "local" becomes. Bill Gates and Warren Buffett have worldwide leverage. The head of the chamber of commerce in a small town has leverage in that town. The ruling elite often have more education, more money, and the ability to self-segregate themselves from problems, as well as perceived problem-makers, and coexist only with those who share certain common roots and values. If they almost totally separate themselves from the rest of societal structure, as Tocqueville observed, they become disturbingly detached from society, with dire consequences for everyone.

In the U.S. today people don't learn how to talk to those who aren't like them. If you're from the educated bourgeoisie, you're comfortable with the word *milieu*. If you're poor, no matter what race, you might use the phrase "The Man" with capital letters implied. It's a gilded trap for our political system, with cul-de-sacs and center-city lofts on one side and trailer parks and and inner-city slums on the other.

Both the right and left are increasingly splitting, and the intelligentsia on both sides perceive something is lost, as we see others only across multiple chasms. Indeed, we need a bridge across every divide.

America is a voluntary song. It has certain rhymes, refrains, and rhythms, and it sounds much better when many voices are raised. Not in discord, but rather when we all understand the music, sing harmoniously, seek perfection in the performance, and bring along the others in our choir.

Our goal in this book is to remind Americans how to sing in tune—voluntarily.

On small things does history turn

When my farm-living grandmother thought the chimney for her wood-burning kitchen fireplace was getting clogged with soot, she would let the fire go out, put a ladder up to the chimney, grab a hen by the ankles, take her up to the top of the chimney, and drop her in. The hen would squawk and flap and scratch all the way down to the hearth where my grandmother had put up an old sheet to keep the soot from billowing out into the room. Grabbing the relieved and sooty hen, Grandma would put her back with the rest of the flock. The hen did not lay eggs for a couple of weeks. But the chimney got cleaned out!

Many Americans feel abused like that hen after a presidential election: dropped down a chimney and covered in filth, but at least now the political system should be working again. As noted, we believe it to be a self-correcting system, though at times it does break down.

One school of thought is that my grandmother's people, landholding farmers, caused the U.S. Civil War and perhaps delayed the ending of slavery by two decades. It isn't so much about what actions they took, but rather that their leaving one part of the country for another destabilized the nation. It isn't a total stretch to say they caused the Civil War by leaving South Carolina for Ohio in 1806, and they took a self-correcting opportunity with them.

In 1806 only 2% of the population voted in elections, as only white males who owned property could vote; in fact, showing your receipt for property taxes paid was your voter identification. There were only 35,000 people represented by each congressional seat, and only about 700 people voted in a typical congressional election.[10] Indeed, for the first 40 years of the republic, those very small numbers determined the direction of the country. The government was both intimate and exclusive.[11]

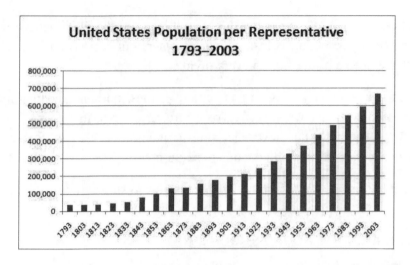

Source: "United States Congressional Apportionment."

Yes, in 1806 my maternal ancestors helped set in motion events that caused the Civil War. It was not that they fired on Fort Sumter, nor did they join John Brown in his attack on the Harper's Ferry armory. Half a century before either of those major moments in American history, my ancestors departed Abbeville, South Carolina, taking their opinions with them. It is on small points like this that history turns.

All my life, I have been able to step out the back door of my family farm in Ohio and see across the fields to the roofline of Hopewell Church,[12] founded in 1808 by my mother's Scotch-Irish ancestors. They moved here after a Calvinist minister named Porter started preaching a simple message in South Carolina: God would soon visit his wrath on the South for the sin of slavery. The repentant should free their slaves and "flee to the Ohio" where they would be safe.

My ancestors listened and left. Although Abbeville was small, a move like this was no small thing. Abbeville was the birthplace of John C. Calhoun, the noted states'-rights advocate, first elected to Congress representing Abbeville and that portion of South Carolina in 1810, just a couple of years after my folks (about 135 families and their 135 property-owning male votes) left town.

Calhoun was later elected to the U.S. Senate and twice elected vice president, under two different presidents. He referred to slavery as a "positive good." Abbeville claims its spot in history as the source of the Southern secessionist movement and as "the birthplace of the Confederacy" with countless plaques, many commemorating the first mass march and petition that was signed supporting secession in November 1860.

Not everybody, though, saw the world as did John C. Calhoun. My ancestors were so firm in their beliefs that when they discovered that one of their number had secretly sold his slaves and not freed them, they held his wife and children hostage and forced him to ride back to Abbeville from Ohio, find the slaves, buy them, free them, and bring back copies of the manumission papers. Then they returned this man's family to him—and summarily expelled them all from the community.

The U.S. Civil War might have been averted and the practice of slavery ended peacefully and earlier, but for the fact that my maternal ancestors and others like them pulled up roots and headed north. In doing so they left behind but one strident voice on the issue of slavery. Unchecked, that pro-slavery voice became stronger, louder, and in the end, the greatest threat the United States of America has faced—so far.

Proving God has a sense of humor, after Robert E. Lee's surrender at Appomattox Court House, Jefferson Davis, president of the Confederacy, fled south to organize guerrilla resistance. The treasurer of the Confederacy caught up with Davis in Abbeville, however, and informed him the movement was dead broke, and no one would lend any money. It was in Abbeville that Davis signed the papers dissolving the Confederacy. Secession began there and died there.

The secessionist movement and its fanaticism could take root in places like Abbeville because people who thought differently had left. Had they stayed and continued to speak up against slavery, they could have moderated the voices defending slavery and perhaps ended that barbaric practice earlier and without bloodshed.[13]

Historian Shelby Foote tells us that the Civil War happened "because we failed to do the thing we really have a genius for, which is compromise."[14]

How do you govern in a manner that respects compromise? You think small, and you consider the humble buckeye.

Ohio as barometer

> Small nations have therefore ever been the cradle of political liberty, and the fact that many of them have lost their liberty by becoming larger shows that their freedom was more a consequence of their small size than of the character of the people.
>
> —Alexis de Tocqueville, *Democracy in America*

> Ohio is special because, in so many political and nonpolitical ways, it is not special. So, every four years, the political parties send their products for testing in the Buckeye State. If the product doesn't sell there, chances are it won't sell nationally either.
>
> –Kyle Kondik, *The Bellwether: Why Ohio Picks the President*

If your state's population is increasing, your individual voice as a citizen is getting harder for politicians to hear. While Ohio is seventh in population, it has one of the smallest legislatures. Combined with the number of large cities and counties, this makes a citizen's individual voice hard to hear and makes compromises more difficult. This is your now or your future in every state with a growing population. In Montana, for example, it's easier for elected officials to stay connected to their constituents—and vice versa—than in California.

Seats in the Ohio House of Representatives have constituencies of about 116,500 people, and Ohio Senate seats are around 350,000 deep, about half the size of a U.S. congressional seat. This means grass-roots organizing is tough, and elections are often money-driven. Cuyahoga County, which contains Cleveland, has a bigger population than nine U.S. states, meaning the county executive in Cuyahoga County has a constituency roughly the same size as that of the governor of Maine.

With the country continuing to grow in population, the governing becomes more difficult, as Tocqueville notes. Watch what happens in Ohio, as it might be the future in your state or region, and compromises that work there might work in your community too.[15] To paraphrase the New York City slogan, if you can make it work in Ohio, you can make it work anywhere.

Healthier Buckeyes

> Social change has long been a characteristic ofAmerican life. This change does not proceed at an even pace; rather, it tends to cluster into periods of intense activity.
>
> –George W. Knepper, *Ohio and Its People*

A legislative hero in the Buckeye State for Bridges and Getting Ahead, Ron Amstutz, was born into a Mennonite family on a small dairy farm in Wayne County, Ohio. In 1980 he was elected to the Ohio Legislature where he served in various capacities for 36 years. It turns out Amstutz is distantly related by marriage to other folks of Mennonite heritage in the Bridges/Getting Ahead universe: Ruby (Krabill) Payne and her sister, Ruth (Krabill) Weirich.

While quite conservative politically, Ron has that distinctive Mennonite outlook on helping the less fortunate. It was while he was chair of the Ohio House Finance and Appropriations Committee, the most powerful committee in Ohio, that he first encountered Bridges/Getting Ahead.

Ron had for several years been looking for some form of "pixie dust," something that could be sprinkled onto the problems associated with poverty to make them less intractable. In short, he was looking for a unified field theory of social science, something that could bust down the "silos" and begin to deal humanely and sensitively with the issue of poverty. The status quo just wasn't cutting it anymore.

For several years Amstutz had been thinking about "Healthier Buckeyes" but wasn't sure what it could be, let alone how he could deliver. He had a label with no substance, but he knew there was something to it, something glinting through at the corner of his eye, a color he couldn't yet quite see.

When he sat down for coffee with Phil and me, it suddenly all clicked. In the Bridges triple lens he found a "methodology" for addressing the issue. Some researchers call this the "whole of government" approach, where all the various silos of the bureaucracy are involved. (In the social services of some states it's called "wraparound.") For example, this approach is currently being explored by the federal government for veterans' issues, such as housing, education, and mental health.[16]

Pushing all his political chips onto the table, Amstutz requested funding in a state budget to "supercharge" existing local-level policy programs that resembled Bridges/Getting Ahead programs. He asked for $50 million and got $11.5 million.

It was enough. Funding 21 projects in Ohio, half of which were directly based on Bridges/Getting Ahead, the Healthier Buckeye Grant Pilot Program created a new dynamic.

The Center for Community Solutions, a nonpartisan think tank based in Cleveland, summed up the program in 2016:

> In the 131st General Assembly, House Bill 64 (the state budget) created the Healthier Buckeye Grant Pilot Program and the Ohio Healthier Buckeye Advisory Council. Local Healthier Buckeye Councils are encouraged to collaborate across employment and community sectors to examine the role that poverty plays in their communities and form solutions to increase financial independence among the individuals

living in poverty. Those applying for the Healthier Buckeye grant dollars were required to form local councils and submit annual reports to the Ohio Healthier Buckeye Advisory Council. Twenty-one local Healthier Buckeye Councils were funded with grant amounts ranging from \$85,872 to \$945,157.[17]

What makes the Healthier Buckeye program so interesting to legislators is Medicaid's drain on state budgets currently, even with federal matching funds—or perhaps because of those funds.

Medicaid haunts state fiscal officers

Medicaid is sometimes referred to as the Pac-Man that eats the state budget, as the expenditures are open-ended. When economic times are tough, more people enroll, and costs go up. For states, however, that is often when revenues decline due to softness in the economy, so states suffer a double blow. The federal government can just print money, but most states have a constitutionally required balanced budget. The states get squeezed. They either increase taxes, or they cut funds to schools—or usually both. Everyone is unhappy.

Also, the overwhelming amount of tax income in the U.S. increasingly comes from the wealthy, and, of that, most of the income is derived from capital gains and stock dividends, which occur mainly when there's activity on Wall Street or a business is sold. During recessions, those activities take a huge hit.[18]

Even states with a blue tint like Vermont, New York, and California have broad experiments going on in efforts to bring down social-services costs.[19]

In short, the increasing costs are causing states, blue and red, to want to innovate. Only by having in place the means to "supercharge" existing and new Bridges/ Getting Ahead programs can states do a more effective job of bringing poverty to heel.

The political hotspot is adult, non-disabled recipients; they receive a little more than a quarter of the Medicaid money and comprise almost a third of the Medicaid population.[20]

While the aged and disabled make up one-fifth of the recipients of Medicaid, they receive half the Medicaid funding.

Medicaid spending has risen from less than .5% of GDP to 2% the past 40 years. The trendline continues to go up. Medicaid indeed threatens to become the Pac-Man that swallows the budgets of a number of states.[21]

The purpose of this brief examination of Medicaid is to help the reader understand that most state elected officials fervently wish the issue of poverty would just go away. The growth of Medicaid and related welfare programs is threatening other aspects of local, state, and federal budgets: the fun stuff.

States are hungry for new and innovative ways of reducing the poverty rate, sometimes for moral reasons, sometimes due to fiscal pressures.

Now that we have outlined the problem, here is how we think Bridges Out of Poverty and Getting Ahead in a Just-Gettin'-By World, plus this book and programs like Healthier Buckeyes, can help. If America is a song, what is this musical composition we call Bridges and Getting Ahead?

Chapter 2

What Is the Bridges Model?
Philip DeVol

It takes time for an organization to absorb fundamental new ways of looking at the world. Introducing new perspectives … when an organization is confronted with the need to act, will inevitably be inadequate. The need to act overwhelms any willingness people have to learn. Thus, well-designed strategic conversations occur long before the moment of decision.

—Peter Schwartz, *The Art of the Long View*

This chapter is a primer on the Bridges model. We explain why a common language is needed to address poverty, as well as identify the elements of the Bridges language. We describe how people learn and apply the concepts. Their innovations are shared through learning communities that can inform policy development.

Poverty is like a hot, thick cloud of smoke that all too often smothers and obscures the skills, gifts, hopes, and dreams of people under it. Lost in the smoke are the causes of the fire. In this chapter we investigate both the realities and the causes of poverty, a complex, systemic problem.

Poverty also has a negative impact on many institutions, starting with organizations that provide prenatal care and traveling through the span of life to hospice care. Poverty is a common denominator for many sectors in society. Its impact is felt by a wide range of entities, including schools, healthcare providers, social services, food services, faith communities, police and other first responders, courts, correctional facilities, workforce development, employers, and government.

The problems of poverty experienced by individuals also are felt by institutions. An employee whose car breaks down feels the pain of lost wages; the employer in turn feels the pain of lost productivity. A child who goes to school hungry has trouble learning her lessons; the school then has trouble meeting educational standards.

Understandably but unfortunately, these sectors come at poverty problems from their own perceptions or mental models of poverty. Each designs its programs, policies, and procedures according to its understanding of poverty. It's the old story of the blind men describing the elephant by touching different parts of its body.

The problem of poverty doesn't respond to simplistic bromides and slogans about "pulling yourself up by your bootstraps" or "teaching people to fish" or telling people to "just get a job." Nor has poverty been solved by the platforms of either left or right. And it hasn't been solved by faith and justice initiatives. While the marketplace has raised millions of people in the developing world out of abject poverty, it also has contributed to the growing divide, even chasm, between the rich and poor in the developed world.

How much better would it be for people in poverty and the organizations themselves if they shared an accurate mental model or perception of what poverty is? What has largely been missing is a common or shared language to investigate and address the complex reality known as poverty.

Bridges offers a common language that includes:

1. An accurate understanding of poverty and economic class that engages people from all classes to work on the problem (Chapter 3).

2. An understanding of the causes of poverty that engages both right and left (Chapter 4).

3. A way to engage people who experience discrimination and barriers to upward mobility (Chapter 4).

4. Information on cues, habits, and language usage so people from different class environments can build relationships and better navigate the worlds of work, school, and community (Chapter 5).

5. A definition of poverty that gives individuals, institutions, and communities something they can do about poverty—something they can take action on (Chapter 6). Sometimes this three-part construction is called the Bridges triple lens, and occasionally the word "organization" is used instead of "institution" as part of the triple lens.

The Bridges model, soon entering its third decade, offers the content and methodology for a comprehensive approach. In this chapter we will introduce you to the model. Naturally, a comprehensive approach will have several elements, and it may appear complicated at first. It takes time to consume and understand.

> The Bridges language becomes common to everyone on the ground. After I taught Bridges to a master class in law ethics and enforcement, I ran into those students later who told me they were able to use the Bridges material right away. We finally understood what we were seeing in the street. It does open people's eyes and helps them make sense of what they see.
>
> –Judge Jennifer Brunner,
> former Ohio Secretary of State

We can't address poverty without changing the mindsets that unwittingly hold it in place. In this chapter we offer a new way to define and analyze poverty and offer thinking tools that can be used to address poverty more effectively.

All we ask of you, the readers, is to give your judgmental mind a rest (you know, the part of your brain that is always sorting out what it is for and against). Please suspend your existing mental model of poverty and economic class so you can take in new ideas. At the end of the book, you may have your mental model back—or you may choose to modify it as you see fit.

How people learn Bridges concepts

The folowing three books and their accompanying workshops are used to introduce the ideas.

- *Bridges Out of Poverty* by Ruby K. Payne, Philip E. DeVol, and Terie Dreussi Smith for those working in institutions that serve people in poverty

- *Getting Ahead in a Just-Gettin'-By World* by Philip E. DeVol for those living in poverty

- *Bridges to Sustainable Communities* by Philip E. DeVol for those working at the community level

Terminology used in the 'Bridges language'

Bridges has developed a language of its own; it often is called "Bridges language." Sometimes it's referred to as "the common language."

When we refer to the book *Bridges Out of Poverty* and the associated trainings, we usually shorten it to "Bridges" and "Bridges training." The context helps the reader understand the usage.

When we describe the initiatives, communities, and collaboratives that have arisen, we use the term "Bridges." Once again the context should make it clear.

Getting Ahead in a Just-Gettin'-By World is a program, workbook, and learning experience that is for people in poverty and others who are struggling to get by. *Getting Ahead in a Just-Gettin'-By World* was published five years after *Bridges Out of Poverty.* Getting Ahead brought new elements to the Bridges work that did not appear in *Bridges Out of Poverty* and thus enhanced the Bridges language.

But Getting Ahead should not happen apart from Bridges because it's important that people in the middle class and wealth be involved in a Bridges initiative in order to understand, support, and work with people in poverty.

Since Bridges is sometimes used without the Getting Ahead program, the term Bridges/Getting Ahead specifies when Getting Ahead is part of the initiative.

NOTE: For more information about and examples of Bridges language, please see the "Glossary of Bridges Terminology" in Appendix A.

As these books and associated workshops are being used to introduce the common language of the Bridges model, we occasionally encounter raw forms of the divisiveness and judgments of one economic class against the others. People inevitably bring their diversity with them to the table: their race, class, religion, land of origin, immigration status, ethnic customs, gender, sexual orientation, individual gifts and skills, and of course their political convictions about a wide range of issues.

In the following pages we describe how diversity, even with its challenges, is both valued and enjoyed—and how people who are very different can work together in mutual respect.

A short course in Bridges concepts

The Bridges model operates on the law of attraction: If you like this approach, then take ownership of the ideas and apply them where you live and work. Your innovations can impact the lives of people in poverty, improve the outcomes of your organization, and help build a broad community initiative. When you share strategies with others, you are creating a learning community—whether it's at the water cooler where you work, within your own discipline, or in a community collaborative.

Bridges initiatives operate on the law of attraction at all levels.

The Bridges model, or pattern, evolved as Bridges communities began organizing their work. Bridges concepts described in chapters 2–6 constitute a common language. They can be used differently in each setting because Bridges is more a set of ideas than a program.

Sectors that are impacted by poverty and work with people in poverty use Bridges concepts to improve their outcomes. No single community has included every sector listed below, but many have engaged several sectors. These learning communities vary in structure and formality.

What we present here is based on realities on the ground, and it serves as a guide to catalysts in communities where Bridges is being introduced.

These 17 sectors have applied Bridges concepts. Poverty, a common denominator for all of them, covers the span of life:

- Prenatal care
- Early-childhood development
- K–12 education
- Postsecondary education
- Housing
- Workforce development
- Businesses/employers
- Banking/lenders
- Health and healthcare
- Faith-based entities
- Arts and entertainment
- Governmental safety-net services
- Nonprofits
- Addiction and mental health
- Courts and corrections
- Law enforcement and first responders
- Elder care and hospice

In the model on the following page, we present only eight of the 17 sectors in order to make the concepts easier to follow.

The Bridges Model

Elements of the model

The center of the model: The common language of Bridges centers on the topics covered in the subsequent chapters 3–7.

- Chapter 3: Mental models of poverty, middle class, and wealth
- Chapter 4: Four causes of poverty, plus barriers due to discrimination
- Chapter 5: Hidden rules of economic class
- Chapter 6: A definition of poverty that gives individuals, institutions, and communities a comprehensive way to address poverty
- Chapter 7: Methodology—how Bridges communities are built

The arrows from the center to the eight sectors represent their use of the common language.

The arrows from sector to sector represent the learning community that is formed locally. Representatives of each sector, along with people in poverty who are served by those sectors, are at the planning and decision-making table of the Bridges collaborative in the community. They form a learning community that exchanges best practices and works to surmount or remove barriers experienced by people in poverty.

The arrows pointing from the sectors to the circle labeled "Policy" represent the work of changing behaviors and policies at the institutional, community, and state levels.

Next we'll review and reflect on mental models of poverty, middle class, and wealth—and ways in which socioeconomic class is a powerful force in our society.

Chapter 3

How Understanding Class Environments
Can Help Solve Problems

Philip DeVol

There is no such thing as a neutral educational process. Education either functions as an instrument that is used to facilitate the integration of the younger generation into the logic of the present system and bring about conformity to it, or it becomes "the practice of freedom," the means by which men and women deal critically and creatively with reality and discover how to participate in the transformation of their world.

–Paulo Freire, *Pedagogy of the Oppressed*

Here we start by developing an accurate Mental Model of Poverty as experienced locally by people who live it. We then compare and contrast that with mental models of middle class and wealth as all three classes come together to work on problems. For example, this approach led a plastics firm to improve the retention rate of new hires from 29% to 69%.

In Bridges it is the people *in* poverty who describe poverty as it is in their community. They are paid a modest stipend to participate in a focus group of 12 people who meet 16 times to use the workbook *Getting Ahead in a Just-Gettin'-By World.*

In the first session of the Getting Ahead learning experience, the group creates a Mental Model of Poverty in their community.

Their investigations into the impact that poverty has on them and their community provide accurate and relevant information about poverty in their city or county. Behind every word and phrase in the mental model (see visual at right) from South Bend, Indiana, is a story from the real world.

The poverty experience is different in every community. What life is like in a doughnut city that has experienced white and middle-class flight is different from life in a frontier county in Colorado

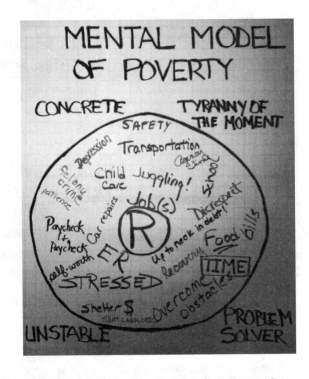

where there are 15 people per square mile. Poverty in Appalachia is different from poverty in the suburbs, and it is different from poverty experienced by Native Americans.

Comparing and contrasting the elements of class

While the details of the poverty and class experience vary by region, state, or race, there are some common elements of class structures that can be identified and studied.

Creating a Mental Model of Poverty for their community is the first way people in poverty inform and help guide Bridges initiatives. Most of the time programs and policies for those in poverty are made by members of the dominant culture—the middle and upper classes. Not having people in poverty at the planning tables may explain why so many poverty programs go wrong and fail to serve people well.[22]

Behind the icons in the three ensuing mental models are stories, data, and historical context. Gillian Tett, managing editor of *Financial Times US,* is an economist and anthropologist. She suggests looking at complex issues from the bottom up, with analysis of micro-level patterns in each economic class. She also advocates an insider/outsider point of view to compare societies, cultures, and systems in order to prevent mental blindness or tunnel vision.[23]

Mental Models of Class

Problem solvers	– Problem solvers
Concrete	– Abstract
Unstable	– Stable
Tyranny of the moment	– Long view
Financial security	– Financial insecurity
Low resources	– High resources
Powerless	– Powerful

Poverty

Middle class

Wealth

Source: All three mental models from *Bridges Out of Poverty Training Supplement.*

These mental models of class represent the hand-drawn models created locally by Getting Ahead investigators. They are used to compare and contrast their class experiences. This helps people from all classes achieve an insider/outsider point of view and have a better understanding of people from different classes. Ideally these same people will gain a better understanding of their own experiences, attitudes, biases, and perceptions.

Many people (of a certain age) feel nostalgic for the strong sense of community that has been lost. They often are thinking about the so-called Golden Age of the middle class, a largely white experience. That period lasted roughly from the mid-1940s to the late 1970s. Robert Putnam in *Our Kids* and Charles Murray in *Coming Apart* both write about that period—from the progressive and conservative points of view, respectively. Nostalgia for that period clearly played a large role in the 2016 presidential election.[24]

Income inequality became quite pronounced in the late '70s and has been growing ever since. That has made it possible for people to move into neighborhoods and live with people like themselves, creating in effect a class divide with clear physical boundaries.

The wealthy live in gated communities or down long driveways, the middle class cluster around the best schools, and those in poverty live wherever they can find affordable (or not so affordable) housing. Residential segregation, according to Richard Reeve in *The Dream Hoarders,* has become increasingly entrenched as the top 20% of Americans separate themselves from the bottom 80%.[25]

Six analytical categories

The three class environments can be analyzed in many ways. For our purposes, however, we will concentrate on six analytical categories seen in the preceding graphic depicting the three mental models:

- Problem-solving strategies
- Concrete and abstract thinking
- Stability factors
- Tyranny of the moment and the long view
- Financial security
- Depth of resources and power

In the first session of Getting Ahead it becomes apparent that the investigators are problem solvers. This realization tends to come with a jolt of pride because all too often people in poverty have been branded by society as "the problem." Unstable, under-resourced conditions demand constant, immediate, daily problem solving just to get by.

People in poverty have firsthand knowledge about poverty and are needed at the planning tables in the community. They know the institutions from the user's point of view. They can help design programs to be more effective, thereby helping to solve institutional and community problems.

Indeed, people from all classes are problem solvers, and all are needed at the table.

We have already established that people in poverty are problem solvers. But in fact people from all classes are problem solvers.

The wealthy are needed as problem solvers because they have connections, the long view, and a willingness (sometimes) to try new things. Plus they have financial resources.

The middle class are needed to organize collaboratives, build and manage programs, monitor and improve what they do, generate achievements that positively impact others, and, of course, check items off their to-do lists.

People in poverty are needed because they have accurate and relevant information on poverty in their community. They know the institutions from the user's point of view and have firsthand knowledge of the barriers to upward mobility. They can help design programs to be more effective, thereby also helping to solve institutional and community problems.

People from poverty, middle class, and wealth are all problem solvers. All three classes must be involved in any initiative that addresses poverty.

Getting Ahead investigators (as the participants are called) tell us that most things in their environment are unstable and likely to break down. This includes cars or transportation systems, childcare arrangements, housing, jobs, health services, and appliances. Seen from an outside, middle-class view, much of this looks like the fault of people in poverty as if they were "the problem." In the ensuing story we learn how people solve problems.

'When the car breaks down, we don't call Triple A; we call Uncle Ray'

When a car breaks down a middle-class man will call Triple A first and then call his boss. His boss will tell him, "Don't worry about being late. You've got comp time coming. Get in when you can." The Triple A driver will drop him off at work and tow the car to a shop to be fixed.

The man in poverty doesn't call Triple A. He calls Uncle Ray. Uncle Ray will put a chain on the car and drag it back to the man's house. Next they will have to find parts (perhaps at a junk yard) and send someone to get the parts. If he's short of cash, he will have to borrow some from Uncle Ray or someone else. Then the man will crawl under the car, perhaps with the assistance of Uncle Ray, to make the repairs himself.

All of this is a major hassle that takes most of the day, but in the end the car is back on the road. The man in poverty is a problem solver. He used his relationships and reactive problem-solving skills. Unfortunately, the car problem could well kick off a negative chain reaction to more problems: Who picks up the kids, missed appointments or being late to work, perhaps losing his job, owing money to another person.

For the middle-class man, the problem is solved with money. He's at work solving abstract problems, not under the car fixing concrete problems. At the end of the day he is reunited with his car. The problem with the car causes barely a ripple in his day.

In the preceding scenarios, both men were problem solvers, but the middle-class man had cushions to soften the experience. Life in poverty is a series of concrete problems that demand concrete solutions that you have to fix now! In the *Getting Ahead* workbook this is called the "tyranny of the moment."

In *Scarcity* the authors refer to this as the tunnel. The concrete problem forces people into the "now" or a mental tunnel that demands all their attention, leaving very little room for abstract thinking. They write:

> When your bandwidth is loaded … you're just more likely to not notice things, you're more likely to not resist things you ought to resist, you're more likely to forget things, you're going to have less patience, less attention to devote to your children when they come home from school.[26]

Others have identified the same phenomena. Economist Milton Friedman found that when people or a society is experiencing torture, natural disasters, or war they tend to be more open to suggestion and direction. In those moments he proposed "shock treatments" that imposed economic policies to his liking. Those who were struggling to get by, trying to keep their heads above water, and dodging bullets (figurative and sometimes literal) were not likely to resist.

Theory of change

In Getting Ahead, investigators learn a theory of change that they can use to free themselves from the tyranny of the moment. They can consciously move to abstract thinking while still living in chaos. Peer-reviewed research on Getting Ahead by the Jindras shows that people do indeed use the theory of change.[27]

One Getting Ahead investigator says it like this:

> When Getting Ahead came into my life, life was in peril pretty much. Things were worse than they had been in a really long time. Before I couldn't think out of the box like we talk about in Getting Ahead. The ability to do that has created so much breathing room, so much mental space. Our life is more stable now literally just from taking this class, just because we have a set way of doing things now. There's no chaos surrounding everything. It's like, this is what our plan is and this is what we're going to do. You know it doesn't have to be a state of mind. It doesn't have to be the continuous peril of your life to be in poverty. There are ways to get ahead.

To solve the steady stream of concrete problems, people in poverty naturally turn to organizations in the community to attempt to get concrete solutions. Poverty could be described as a never-ending hunt for resources to meet immediate needs: food, shelter, health and dental services, work, cash, addiction and mental-health services, childcare, etc.

Most individuals in poverty aren't looking for long-range, abstract solutions in the form of education, programs, and treatment plans. When car repairs result in not having money for the next meal, the family needs food—not a class on money management. Concrete problems demand concrete solutions.

Informal surveys of Getting Ahead investigators puts the number of organizations people in poverty go to in the course of a year at between three and 10. Getting Ahead investigators call this "agency time."

A Getting Ahead graduate in Oklahoma said:

> If you have gone to an agency, they have their processes. They find these processes to be beneficial, but in those processes what happens is you become like a herd of cattle and not like an actual person. You are just treated differently in poverty.

For people in poverty, the hassles build up. Transportation is rarely as simple as jumping in the car and driving off to an appointment. It can be two buses and a half-mile walk from the bus stop to the agency. Or maybe there's no bus service, so trying to borrow a car or calling someone for a ride is the only way to go.

Getting time off from work isn't just a matter of using comp time, it can mean losing income and perhaps the job itself. Paying fees and bills isn't as simple as writing a check if you don't have a bank account. There are check-cashing fees, money-order fees, and the added problem of inconsistent pay schedules. People in poverty may be the masters at stretching a dollar, but the inconsistent flow of income means that it's not easy to pay bills on time.

The concrete costs in time and money drain the mental energy that people could be giving to things of the mind, the abstract. The tyranny of the moment runs in a cycle from concrete problem to concrete solution on to the next concrete problem. A Dutch abstract expressionist named Willem de Kooning was literally a starving artist on the streets of Rotterdam in the 1920s before moving to the United States and making a name for himself. Of those hard years in the Netherlands, he said, *"The trouble with being poor is that it takes up all your time."*

Benefits of doing 'life cycles'

For those who design internal processes, programs, and procedures, we strongly suggest conducting a Client Life Cycle (see James Champy's *Reengineering Management* and Paco Underhill's *Why We Buy*). When doing a Client Life Cycle, or an Employee Life Cycle, as in the Cascade Engineering example below, the staff examines every step in the process the client/employee goes through in the organization from the first contact to the last. This must be done from the client's or employee's point of view. The process, matched with what we know about poverty, reveals the many well-intentioned "steps" that were more like hurdles for clients or employees.[28]

Cascade Engineering, a $400 million, Michigan-based manufacturer of plastic systems, was one of the first Bridges sites to utilize the Employee Life Cycle. The day after a workshop on Bridges concepts, Fred Keller, the president and CEO, told middle managers and supervisors to come to the management team with a proposed plan to implement Bridges concepts in employment procedures. This was driven by the high cost of turnover. The company was losing most new hires within the first two weeks, so the Employee Life Cycle had to be done only for those two weeks. Within a year of establishing its Bridges workforce stability solution in the late 1990s, Cascade improved its retention rate of new hires from 29% to 69%. This trend has continued to the present.

Later Cascade issued the following statement: "The company recognized that former welfare recipients often lacked access to reliable transportation, stable housing, childcare, short-term credit, and other support systems essential for successful job performance that most employers routinely assume to be in place."[29]

The following chart describes the actions that were taken, along with savings to the employees in time, money, and cognitive overload.[30]

Actions resulting from an Employee Life Cycle	Temporal	Financial	Cognitive
Shortened orientation.	X		X
Gave cab vouchers to everyone in the plant; no need to miss work if the car doesn't start.	X	X	X
Persuaded city council to extend bus route to the street where Cascade Engineering is located, one block outside the city limits.	X	X	X
Faith-based group offered transportation to and from work if the car was in the shop for a few days. There was a cost for this, but it didn't cost the employee their job.	X	X	X
Issued paycheck weekly instead of biweekly so employees didn't have to go to payday lenders.		X	
Brought TANF [Temporary Assistance for Needy Families] worker trained in Bridges into the plant to work full time with eligible employees to find [and] manage government resources and link employees to all community resources. This combined the driving force of relationships with achievement. This was an early public/private partnership.	X	X	X
Broadened acceptable reasons to miss work to include sick children and parents.	X	X	X
Offered short courses in plastics. Certification resulted in pay raises.	X	X	X
Financial classes offered by a community partner led to direct deposit of paychecks.	X	X	X
Local college offered classes onsite.	X	X	X
Started a non-profit that serves 12 companies to provide case management and wraparound services: a more sophisticated public/private partnership.	X	X	X

Source: Cascade Engineering, Grand Rapids, Michigan.

According to an October 2017 company statement:[31]

> Cascade was able to decrease turnover from 62 percent to 2 percent over a period of nine years. The turnover costs also decreased from $3.6 million in 2000 to $493,000 in 2008. Employees in the program, almost half of whom are people of color, have become financially self-sufficient, thereby saving the state of Michigan almost $1 million in cash assistance, food stamps, and child care vouchers.

The most profound change, the transformation of relationships within the plant, could not be quantified. Cascade Engineering advances racial and class equity in such a way that many visitors report that they can feel the warmth of a healthy, "everyone belongs" organization when walking through the door.

Before we address other types of transformation and change—even to policy in this country—let's step aside for a few moments and consider factors that cause the condition called poverty.

Chapter 4

What Causes Poverty? An Explanation That Both Conservatives and Progressives Can Support
Philip DeVol

The character flaw versus impoverished environment theories are essentially a version of the old nature (character flaws) versus nurture (environment) debate. Like any nature versus nurture discussion, it misses the larger point: Nature and nurture always work together ... they react to changes in the environment.

–Keith Payne, *The Broken Ladder*

Understanding four clusters of research on causes of poverty allows progressives and conservatives to take a both/and approach rather than an either/or approach. The Bridges model is very different from right and left ideologies espoused on cable TV. In this chapter, examples from Bridges communities illustrate how a thinking tool can provide comprehensive solutions with people who experience discrimination and other barriers to upward mobility.

Given the political divisiveness of our time, it seems like an improbable claim to say that people from the left and right come together to work on poverty issues. And yet, it already has been happening for nearly two decades.

To understand how this can be, we need to examine what brings people to work on poverty issues. For some it is their religious faith, and for others it a matter of social justice. Some are in poverty or were raised in poverty and want to do something about it. Others, concerned about the community, recognize that high levels of poverty are incompatible with community sustainability.

And, of course, many individuals work in organizations that serve people in poverty: government and social services, health and healthcare, education, workforce development, addiction and mental health providers, and many more. These latter folks are motivated both to improve the outcomes of their organization and better serve their clients.

Among these people all the divisive issues of the day may be present: religious and social issues, including abortion and a woman's right to choose, guns, race, women's rights, sexual orientation, and immigration. In these times even social issues have been politicized.

The good news, however, is that when individuals and groups are focused on working with and helping people in poverty, social and political issues rarely come up. The political divide has seldom interfered with the work of Bridges communities. We have been told that this is largely due to how we view the research topics on the causes of poverty.

Causes of poverty

In the Bridges approach, research topics fall into four categories: (1) individual behaviors, choices, and circumstances; (2) community conditions; (3) exploitation; and (4) political/economic structures.[32]

The Four Causes of Poverty

Individual behaviors and circumstances	Community conditions	Exploitation	Political/ economic structures
Definition: Research on the choices, behaviors, and circumstances of people in poverty	*Definition:* Research on resources and human and social capital in the city or county	*Definition:* Research on the impact of exploitation on individuals and communities	*Definition:* Research on political, economic, and social policies and systems at the organizational, city/county, state, national, and international levels

(continued on next page)

(continued from previous page)

Individual behaviors and circumstances	Community conditions	Exploitation	Political/ economic structures
Sample topics: ~ Racism ~ Discrimination by age, gender, disability, race, sexual identity ~ Bad loans ~ Credit-card debt ~ Lack of savings ~ Skill sets ~ Dropping out ~ Lack of education ~ Alcoholism ~ Disabilities ~ Job loss ~ Teen pregnancies ~ Early language experience ~ Child-rearing strategies ~ Bankruptcy due to health problems ~ Street crime ~ White-collar crime ~ Dependency ~ Work ethic ~ Lack of organizational skills ~ Lack of amenities	*Sample topics:* ~ Racism ~ Discrimination by age, gender, disability, race, sexual identity ~ Layoffs ~ Middle-class flight ~ Plant closings ~ Underfunded schools ~ Weak safety net ~ Criminalizing poverty ~ Employer insurance premiums rising in order to drop companies with record of poor health ~ Charity that leads to dependency ~ High rates of illness leading to high absenteeism and low productivity ~ Brain drain ~ City and regional planning ~ Mix of employment/wage opportunities ~ Loss of access to high-quality schools, childcare, and preschool ~ Downward pressure on wages	*Sample topics:* ~ Racism ~ Discrimination by age, gender, disability, race, sexual identity ~ Payday lenders ~ Lease/purchase outlets ~ Subprime mortgages ~ Sweatshops ~ Human trafficking ~ Employment and labor law violations ~ Wage and benefits theft ~ Some landlords ~ Sex trade ~ Internet scams ~ Drug trade ~ Poverty premium (the poor pay more for goods and services) ~ Day labor	*Sample topics:* ~ Racism ~ Discrimination by age, gender, disability, race, sexual identity ~ Financial oligarchy—the military, industrial, congressional complex ~ Return on political investment (ROPI) ~ Corporate lobbyists ~ Bursting "bubbles" ~ Free-trade agreements ~ Recessions ~ Lack of wealth-creating mechanisms ~ Stagnant wages ~ Insecure pensions ~ Healthcare costs ~ Lack of insurance ~ De-industrialization ~ Globalization ~ Increased productivity not resulting in more compensation to workers ~ Minimum wage, living wage, self-sufficient wage ~ Declining middle class ~ Decline in unions ~ Taxation patterns

Source: *Getting Ahead in the Workplace* by Philip E. DeVol.

Conservatives tend to focus on individual behaviors, choices, and circumstances, including personal responsibility. Progressives tend to focus on political/economic structures and policy solutions. Most people in the U.S. are very familiar with the either/or political narratives of the left and right. Most politicians, think tanks, media outlets, commentators, and columnists create and feed off the either/or approach to poverty. This zero-sum—"We're right, you're wrong"—approach to poverty serves primarily those with political agendas and profit motives.

The causes of poverty are more accurately seen as *both/and* rather than *either/or*. Poverty is caused *both* by the choices, behaviors, and circumstances of the poor on the one hand *and* by political/economic structures on the other. Honoring good research from both right and left allows people in Bridges communities to work on poverty issues together.

Bridges addresses all the causes of poverty

In Bridges we address *all* the causes of poverty: individual responsibility and political/economic structures and everything in between. Bridges communities want people from both sides of the political aisle—and from all three classes—to be at the table.

The second column in the chart is about community conditions that cause poverty. Getting out of poverty has a lot to do with where one lives. In fact, sometimes the way to get out of poverty is to get out of town. Some people do relocate, but others just don't want to leave the area they call home.

> ### The work on poverty from a Bridges perspective attracts people from both left and right—and addresses all causes of poverty.

Studies on upward mobility, which is the probability of climbing the ladder from one quintile to the next—for example, moving from the second quintile (near poverty) to the third quintile (middle class)—cite data on commuting zones. These are defined as driving distance to a well-paying job; the studies will tell you the chances of upward mobility in your location.[33]

For example, Bucks County, Pennsylvania, where there is a strong Bridges initiative, is ranked fourth in the nation in commuting zones; Tucson, Arizona, another city with a strong Bridges initiative, is ranked 99th. The outcome studies from Bucks County bear this out; Getting Ahead graduates are doing very well. (Upward mobility also is addressed later in this chapter.)

A key secret to the success of Bridges is that it attracts people from all classes, races, sectors, and political persuasions. Most importantly, people form relationships while working on poverty issues. Once those are in place, it isn't likely that social and political divides will interfere with the initiative. In short, relationships across class lines make it possible to resist the pull of extreme political narratives.

Exploitation is often overlooked as a cause of poverty. For those in poverty, predators are a major destabilizing force. They are vulnerable to predators because they have concrete problems that demand immediate concrete solutions. Predatory lenders—such as payday lenders, check-cashing shops, buy-here/pay-here car dealers, lease-purchase outlets, and pawn shops—operate on a business model that takes advantage of people who are living in the tyranny of the moment. They are less likely to analyze the contracts they are signing than people not in the tyranny of the moment.

A less-recognized form of exploitation is fee-collecting strategies sometimes used by local governments and contractual for-profit providers. For example, charging a $75 booking-in fee at the local jail, plus a daily rate of $50, is seen as a revenue source for the county, but this practice harms the poorest offenders the most.

Other destabilizing fees include having those on probation pay a fee for probation services, or pay to talk with an imprisoned family member using video conferencing, or water fees and late-payment fines that fall heaviest on those who move the most: people in poverty.

The Bridges initiative in Burlington, Vermont, helped create a thinking tool (chart on next page) based on the four causes of poverty. It is used to address all the causes of poverty when dealing with specific barriers. It has been shared with other Bridges communities across the United States.

In the following example from Muskogee, Oklahoma, Mary Hicks, a Getting Ahead graduate, was helping a young mother who had run into a problem with her water bill. Mary tells the story:

> We had a purchase order from a social-service agency to pay the bill (the Department of Human Services had threatened to remove her child from the home if her water was shut off). The water department refused to accept the purchase order for payment. I didn't know what to do, but I wasn't going to leave that building until I found a way for that water bill to get paid; I had the "money" right there in my hand!
>
> That's when Mayor Bob Coburn walked into the foyer and saw me—with whatever look I had on my face and that purchase order in my hand. The mayor went with me back to the water department and had them accept the money order right then and there. After that, Mayor

Coburn and City Councilman Wayne Johnson, a Bridges Steering Committee member, conducted an investigation into the reasons behind them not accepting the purchase order.

The mayor saw her in the city's utilities office and, knowing her from Getting Ahead, asked what the problem was. The chart below describes the actions taken by the Getting Ahead grad and the City of Muskogee on all four causes of poverty. In the top-left corner the barrier is named: "Water fees and late-payment penalties." In the column below are four levels at which the problem can be addressed: individual, organizational, community, and policy. The Muskogee problem was addressed at the community level, i.e., the community row.

In the following four columns, please note the action on all four causes of poverty: individual, community, exploitation, and political/economic.

Address All Causes: A Thinking Tool

Barrier: Water fees and late-payment penalties	Individual	Community	Exploitation	Political/economic
Individual				
Organizational				
Community	Mary, a Getting Ahead graduate who returned to school and got a job at a social-services agency, helped a young mother who was living in unstable conditions. Mary identified the problem. The mayor, who is on the Bridges Steering Committee and a member of AIM (Action In Muskogee) and knew Mary, got involved.	Bridges training was provided to city officials and staff. Members of the chamber of commerce, the City of Muskogee, the courthouse, and the colleges in the county, along with other Getting Ahead grads, took two years to find a solution. Several departments had to completely redesign their paperwork and computer systems, including the payroll department. This took almost a year to accomplish, but policy was changed to benefit all residents of Muskogee.	This addressed the problem that had the poorest people paying the largest portion of the $1.4 million generated from the fees.	Muskogee officials found a fair solution. Policy changes: a. The water billing cycle now goes from 7–9 days to 12–14 days. b. Renters pay the same deposit as homeowners. c. Deposits can be paid out one-half at time of initializing service and the rest in monthly increments of $20.
Policy				

Source: Bridges initiative, Burlington, Vermont; adapted by Philip DeVol for Muskogee, Oklahoma.

This thinking tool ensures that each barrier encountered by a person in poverty is addressed thoroughly and keeps us from defaulting to our "favorite" cause of poverty. Conservatives are encouraged to look beyond individual choices and responsibility. And progressives are urged to look beyond systemic approaches.

Tom Martindale, the first director of the Bridges initiative in Muskogee, notes that this was possible because the Muskogee mayor and most of the city officials had Bridges training and shared a common language with the Getting Ahead graduate. Just as importantly, the graduate and the mayor knew each other personally. Relationships of mutual respect are at the heart of this work.

As a thought exercise, imagine using the "Address All Causes" thinking tool to speak to the following situation described by a Getting Ahead facilitator:

> One of the people in the class is a Hispanic woman, married, seven kids. She is documented. Her parents were probably immigrants, but she was born here. She grew up in the United States but in a very isolated community. We were talking about minimum wage and about the gap between minimum wage over the period of time with the cost of living.
>
> When we talked about the minimum wage, what it was, I'm sitting across the table from her and she just got this really troubled look on her face and I thought, "OK, something is going on." She sat there for a few minutes and then she just blurted out, "I had no idea there was a minimum wage." She said, "I have been working for this motel in housekeeping for five years. I was promoted to manager a year ago." She said, "I only make $4 an hour."

In my opinion, there isn't anything better than Bridges material and the research around poverty in Getting Ahead. I proposed to our group that we use the "Four Causes of Poverty" as the cornerstone for our work. Having these focus areas defined will clarify and simplify the process for counties that want to develop plans or strategies around reducing poverty. We plan to use the four areas to challenge conventional approaches, establish new cross-sector collaboration, and support collective action to impact state policies.

–Toni Brown, community support specialist, Georgia Family Connection Partnership

Bridges: A way to engage people who experience discrimination and barriers to upward mobility

Some people face more barriers on the journey out of poverty than others. For the woman who was paid only $4 an hour, poverty is interwoven with threads of racism, discrimination, gender bias, and isolation. In Getting Ahead she could examine her personal experience specifically. Her experience and the experiences of other investigators becomes the material from which their learning springs.

For Getting Ahead sites that choose to address the intersections of race, discrimination, exploitation, and poverty, there is an optional supplement provided by MCARI (Minnesota Collaborative Anti-Racism Initiative) that is available on the website.[34]

There are many lenses through which poverty can be examined beyond economic class: race, gender, immigration status, disability, age, sexual orientation, and others. In Bridges the lens of economic class is used because it offers the most panoramic view of the topic. When recruiting for Getting Ahead, the organizers are instructed to develop the most diverse group possible. We have found that the more diverse the group, the deeper the learning. Getting Ahead investigators bring with them their personal experiences and views about all the lenses.

Naturally, the makeup of groups follows the demographics of the community. The national study of Getting Ahead conducted by Elizabeth Wahler, Indiana University School of Social Work, provides this information about those who take part in the 16 sessions of Getting Ahead: 65.6% whites, 15.8% African American, 8.8% Latino, and 9.3% other.[35]

In the chart that lists four causes of poverty it's no accident that racism and discrimination appear at the top of the list in each of the four categories: individual behaviors, community conditions, exploitation, and political/economic structures. Bridges initiatives are expected to address racism and discrimination just as they would any other barrier.

Early in Bridges history, Jodi Pfarr began addressing these issues as the "isms" (racism, sexism, ageism, etc.) in her workshops, thus opening the door for many more people to utilize the Bridges ideas. Her book *The Power of Diversity: Unlocking Potential in Individuals and Organizations,* coauthored with Allison Boisvert, offers communities a way to address race and discrimination that is consistent with and expands on Bridges concepts.

In *The Power of Diversity* readers become aware of "normalized" groups, such as middle-class white males who represent established societal "norms" of behavior that don't take into account the rich diversity in our nation. With this awareness,

Pfarr and Boisvert offer tools that allow individuals and groups to analyze their institutions and communities to better see how normalized groups impact poverty. We explore this topic further in chapters 5 and 10 of *Bridges Across Every Divide.*

The work of poverty must include people who have experienced discrimination, poverty, and economic class differently from those in the dominant culture.

In the coming years Bridges will be focusing more on the "isms" that divide us. The notion of a post-racial society imploded during and after the 2016 election. In fact, a post-racial period never really existed. In his article "White Economic Privilege Is Alive and Well," Paul Campos writes: "The income gap between black and white working-class Americans, like the gap between black and white Americans at every income level, remains every bit as extreme as it was five decades ago." He goes on to conclude:

> Consider that in the mid-1960s, Jim Crow practices were still being dismantled and affirmative action hardly existed. Yet a half-century of initiatives intended to combat the effects of centuries of virulent racism appear to have done nothing to ameliorate inequality between white and black America.[36]

In response to racism and discrimination, Bridges communities must stand with Getting Ahead graduates and all people in poverty. The role of the organizations that form Bridges collaboratives is to remove barriers and clear pathways for those making the journey out of poverty. The climb is hard, even for those in the dominant culture—and much harder for those who face racism and other discrimination.

One struggle is knowing the hidden paths, the hidden rules, for such a climb.

Chapter 5

Pulling Back the Curtain on 'Hidden Rules' of Class: Replacing Judgment with Understanding

Philip DeVol

Pierre Bourdieu analyzed how a mundane action, such as deciding to order bouillabaisse in a restaurant, creates social labels and markers that sort people into different groups. The tiny decisions that people constantly make in their lives are never irrelevant or meaningless.

–Gillian Tett, *The Silo Effect*

In this chapter we learn how Bridges provides insight into "hidden rules"—cues, habits, and language usage—so people from all classes can better understand each other, build relationships, and together navigate the worlds of work, school, and community more skillfully.

We have established that income inequality leads to residential segregation that in turn leads to class-based living environments. Now we look at what it takes to belong and survive in the environments of poverty, middle class, and wealth.

The demands of the environments generate social norms, attitudes and habits. These norms are used to fit in, to belong, and to survive. And, unhappily, these norms are sometimes used to exclude the poor. In *Dream Hoarders* we learn that zoning has been used by the top 20% to isolate themselves from the "other."[37]

In their paper "America Can't Fix Poverty Until It Stops Hating Poor People," john powell and Arthur Brooks note: "Well-to-do Americans have almost no meaningful cultural contact with anyone from economically marginalized communities—from struggling inner cities to decaying suburbs to depressed rural counties."[38]

Economic and social class structures have been part of U.S. history just as they have been in other countries. Pierre Bourdieu wrote about his exhaustive study of class structures in France in *Distinction: A Social Critique of the Judgement of Taste.*[39] Paul Fussell took a sometimes humorous look at the topic in *Class: A Guide Through the American Status System* and, more recently, Elizabeth Currid-Halkett wrote *The Sum of Small Things: A Theory of the Aspirational Class.*[40]

In her first book, *A Framework for Understanding Poverty,* Ruby Payne called these unwritten social cues and habits the hidden rules of class. Knowledge of the hidden rules of poverty, middle class, and wealth gives us an understanding of how others live. It is also an opportunity to reflect on our own class experience and how we came to the rules we live by.

People typically begin their journey into Bridges ideas by examining the "others." Many middle-class and wealthy people are interested to know why people in poverty behave the way they do. And, in turn, many individuals in poverty wonder why the middle class and wealthy behave the way they do. We often call these "aha" moments—when understanding about another class dawns on us.[41]

For what do we live, but to make sport for our
neighbors, and laugh at them in our turn?

—Jane Austen, *Pride and Prejudice*

In a way, that's the easy part of working on class issues. The harder work begins when we examine our *own* class experience. How did we get where we are? What are the causes of poverty? How were the three distinct economic classes formed? What is our class history? This is when we move from the "aha" moments to "insights" into our own experiences and family histories. What advantages or disadvantages did our birth give us? What opportunities to live healthy, financially secure lives were earned, and what came from our birth?

Hidden Rules of Class (abbreviated)

	Poverty	Middle Class	Wealth
Driving forces	Survival, relationships	Work, achievement	Financial, political, social connections
Food	Quantity is important	Quality is important	Presentation is important
Destiny	Believes in fate; cannot do much to mitigate chance	Believes in choice; can change future with good choices	*Noblesse oblige*
Education	Valued and revered as abstract, but not as reality	Crucial for climbing the ladders and making money	Necessary tradition for making and maintaining connections
Language	Casual register and circular story patterns are used more often; nonverbals are emphasized	Formal register and linear story patterns are used more often; language is used for negotiation	Formal register is used for networking
Power	Personal power is linked to respect and sometimes to survival	Institutional or societal power is linked to negotiations, positions, influence on decisions	Community power is linked to networks that influence institutions and policies
Money	To be used, spent	To be managed	To be conserved, invested
Social emphasis	Inclusion by those who are liked and needed	Emphasis on self-governing and self-sufficiency	Emphasis is on social exclusion

Source: *A Framework for Understanding Poverty* by Ruby K. Payne.

Decoding three hidden rules: Food, driving forces, and power

Let's more closely examine three of the eight hidden rules listed here, starting with the rules on food because they clearly illustrate how the environment creates the rule.

Food

Many people in poverty experience food insecurity and hunger. It stands to reason that having enough to eat (sufficient *quantity*) is more important than how nutritious the food is—or how beautifully and aesthetically the food is presented.

By contrast, the more income and food security people have, the more likely they are to value the nutritional value of the food. So *quality* is the most important to the middle class. And if food is merely a small fraction of a family's income (and both quantity and quality are ensured), individuals in wealth are more likely to place the greatest emphasis on the *presentation* of the food.

At a much deeper level for people in poverty in particular are issues of obesity and diabetes. The ramifications of these for workers in our institutions and community who deal with food insecurity, health, and education cannot be overstated. These and other health-related issues are explored in detail in *Bridges to Health and Healthcare*.[42]

Navigating the worlds of poverty, middle class, and wealth requires knowledge of those environments and the hidden rules of class that arise from them.

Driving forces

Decoding hidden rules on the driving forces of poverty, middle class, and wealth could fill a book by itself. Earlier we established that people in poverty are problem solvers who usually use their relationships rather than money to solve problems. It's a world of reciprocity, of people doing for and caring for each other. And it's a form of philanthropy.

Individuals in the middle class, because they have enough income to be self-sufficient, generally solve their problems with money. That financial cushion allows them to attend to achievement in school and the workplace. You only need to ask how people in middle class greet each other to know how driven they are by work and achievement. The first question after exchanging names invariably is "What do you do?" This question is even part of the mating ritual, the answer to which will reveal the person's level of education and income, i.e., accomplishments. And this could mean the beginning or the end of the relationship. In wealth, achievements are nice, but things go best when you are well-connected to others who also are well-connected.

Most U.S. institutions run on middle-class rules and norms. You might say that the rules of the middle class have been normalized in our society. This is analogous to saying that right-handedness has been normalized in our society (much to the annoyance of left-handed people). Or that white, male, Western, European culture has been normalized into the power structures of our society. Or that Standard American English has been normalized.

Those who are right-handed, white, males, who use the formal register of language and adhere to Western, European cultural assumptions don't have to give much thought to their advantages. Their situation or status may be "invisible" to them; it's just "normal." This isn't to blame them or to set up another divide, but to make the point that the middle-class norms tend to be largely invisible to those in the middle class. They are simply playing out the hand they were dealt; this, they think, is simply the way society works.

> Small signals constantly express and reinforce power relations. Our ideas about what is pretty, ugly, tacky, trendy, or cool classify people (and things) into particular mental and social buckets.
>
> –Gillian Tett, *The Silo Effect*

One of the most damaging features of invisible status is what Robert Fuller calls rankism.[43] This results in middle-class people often (intentionally or unintentionally) pulling rank on people in poverty, a relationship-damaging behavior. This helps explain why programs for people in poverty are often designed without them being at the table. Or deciding what resources people get or don't get, or doing for others what they can do for themselves, or assuming that your judgments are more accurate than the judgments of another. Rankism, which will be explored in greater depth in Chapter 10, comes from a power imbalance that seems natural but isn't.

Bridges and Getting Ahead make these norms explicit. Once there is an understanding of the hidden rules of class, individuals in poverty can navigate the rules as they see fit.

The hidden rule about driving forces becomes important when people in poverty encounter the institutions that are run on middle-class rules, which is virtually all of them. For employees or volunteers in organizations that work with people in poverty, knowledge of the hidden rules can even lead to the redesign of procedures and programs.

For example, before learning about the driving forces of class and other hidden rules, the author's former organization, an addictions treatment center, was focused entirely on work (efficiency) and achievement (sobriety and recovery). Every procedure and policy was designed to get people into treatment quickly because insurance paid for only 13 sessions. After learning about the environment of poverty and the norms that grew out of it, we began to understand why treatment wasn't as effective with clients who were in poverty as it was for those who were middle class.

Knowledge of hidden rules helped us redesign practices that led to better outcomes. First, we combined the driving forces of relationships from poverty with the driving force of achievement from middle class to improve treatment and prevention outcomes. Second, we gave up our reliance on the formal register of language and began using the casual register where we could.

At the front desk we put a receptionist who was bilingual, meaning she could speak in both formal and casual (street language) registers. She was a "relationship"-based person, having been raised herself in poverty, and she just loved people. Our orientation was shortened, and a video (in casual register) was used to explain what was done at the agency. We also redesigned educational materials and presentations.

We made the waiting room friendlier, offered coffee and juice, set up a children's corner with toys and books, changed the notices on the walls to pictures, and removed the desks in the counselor's offices and added tables so counselors and clients could sit side by side.

This simple beginning led to an immediate drop in "no-shows" and eventually resulted in many other changes at the agency.

Power

Knowledge of the hidden rule on power has been very helpful in the workplace. New hires from poverty have been known to walk off the job after being reprimanded by a supervisor. To understand this, it's important to know that people who don't have much power tend to be hyper-vigilant about power and sometimes hyper-sensitive about it. This is made worse by the fact that power, for those who have it, is often invisible to them.

For the middle class the supervisor's power comes with the position. But people who don't have much power can feel disrespected when spoken to about a problem.

For some individuals in poverty the only way to maintain self-respect is to walk off the job—or to punch out the foreman or supervisor and *then* walk off the job.

A supervisor and a front-line worker in a clothing warehouse in Geelong, Australia, were able to use their new understanding of the hidden rules of power to save the front-line worker's job. The supervisor was trained in Bridges, and the front-line worker was a Getting Ahead graduate. The front-line worker was insulted, not by the supervisor, but by a co-worker. His immediate reaction was to fight, but he recognized the impulse and sought out the supervisor instead. The supervisor congratulated him on his restraint because fighting was a firing offense.

The two of them then worked on a plan for dealing with similar situations. Naming the hidden rule of power gave the supervisor and the front-line worker a way to process the experience *and* strengthen their relationship.

In addition to knowledge of hidden rules, it's important to have a shared understanding of poverty and how it's defined. Hint: It's not just about money.

Chapter 6

How a Shared Definition of Poverty Leads to Action at Multiple Levels

Philip DeVol

The focus on poverty only as a financial struggle greatly undervalues the human experience.

–Brad Essary, quoted in Keys, "Getting Ahead
Helps People to a More Fulfilling Life"

The Bridges definition of poverty gives individuals in poverty—as well as those in institutions and communities, along with policymakers—something they can do about poverty: Build 11 resources! A thinking tool helps distinguish between resources that simply maintain people in poverty and those that help people get ahead.

In the United States poverty is defined by individual and family income as determined by federal and state guidelines. That definition suggests that the only solution to poverty is to increase monetary incomes.

Yes, jobs and work—and the money derived from both—are important for all the obvious reasons: self-sufficiency, a sense of direction and worth, and the contribution to family and community. But information on incomes doesn't begin to describe the other factors that people can act upon. And it doesn't cover what it takes to build a truly stable life for individuals or the community as a whole.

In *A Framework for Understanding Poverty,* Ruby Payne defined poverty as "the extent to which an individual does without resources." The Bridges model expands her original definition to say: "the degree to which we, as individuals, institutions, and communities, do without 11 resources." This comprehensive definition means that we can take action in relation to poverty in many ways and at three levels.

The definition of poverty must focus on much more than just raising incomes.

The resources that individuals need to live and create stable lives are:

- Financial
- Emotional
- Mental
- Spiritual
- Physical
- Social capital/support systems
- Language
- Relationships and role models
- Integrity and trust
- Motivation and persistence
- Knowledge of hidden rules of class[44]

If our communities, institutions, and individuals are rich in these areas, people will be more likely to be included, engaged, and empowered. Social cohesion is the glue that holds people together over the long term, making it possible to pass on a better life to our children.

A definition of poverty that focuses on building resources

The table on the next page makes it easy to conceptualize the importance of having individuals, institutions, and communities involved in building resources. It's much easier for an individual to make the climb out of poverty when the institutions and community also are intentional about building resources.

Definitions of Resources

Individual	Institutional	Community
Financial		
Having the money to purchase goods and services, save for emergencies, and invest. Understanding the rules of money and wealth creation.	Employment opportunities include many well-paying, full-time jobs with benefits and opportunities for advancement.	Collaboratives exist that offer fair loans. Available are transportation, childcare, and health services that reduce the time and trouble it takes to get to work and agencies. Wealth-creating opportunities are offered.
Emotional		
Being able to choose and control emotional responses, even in negative situations. Having emotional competence to work with people from many backgrounds.	Institutions provide the environment, trainings, programs, and processes that are safe, healthy, positive, and supportive for everyone.	The community is a safe place where diverse people and groups are included— where there is a free exchange of ideas.
Mental		
Having the mental abilities and skills to deal with daily life. Having the education and training to compete in the workplace for well-paying jobs.	Equitable educational opportunities are available for people of all ages, genders, classes, races, religions, cultures, and ethnicities.	Communities have safe, healthy, affordable access to the development of the brain from pre-conception to old age.
Spiritual		
Having purpose and guidance and/or culture that provide purpose and guidance.	Institutions consistently adhere to ethical standards, policies of tolerance, inclusion, and a cultural environment that is supportive of spirituality.	Communities are a safe haven for people of all faiths, as well as those who espouse no religion.
Physical		
Having physical health and mobility.	Institutions adhere to policies and practices that support prevention, early intervention, and treatment for their employees and clients and customers.	Communities protect and preserve the water, air, soil, plants, other natural resources and animals in sustainable ways. And make health and healthcare affordable for all.

(continued on next page)

(continued from previous page)

Individual	Institutional	Community
Social capital		
Having plentiful bonding and bridging social capital.	Institutions design the environment, procedures, and policies that promote and support the development of bridging social capital.	Communities design housing and transportation to provide a highly resourced environment that is inclusive and invigorating for all people.
Language		
Having the vocabulary, language ability, and negotiation skills to succeed at school, at work, and in the community.	Institutions offer access to people with differing languages and registers of language, as well as communication needs.	Communities offer all people and groups access to planning and seats at decision-making tables—and encourage inclusion in all aspects of society.
Relationships and role models		
Having frequent access to others who are appropriate and nurturing in positive ways.	Institutions promote supportive, relationship-based learning, problem solving, and decision-making pathways for employees, clients, and customers.	Communities engage people from all classes, races, sectors, and political persuasions in problem-solving roles.
Integrity and trust		
Being consistently honest and having strong principles and ethical standards.	Institutions adopt and adhere to policies that require the highest standards of behavior.	Community leaders set high standards for ethical behavior and adhere to them.
Motivation and persistence		
Having the energy and drive to prepare, act, and follow through.	Institutions develop and adhere to clear statements of purpose that identify the motivation of the whole enterprise.	Communities use data, establish best practices, and encourage innovation in order to make their quality of life sustainable.
Knowledge of hidden rules		
Knowing the unspoken cues and habits of all economic classes. Being able to navigate class systems.	Institutions design their practices and environments to help people from all classes and races succeed.	Communities come together to build a sustainable community where everyone can live well.

Source: Definitions in all three columns developed by Jodi Pfarr and Philip DeVol, 2017.[45]

The meaning and value of most of these resources are self-evident. Social capital, however, is nuanced and requires a brief explanation.

In Robert Putnam's *Bowling Alone* (2000) we learn that bonding social capital is what we have with people closest to us and people from similar environments. Bridging social capital is something we may have with people who come from different classes, nationalities, and educational backgrounds (in other words, people different from us).[46]

Bonding capital is good for "getting by," while bridging capital is good for "getting ahead." People from settings different from ours can open doors to new opportunities and resources. Many people of all classes can name individuals who helped them advance in their education or careers. Building bridging social capital is one of fastest ways out of poverty.

In Bridges communities, middle-class and wealthy people readily make themselves available as bridging social capital to Getting Ahead graduates. In Reno, Nevada, a young mother and Getting Ahead graduate who was participating in a workshop mentioned that she was finding it very difficult to enroll in a community college. Two professors from that college who also were attending the workshop got up and gave her their business cards saying, in effect, "We will help you get through the system. Give us a call." Instant bridging social capital.

> The most impacting part was identifying 11 key resources for a healthy life, including finances, motivation, role models, emotional health, and a support system. I'm walking away a better person, with a better life for my son.
>
> –Veronica Rodenkirchen, paraphrased in Hazelton, "'Getting Ahead' Offers Big Step in Right Direction"

The Bridges definition of poverty gives individuals something they can do about poverty: Use their higher resources to build their lower resources. In Getting Ahead, investigators do a self-assessment of their resources on a five-point scale. This leads to creating SMART (specific, measurable, attainable, realistic, and time-specific) goals that will lead them to what are called their future stories.

Getting Ahead can be hard intellectual and emotional work. The examination of one's own life and the impact that poverty has had on each individual often leads to people taking charge of their lives in a new way.

This definition of poverty also gives leaders in the institutions and community a way forward. The challenge to our institutions and community is to do the same level of analysis in regard to their role in helping to build resources of people in poverty. What our institutions and communities generally do is simply maintain the status quo instead of working with people who are taking their own steps to get out of poverty.

The Implied Promise

When people in poverty come to our institutions and community programs, an implied promise is made to them. It is: "By coming here things will get better for you." As noted earlier, people in poverty typically go to 3–10 agencies a year in an effort to make things better. How many people have passed through and completed our programs and yet their lives remain virtually the same?

The term "resources" needs to be clarified further. One use of the term describes resources as water, food, money, shelter, clothing, etc. These are immediate daily needs. Think of someone being released from prison. The returning citizen's needs are immediate, including: cash, food, a place to stay, a ride, medication, an ID, a job.

Sometimes the term "resources" is used to describe the institutions in the community—as in "Our community has many resources for returning citizens who are in poverty: mental health agencies, hospitals, workforce development programs, and the like." The institutions themselves are called resources.

In Bridges the term "resources" refers to the *matrix* of 11 resources that can be built to transform a person's life. It's much more than simply meeting immediate needs.

The thinking tool on the next page distinguishes among resources that maintain Getting Ahead investigators in poverty (in other words, getting-by resources) and resources that lead to getting ahead.

Resources

	Financial	Emotional	Mental	Spiritual	Physical	Social capital	Language	Relationships and role models	Integrity and trust	Motivation and persistence	Knowledge of hidden rules
Getting-by resources											
Getting-ahead resources											

Source: Created by J. Pfarr Consulting,[47] adapted by DeVol Associates, LLC.

This tool is used to impact poverty at the three levels of the Bridges triple lens—individual, institutional, and community. But it also is used with a fourth entity: funders.

Individual use of the tool: A Getting Ahead investigator who lived in subsidized housing determined that her housing was a getting-by financial resource because, should she get a job that "paid too much," she would lose her housing. This sort of benefit, while a positive way to stabilize one's environment, is at the same time a "cliff effect" benefit. For every two steps up the ladder there is a benefit cliff that often means a step or two back down the ladder.

If she takes the better-paying job, her housing goes from 30% of her income to as much as 60%. Encouraged by her fellow investigators, she took the job, saying, "The scariest thing was stepping from a shaky safety net to a shaky ladder (the job). Who knows if the job will be there next year?"

These are the difficult decisions that people in poverty face as they struggle to climb the ladder. As noted previously, the challenge to institutions, communities, and funders is to do the same hard analysis.

Institutional use of the tool: Using the Bridges triple lens approach, institutions use this tool to evaluate the resources they provide. The purpose of some organizations is to provide a safety net, in which case getting-by resources make sense. Civilized societies do need to support those who are sick, old, and under-resourced.

For many organizations the purpose is mixed: providing some support for immediate needs and some support for climbing the ladder. A good example of institutional change is given to us by St. Vincent de Paul (SVdP), a Catholic group that has been helping people in poverty for 400 years.

SVdP's primary activity is to make home visits to those in poverty to befriend them and bring them the supports or resources they need—essentially a getting-by strategy. In 2011 program officials began to add Bridges concepts as part of a plan to take a more systemic approach to poverty. The first woman elected to head up SVdP in the U.S., Sheila Gilbert, led the initiative by offering Bridges training to approximately 150 sites and 80,000 volunteers, thus tipping the scales of their work toward also helping people get out of poverty.

Community use of the tool: Communities use this thinking tool to assess the balance of resources available in the community. Many communities serve as examples of Bridges concepts at work. Schenectady, New York, is one of them. Eight sectors are involved in the Bridges initiative: arts/entertainment, business, education, faith-based, government, healthcare, media, and social.

The chair of a local foundation, when asked about how the foundation grants funds, stated, "We make grants to organizations that are part of the Bridges initiative. That way we know that the balance between getting-ahead and getting-by resources is taken into consideration."

Funders' use of the tool: Foundations, United Way, private donors, and granting organizations wrestle with how to fund projects that deal with poverty. Bridges initiatives that operate at the community level are attractive to funders because a collaborative is already in place, thus solving the problem of organizations competing for the funding. Some Bridges sites are now being awarded million-dollar grants over 3–5 years.

Many government programs that access the typical funding streams use Bridges training and strategies. And in a few cases government-funded programs have acted as the catalyst for implementing Bridges and Getting Ahead. In the state of Washington, Susan Kempf spearheaded an initiative that offers Getting Ahead to people in workforce development programs. Post-Getting Ahead support was provided by local area planning groups at the community level. In Howard County, Maryland, Bridges and Getting Ahead were integrated into typical programming with considerable success by Quinton Askew.

To sum up: Bridges has been called a movement by people who have seen it spread across the U.S. and by those who have taken part in building an initiative in their community. If you were to attend an annual national Bridges conference, you would see the Bridges movement at work.

What is happening in Bridges communities fits a definition of *movement:* "a group of diffusely organized people or organizations striving toward a common goal relating to human society or social change, or the organized activities of such a group."[48]

In the next chapter we describe the Bridges methodology that evolved as the movement was forming and developing.

Chapter 7

Methodology: Ways That Bridges Communities Grow

Philip DeVol

Acting should precede planning ... because it is only through action and implementation that we create the environment. Until we put the environment in place, how can we formulate our thoughts and plans? ... We create the environment through our own strong intentions.

–Margaret Wheatley, *Leadership and the New Science*

Previous chapters were about achieving a new understanding. This chapter is about how that happens and how people take ownership of the concepts. Bridges is not a program, it is a set of ideas that can be applied in many ways. This methodology leads to remarkable innovations.

In the previous chapters we introduced core ideas that attract people to this work. Coauthor Gene calls Bridges ideas an earwig: something that gets into your head that you can't get out. There must be a less horrifying metaphor. Some people say, "I drank the Kool-Aid." That's not much better.

More positively, many speak of having an "aha" moment or an awakening. Pick your metaphor, but whatever it is, once your thinking has changed, you can't go back to the way you used to think. As in: "Now that I see people in poverty as problem solvers, I can't go back to thinking of them as 'the problem.'"

As Bridges communities have sprouted across the United States, a development pattern has taken shape—something we call the Bridges methodology. It began with eight sites from Indiana, Ohio, and Wisconsin that had heard about one another and wanted to meet. They conducted a few conference phone calls to share what they were doing and then decided they wanted to meet in person.

This led to eight sites gathering for the first "national conference" in Columbus, Ohio, in 2006. Judge Jennifer Brunner was the first speaker at the first Bridges conference. The point is that people like to learn from each other. Most conversations led to new ideas and eventually to definable best practices. We've discovered that people are attracted to the Bridges methodology almost as much as they're attracted to the Bridges concepts.

In this chapter we will:

1. Explore how the transfer of knowledge methodology sparks innovations.
2. Describe the process of exposing the community to Bridges language.
3. Define the roles and structures needed to develop a sustainable initiative.
4. Discuss the guiding principles at the heart of the methodology.
5. Review studies and research papers about the effectiveness of Bridges and Getting Ahead.

The Vision
Bridges brings people together from all classes, races, sectors, and political persuasions to create communities where everyone can live well.

1. Exploring how the transfer of knowledge methodology sparks innovations

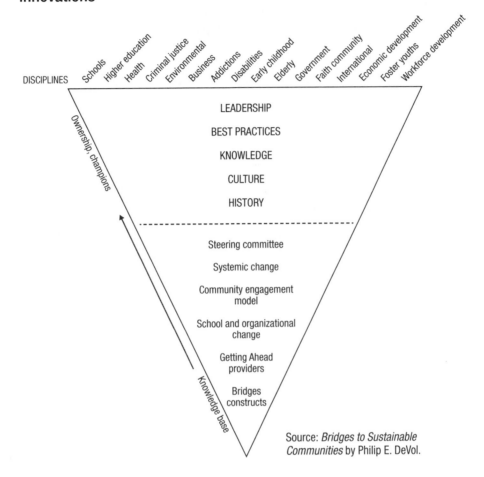

Source: *Bridges to Sustainable Communities* by Philip E. DeVol.

We've found that one of the main reasons people like Bridges is because it's *not* a program. Instead it's a set of ideas and tools that can be applied as needed to fit local situations and conditions. Once the concepts are understood, people are encouraged to apply the ideas in their settings, to innovate, and (eventually) to create new models.

We've found that most people love being innovators, and they enjoy sharing their models with others. It means we're always learning, adapting, and finding new solutions. When the ideas and models are "owned" by the people and organizations that created them, the initiative is more likely to be embedded and sustained.

In the preceding mental model, the arrow running up the left side of the triangle depicts the transfer of knowledge.

Everything below the dotted line in the triangle is the training component found in the books and workshops provided by aha! Process. The core ideas, covered in chapters 2–6, are presented by national Bridges trainers, local certified Bridges trainers, and local certified Getting Ahead facilitators.

Over the past dozen years or so, the Bridges books and trainings have changed mindsets. First, people grasp the ideas, then they gain mastery of the concepts—and apply them in personal and organizational ways. Their innovations contribute to the knowledge base when the ideas are shared with others.

The Joy of Innovating

People are attracted to both the Bridges concepts and the Bridges methodology. Bridges is not a program; it is a set of ideas and tools that can be used to innovate.

In new Bridges communities everything above the dotted line (leadership, best practices, knowledge, culture, history) must be created locally in the disciplines named above the triangle.

Individual responses to the concepts

During the transfer of knowledge, *the ownership of the ideas shifts from the "experts" to the listeners and readers*. The "aha" moments that people experience when they first learn about class differences is often the beginning of deep learning experience. This phase is analogous to taking a trip up the Amazon River to observe tribal people. Learning about the "other," people who are different from "us," is important. We learn how the environment of the Amazon shapes the norms and culture of the people there, the hidden rules that govern their society, and the impact that globalization and climate change has on them. Ideally this experience will lead to changes in the learner's behavior relative to, and in support of, the tribal people.

As we also discussed in Chapter 5, the step from an "aha" moment to an insight happens when we shift the focus of our examination from the *other* to *ourselves*. We examine our own class environments and experiences. We analyze our own journey through the class system. How did our family acquire wealth and power? What resources were passed to us by our families, institutions, and communities? How does our experience shape our attitudes and interactions with people from other economic backgrounds?

Ideas turn into reality as we apply the concepts in our personal and professional lives. We accept the need to make changes, with the focus moving from "them" to "me."

People in Bridges communities tell us that having applied Bridges ideas and seen the outcomes, they realize that a paradigm shift has taken place. Their view of how poverty works in the world has changed. Now their use of Bridges concepts has become rooted in deep understanding.

Institutional/organizational responses to the concepts

An individual can have a paradigm shift, but so can an institution and community. This is when the Bridges ideas have reached critical mass, meaning that enough people are familiar with Bridges to start and maintain an initiative.

The fact that Bridges is not a program is attractive to front-line staff persons who are familiar with the feeling of dread or at least apprehension that comes with the news that the CEO has decided to implement a new program. Knowing that Bridges isn't a prescription but something that can be utilized in pragmatic ways is both a relief and a challenge.

Bridges is sustainable when the solutions are adapted by local catalysts and champions. They take into account the knowledge, culture, history, and best practices in their organizations and community. While programs are imported to many of those on the "outside," Bridges solutions are locally grown, pertinent to "what's happening here" and invariably relevant.

This methodology evolved into a pattern as one organization and community after another became champions. They made site visits to learn from early adopters. And people in particular sectors, like the courts and employers, began to share best practices. New ideas generate energy that in turn builds new programs.

This process evolved into learning communities at institutional, sector, and community levels, as well as state, national, and international levels.

Learning communities at the institutional level

It's natural for people to enjoy sharing ideas. Learning communities form around the water cooler or coffee station with two or three people talking about how to use Bridges concepts. Anyone in the organization is a potential catalyst for change. The ideas may be as simple as putting toys and children's books in the waiting room and replacing desks, which staff sit behind, with tables where staff sit beside people they serve.

Learning communities at the sector level

Bridges sites that work in education, health, reentry (from incarceration), and courts conduct conference calls to share best practices, host webinars, and make presentations at the national conference. Several Bridges communities have a workplace stability initiative in place and a budding learning community. The public/private partnerships in each community include private employers, nonprofit organizations, banks, credit unions, and employer resources networks that use books and training based on Bridges concepts.

Learning communities at the community level

In Schenectady, New York, eight sectors are using Bridges. A centerpiece to the learning community is the "champions" assigned by and reporting to the CEOs of 30 organizations. They meet monthly to brainstorm best practices, identify local leaders, and work to remove common barriers that people in poverty encounter.[49]

Learning communities at the state level

In Oklahoma the Salvation Army serves as the hub of a statewide learning community. Regular meetings are held for Bridges trainers and Getting Ahead facilitators to share best practices and encourage new learning. The next goal is to influence policies at the state level. In Ohio, learning community calls are made with more than 30 counties that have Bridges initiatives in place.

Learning communities at the national and international levels

aha! Process hosts an annual international conference at which practitioners from all sectors present best practices. aha! Process also supports the learning community with a website, free webinars, and social-media support.

Emerge Solutions is a national learning community focused on poverty solutions and advancing economic equality. Bridges is often featured in its work.

2. Process of exposing people to Bridges language

- National or local certified trainers introduce Bridges to the organization or community.

    Tip: Invite as many people as you can; make full use of the opportunity. Collect information from the audience about how they would like to follow up. A database of those interested means not losing a single person who is drawn to Bridges.

> **Tip:** Train administrators and board members. If the leadership isn't attracted to Bridges, it probably won't fly.

- Develop a team of certified Bridges trainers and certified Getting Ahead facilitators in your organization and/or community.

  > **Tip:** Training is an ongoing necessity to cover turnover in the organization, reach new groups and organizations, and create critical mass of the shared language. Certified trainers become local experts. Engage people in poverty through Getting Ahead. There are specific certifications for K–12, Bridges, and other sectors (workplace, postsecondary, health and healthcare, reentry, youth, etc.).

- Each organization and/or sector collects data to report on outcomes that pertain to their mission: retention rates, completion rates, graduation rates, recidivism rates, and so on. For those who participate in the Getting Ahead series, data are captured about the increases in stability, growth of the 11 resources, and the financial return on investment (ROI). Contact aha! Process about national data-collection providers who have cloud-based data management systems.

  > **Tip:** Start with the end in mind and collect data from the beginning. Data are crucial to continued funding, informing the community, and quality-improvement activities.

- As organizations become involved, invite them to be part of a collaborative. This is the beginning of a learning community and a way to operate above the "silos" in order to impact barriers faced by people in poverty.

  > **Tip:** Include Getting Ahead graduates on the committees and panels, as well as working groups, of the collaborative. Offer them leadership training opportunities that prepare them to serve on executive boards.

  > **Tip:** Send a team to the Bridges conference. It won't be long before your organization or community will be presenting at the conference.

3. Roles and structures needed to develop a sustainable initiative

There are patterns in the ways Bridges sites evolve and operate. There are key roles played by individuals and organizations. And there are different organizational structures to consider. It's hard to control for all the variables, but the good news is that there are many ways for Bridges initiatives to work.

The roles

Catalyst: This is the person who ignites an interest in Bridges in the organization or community. Who this person is has a lot to do with how quickly and effectively the initiative gets off the ground. When the head of a foundation or a banker or judge calls a meeting, lots of people will show up. That stands to reason, but how do judges get involved?

Melissa Knopp, who headed up the Specialized Dockets division at the Supreme Court of Ohio, learned about Bridges and knew that it would help with drug courts and mental health courts. She said, "I got about 15 courts interested in Bridges and approached [Ohio Supreme Court] Justice Moyer about a four-year project to integrate Bridges into the trial court process."

This in turn led to about 80 court personnel, including a number of judges, becoming certified Bridges trainers. Judge Teresa Ballinger from Marion County and Judge Carol Robb from Columbiana County were two of those trained. They became catalysts when they returned to their counties and called people together for the purpose of starting Bridges collaboratives in their counties. The ripple effect from Melissa Knopp as a catalyst is still being felt in Ohio.

Institutional leaders: Mike Saccocio, executive director of City Mission, in Schenectady, says, "A small reality is more compelling than a grand theory." In most cases, a countywide Bridges collaborative begins with one organization creating a "small reality." The reputation and connections of a well-run organization go a long way toward lifting off a communitywide initiative.

Community leaders: The catalyst for a community-level initiative in South Bend, Indiana, was a women's group, Women in Leadership in Community Organizations. They worked through the Center for Intercultural Leadership of Saint Mary's College. The guiding principles were: Don't duplicate what someone else is doing well in the community, and do move beyond service delivery to systems change.

The outgrowth was the creation of the St. Joseph County Bridges Out of Poverty Initiative. By 2008, under Bonnie Bazata's leadership, it had become a destination site. People from across the U.S., as well as from Slovakia and Scotland, have made "pilgrimages" to South Bend in order to see for themselves how such a Bridges collaborative works.

**Bridges communities grow more
from a succession of achievements
than by following procedural steps.**

Backbone organization: This is the organization that provides the administrative and fiscal functions in order to support a community collaborative. The organizations that step up to do this vital work have come from a number of sectors, including: courts, faith, food banks, foundations, government, municipalities, nonprofit service providers, prevention services, schools, and United Ways. Some sites, such as South Bend, organize themselves into a not-for-profit 501(c)(3) for the purpose of managing a Bridges initiative.

Characteristics of a backbone organization include:

- Willingness to serve the Bridges collaborative and coordinate activities of the collaborative

- Doesn't brand Bridges to itself, but is willing to share ownership with other organizations

- Its leadership is totally bought into Bridges

- Getting Ahead grads serve on boards and at the planning tables

- Bridges concepts are being applied in the organization

- All levels in the organization are trained in Bridges

- Has the administrative capacity to provide the necessary support (perhaps by sharing some roles with other organizations) to:

- Manage grants

- Maintain database of member organizations and community members

- Manage data collection, reporting systems, research, CQI (continuous quality improvement)

- Coordinate learning community at county level

- Act as historian

- Willingness to work with statewide Bridges learning community

Need for structure: The backbone organization can play a big part in adding structure to a movement.[50] We recommend that backbone organizations use the Collective Impact approach, often utilized by United Ways. The approach is consistent with Bridges methodology. What Bridges adds to Collective Impact is a common language for those organizations.

Member organizations: The membership of a Bridges collaborative includes those organizations that apply Bridges concepts in their work.

Not many Bridges collaboratives have 88 member organizations like the Santa Rosa Bridges Coalition in Florida. The schools were the catalyst there. With 41 local certified trainers, they reached critical mass quickly. Reaching out to the wider Bridges learning community, they received advice from Marion Matters in Marion, Ohio.

In Santa Rosa, seven working committees are staffed by representatives from the member organizations. The committees focus on awareness/public relations, government/planning, educational training, finance, advocacy, employment, and government/transportation. Karen Barber, Santa Rosa Bridges board member, reports:

> In hindsight, progress has been both swift and significant. Although the lack of resources and support for the citizens of Santa Rosa appeared daunting, there was actually an abundance of groups working to support our citizens. Santa Rosa Bridges has provided the conceptual structure each organization needed to combine our talents and treasure, and the Getting Ahead classes and graduates have provided our community with the confidence and insight that all our citizens have much to give our community.[51]

4. Guiding principles at the heart of the methodology

Bridges initiatives need specific and measurable goals. Naturally the goals aim at working with people to get out of poverty, typically around raising incomes and getting off public assistance.

In Bridges, however, the goals include stabilizing one's environment and building the 11 resources. Each member of the collaborative and every individual graduating from Getting Ahead will have goals that are in line with their missions and plans: to attend and graduate from schools, to improve health outcomes, to reduce recidivism for citizens returning from incarceration, to improve productivity, and to reduce turnover for those in the workplace.

It should be noted that in Bridges and Getting Ahead the goal isn't to bring about conformity to and compliance with the system, but to "… be the means by which men and women deal critically and creatively with reality, and discover how to participate in the transformation of their world."[52]

We want Getting Ahead graduates to become fully engaged in society; to gain a sense of control, power, and self-efficacy; and to have confidence that they have achieved their goals.

The lessons learned from the innovators can be passed on through the learning communities. The way we work with people is central to our success. We found that adhering to the law of attraction and trusting people in poverty are the keys to success.

In Bridges and Getting Ahead we work through attraction and not by imposing our agendas on people in poverty. We've already noted the need for goals, but the main thing is to avoid imposing our goals on others—and to avoid becoming too attached to our own goals. Paradoxically, it's our drive for those goals that often interferes with people in poverty making their own arguments for change, for owning their own plans and journey.

Just as each institution and community must create its own version of Bridges, so must each individual create their own future story.

What follows is a discussion of how to apply the laws of attraction at the individual, institutional, and community levels.

Law of attraction at individual level

People in poverty who are recruited to take part in Getting Ahead should never be coerced or mandated to attend Getting Ahead. To do so would be inconsistent with asking people in Getting Ahead to serve on a focus group that provides accurate information about poverty to the community.

One of the best ways to recruit people for Getting Ahead is to ask if they want to help people who are in poverty and help their community become a better place to live. We've found that people in relationship-based worlds want to give back, to help others, to be philanthropists. This is supported by a study showing that the bottom 20% of Americans gives more than 3.2% of their income to charity while the top 20% gives 1.3%.[53]

When we operate on the law of attraction we can be agenda-free. We can let go of imposing our goals on others.

> Nothing destroys a relationship faster than an agenda.
> Having a goal in mind makes us try to extract something
> from our partner. People keep trying to work at
> the end result. Goals are our undoing.
>
> –Allan J. Hamilton, *Lead with Your Heart*

In Getting Ahead the investigators quickly discover that Getting Ahead is agenda-free. That the relationship between the investigators and the facilitator comes before achievement: the facilitator is not trying to "extract" anything from the investigator.

This means that no one is telling investigators what to do. There are no right and wrong answers for what they investigate in Getting Ahead. Facilitators don't impose their personal agendas on the group, but allow the individuals to make what they will of the content—to make their own argument for change. This is a huge relief to people who are used to being bombarded by the agendas of the organization they go to.

Inmates of a prison in Marion, Ohio, were in the first Getting Ahead while Getting Out group. One of them said, "This prison offers 44 programs and we have been to most of them. This is the first class that didn't have a middle-class guy standing at the front of the room telling us what to do."

Law of attraction for middle-class staff and volunteers

The principle of attraction applies to people who work in organizations that serve people in poverty. Requiring employees to attend educational events is a normal way to introduce new ideas to employees. But, in Bridges, once the ideas have been introduced, the principle of attraction applies. Only the staff members who like the ideas should be invited to apply the concepts and change procedures, program designs, and policies.

In "Why Diversity Programs Fail," Frank Dobbin and Alexandra Kalev report:

> In analyzing three decades' worth of data from more than 800 U.S. firms and interviewing hundreds of line managers and executives at length, we've seen that companies get better results when they ease up on the control tactics. It's more effective to engage managers in solving the problem, increase their on-the-job contact with female and minority workers, and promote social accountability—the desire to look fair-minded.[54]

They offer a telling example:

> In one study white subjects read a brochure critiquing prejudice towards blacks. When people felt pressure to agree with it, the reading strengthened their bias against blacks. When they felt the choice was theirs, the reading reduced.

Debora McDermed, a national Bridges trainer from Portola, California, puts it this way:

> If someone sees or hears something in the Bridges information that is coming from their own inner knowing (otherwise referred to as an insight … sight from within), then behavioral change is easy, natural, and organic. You couldn't stop it from happening. All the things you have seen happen in Bridges—innovation, program design changes, initiative building—begin to occur as if spontaneously.

On the other hand, if people hear the information as coming from outside of their knowingness or wisdom—more like interesting, entertaining, etc.—then you have a 50/50 chance of seeing change, and it will have a characteristic of "effort" about it. The initiative will not quite get off the ground or, if it does, it dies off after the energy of the effort dissipates.

In an early experience in Columbiana County, Ohio, we too found that "control tactics," such as evaluating employees on their command of Bridges skills and strategies, actually created backlash against the Bridges approach in general. Being agenda-free means not trying to control the outcomes—in this case, even how the staff would use Bridges. It's paradoxical but true that less insistence on achieving a goal can result in better achieving the goal.

We learned that Bridges is best developed by people who like and want to use the ideas. Administrators can work with them to design new procedures, changes the environment, and develop new programs. During that process the entire staff can be engaged—and later be expected to operate, generally speaking, within the new environment and structure.

Law of attraction and community work

Leaders of two successful Bridges communities use the law of attraction and the agenda-free approach to build collaboratives. Mike Saccocio and Chuck Holt, president of Factory Ministries in Lancaster County, Pennsylvania, represent the backbone organizations in their communities. They don't approach their peers with a plan in hand. *They begin by listening, by building relationships with leaders from other organizations.*

One of the Bridges principles that evolved from the school of hard knocks is: "Everybody owns it, and nobody owns it." This means that the Bridges initiative should not be "branded" to the backbone organization. Branding Bridges to a particular organization has two negative consequences.

1. First, other organizations in the community don't feel they "own" Bridges. Rather they feel they must go to the backbone organization to get guidance, answers, or permission. They aren't as likely to innovate, and they're more likely to look for solutions to be handed to them.

2. Second, the whole collaborative suffers if the CEO of the organization that claims ownerships of Bridges leaves. How many times have communities seen good initiatives come and go with a CEO? If all organizations "own" Bridges, it will be sustainable and able to survive the departure of a CEO.

Everybody owns it, and nobody owns it.

Building a Bridges initiative by letting go of your own agenda

Saccocio says: "A movement is like a river; it cannot be controlled, but it can be influenced." Giving up control starts with finding out the personal and organizational agendas of others in the community. "The other person's agenda is your *true north* in building relationships," he adds.

Holt says: "If I get something out of it, it's an agenda. Rather, we should care about people before caring about our programs." He starts with having breakfast with community leaders. He asks, "What are you doing? What problems do you run into? What can I do to help you?" He reports: "We come to care about each other and are not worried about our agendas." This, he says, is basic Bridges thinking: "The middle class, being driven by achievement, builds programs. In Lancaster County we choose to use the driving force of people in poverty; we build relationships."

Ultimately the question becomes "What can we do for the good of the community?" Holt does what he can to help others solve their problems. "To be agenda-free, you must be willing to give away autonomy," he says. His ideas must be working; there are 17 organizations in the Together Initiative in Lancaster County, and United Way has given TILC $300,000 a year for three years to pursue their goals.

The philosophy of being agenda-free and relying on others to be attracted to this work is deeply rooted in the work in these two Bridges sites. The practice of letting go of control and trusting others as problem solvers can be messy and is spotted with failed pilot projects, but the trend line of progress is upward to such a degree that funding flows, and the initiatives become sustainable. As Saccocio points out, "If we shift from seeking control, we can gain influence."

For example, the downtown businesses in Schenectady had a problem with drawing people back into the downtown partly because of the number of homeless people on the sidewalks in front of many of the businesses. The City Mission, a faith-based housing program headed up by Saccocio, piloted a program to have people from the shelter meet and greet people as they parked in the downtown area.

This grew into having Getting Ahead graduates trained as Ambassadors, wearing red jackets, welcoming visitors and helping them navigate the downtown area. The Ambassadors worked 8,000 hours in 2016 alone. The Getting Ahead grads and the Bridges initiative have truly changed the character and feel of the downtown area. Their innovation has led to the Ambassadors program being duplicated in two other New York cities: Albany and Saratoga.

To make evidence real, we need to see it, hear it, feel it, and verify it.

Data to be seen.
Stories to be heard.
Relationships to feel.
Verification to know it's real.

5. Reviewing published articles on Getting Ahead and outcome studies from Bridges sites

Stories are one thing, data are another. The Bridges movement is rich in the first and busy growing the second.

Here we provide links to published peer-reviewed research studies of Getting Ahead and provide links to the less formal, but informative, studies done by a number of Bridges sites.

Differences between studying Bridges and studying Getting Ahead

Getting Ahead lends itself to evaluations and research studies because it is a program. It is a learning experience based on a curriculum that requires model fidelity of those who use it. It is used in a consistent manner across all sites. A number of scholars have stepped forward to study Getting Ahead.

Bridges concepts, however, are applied differently by each organization and each community collaborative. Of course, these organizations report on their outcomes, which is necessary and valuable. Those studies can be found here.[55]

At the time of going to print, the following two Getting Ahead research studies have been peer-reviewed and published.

Two peer-reviewed studies

1. Elizabeth A. Wahler, from Indiana University School of Social Work, Indianapolis, Indiana, did a national study of Getting Ahead titled "A Group-Based Intervention for Persons Living in Poverty: Psychosocial Improvements Noted among Participants of 'Getting Ahead in a Just-Gettin'-By World.'" It was published by Social Work with Groups.

    The abstract reads:

    > This study reviews the results of a national study of Getting Ahead in a Just-Gettin'-By World ("Getting Ahead"), a widely used group-based intervention for helping persons in poverty assess their resources and create a plan for increasing them. Findings from a national study of a diverse sample (N = 215) suggest that the program is facilitating positive changes in poverty-related knowledge, perceived stress, mental health and well-being, social support, hope, and goal-directed behavior and planning. Implications of these findings for practice and future research are discussed.[56]

    Please refer to the Bibliography for a link to this article online.

2. Ines W. Jindra and Michael Jindra, with the Center for the Study of Religion and Society, University of Notre Dame, South Bend, Indiana, and later with the Department of Sociology and Social Work, Gordon College, Wenham, Massachusetts, published an article in the *USA Journal of Poverty.*

    The abstract reads:

    > This article highlights how one nonprofit organization deals with the controversial issue of culture and poverty through its interactions with low-income individuals. Through interviews and participant observation, we analyze its curriculum and process, which focuses on helping participants become more reflexive by analyzing their past life and potential futures through a social class analysis. At the same time, we discuss a key theoretical debate over culture and action/agency. Specifically, we examine

the distinction between practical and discursive consciousness (or declarative and non-declarative culture), and issues of agency. We show how this theoretical process is accomplished in the organization by providing people with the opportunity to change their habits, skills, "cultured capacities" and "repertoires," which can help them get out of poverty. We also show [that] other factors, such as social support, are crucial and how the overall process works more for some than for others.[57]

Reports from Bridges learning communities

Reports: There is also a growing collection of reports, evaluations, and studies coming from Bridges communities. These contributions are from various sectors, many states, and other countries. They can be viewed online at the address listed in the Bibliography.[58]

Webinars: Members of the larger Bridges learning community provide free webinars that can be viewed online.[59] The web address can be found in the Bibliography.

Publications: Publications for many sectors are available online.[60] The web address can be found in the Bibliography.

And two publications of collections of papers from the field: *From Vision to Action* and *From Vision to Action II.*[61]

Web-based data collection and reporting systems used by Bridges and Getting Ahead sites

Local providers of Getting Ahead need and want to collect local data about the progress being made by Getting Ahead graduates.

There are two providers that Bridges and Getting Ahead sites use: CharityTracker and Charity Check.[62] For the sake of consistency both collect information on stability in the graduate's life, the development of the 11 resources named in Bridges and Getting Ahead, return on investment (ROI), and model fidelity.

CharityTracker and Charity Check reports are consistent with Bridges and Getting Ahead theory.

Model fidelity is monitored to ensure that Getting Ahead is being delivered consistently, and so the data are based on consistent use of the curriculum.

During Getting Ahead, investigators do self-assessments of stability factors and resources that become the baseline for measuring changes in both. The providers also collect ROI data on income, debt, asset development, and the utilization of public assistance. Getting Ahead sites contact graduates to conduct follow-up assessments at regular intervals.

Each site can access reports on their own initiative. For comparison purposes, aha! Process provides state and national reports to the local sites. A sample national report from CharityTracker is provided below.

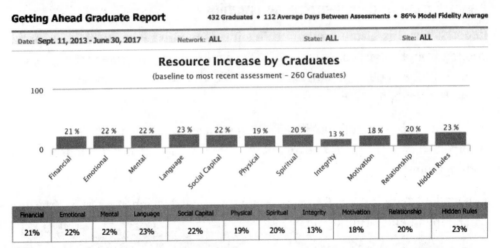

Getting Ahead Graduate Report   432 Graduates • 112 Average Days Between Assessments • 86% Model Fidelity Average

Date: **Sept. 11, 2013 - June 30, 2017**   Network: **ALL**   State: **ALL**   Site: **ALL**

Resource Increase by Graduates
(baseline to most recent assessment – 260 Graduates)

Financial	Emotional	Mental	Language	Social Capital	Physical	Spiritual	Integrity	Motivation	Relationship	Hidden Rules
21%	22%	22%	23%	22%	19%	20%	13%	18%	20%	23%

© DeVol and Associates, LLC • Published by aha! Process, Inc. • Report portal funded by aha! Process, Inc in partnership with Simon Solutions (Developers of CharityTracker™)

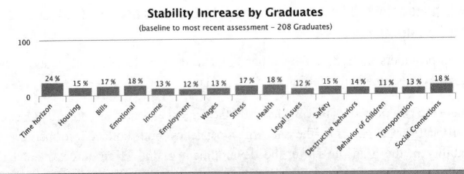

Stability Increase by Graduates
(baseline to most recent assessment – 208 Graduates)

Time horizon	Housing	Bills	Emotional	Income	Employ-ment	Wages	Stress	Health	Legal issues	Safety	Destructive behaviors	Behavior of children	Transportation	Social Connections
24%	15%	17%	18%	13%	12%	13%	17%	18%	12%	15%	14%	11%	13%	18%

© DeVol and Associates, LLC • Published by aha! Process, Inc. • Report portal funded by aha! Process, Inc in partnership with Simon Solutions (Developers of CharityTracker™)

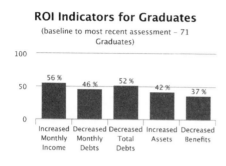

ROI Indicators for Graduates
(baseline to most recent assessment – 71 Graduates)

	Baseline	Most Recent Assessment	Difference	Percentage of Difference
Increased Monthly Income	$77,270	$82,586	$5,316	6 %
Decreased Monthly Debts	$57,251	$55,024	$-2,226	-3 %
Decreased Total Debts	$603,507	$543,673	$-59,834	-9 %
Increased Assets	$301,280	$365,112	$63,832	21 %
Decreased Benefits	$24,689	$27,150	$2,461	9 %

We have learned that telling people what to do to fix their own problems is like pouring water over a rock; it looks wet, but next to nothing soaks in. They must be attracted to *their* solutions and take ownership in them.

And how do we tell our elected officials what policies are needed and not end up with another bunch of wet rocks? How do we get real results back from the elected officials and not just platitudes? How do we attract them to be our champions? And how does leverage play a pivotal part in impacting policies?

Chapter 8

How to Gain Leverage to Move Policy
Gene Krebs

*In the life of a nation, when the old customs of a people are
changed, public morality is destroyed, religious beliefs shaken,
and the spell of tradition broken ... the country then assumes
a dim and dubious shape in the eyes of the citizens.*

—Alexis de Tocqueville, *Democracy in America*

In this chapter we learn that power and influence are different. Influence can be gained for the price of breakfast. Constituency size distorts the democratic model. Relationships rule in politics, and that fact guides policy.

In the United States on a certain Tuesday in early November, many of us pull voting levers. Although the levers we pull are small, if a majority of us pull, then the country, state, or our community changes directions—or else it continues on the same path as before.

Greek scientist Archimedes said that if given a large enough fulcrum and a long enough lever, one could move the world. You also can move policy and political discourse with levers and fulcrums. You can increase your leverage with longer levers and bigger fulcrums.

How, you may ask, do you and your policies get a larger lever and bigger fulcrum?

Amassing a lot of money is one way, but this isn't foolproof. Simply possessing and maintaining great personal wealth, whether you were born into a wealthy household or you created a bestselling app, may not mean you understand public policy or have the political means to move voters. Unfortunately for them, the wealthy often fail to understand this, and they sometimes throw vast sums at problems or policies without success.

At the same time, ordinary citizens have a hard time beating big money when its influence is well-managed. That is because very few ordinary citizens understand the hidden rules of big money. Spending money is basically the only way to scale the distribution of your message to reach more people. The bigger the population you want to appeal to, the bigger (and more expensive) a lever you may need.

To get you into the mind of an elected official, let's first pretend there is a city made up of you and you alone. You are the mayor and the only voter. As long as the funds are available, deciding whether to replace vital infrastructure, like a broken refrigerator, is easy; it's all about you. You "vote" to spend the money (in effect, you tax yourself), and then you have the new refrigerator delivered. Life is easy with a constituency of one.

But now let's pretend you are the mayor of a town of 1,000 people.

The mayor of a town of 1,000 people, where two-thirds are of voting age, has 667 potential voters. At best 80% (533) of the eligible citizens register to vote, but only half of those registered actually come out to vote (267). That means 267 people "control" that town.[63]

In such conditions, the mayoral candidate needs the votes of just 134 people to guarantee a win. If every Saturday morning you have breakfast with three citizens, hear their issues, and develop a relationship with them, within a year you will have broken bread with everyone you need to vote for you, and you should win. In your second year as mayor, you have breakfast with the other half of the people who vote.

When it comes time for your reelection as mayor, you run unopposed. Everyone in town who votes has had food and coffee with you. They all know you listen. And because you listen, you know just how far you can push the community for needed reforms and new investments.

Now let's take this up a notch; your municipality grows tremendously. Your town has become a city of 100,000 people; it is 100 times bigger. In order to develop those personal relationships with all your voting constituents, you need to have breakfast with 300 people every Saturday morning—and listen to them all. Obviously, you can't do this.

How do you get your face in front of the voters? This is where big money helps you scale your messaging.

In larger voting districts, it all comes down to name recognition, so you rent a billboard featuring just your last name. People can't really get to know you personally like they did in the city of 1,000 people, but the billboard gives them a vague idea of who you are.

Psychologists refer to this as "cognitive ease." If you hear a name, even just in passing, you will have a modest fondness for people with that name. They seem familiar to you, even though you've never met.[64]

People go into the voting booth and see your name. If they have seen it somewhere before, they experience cognitive ease, and they pull the lever for you. This vote has nothing to do with your qualifications.

As pundit George Will often notes, people spend more time deciding what coffee to order than how to vote, especially for down-ticket candidates. It takes a unique candidate to break through the noise. Even though your mother always told you how wonderful you are, it isn't self-evident to the rest of the world.

Aside from donating huge sums of money to politicians, how do you influence them? By building relationships. We all live in tribes, whether in politics, in poverty, or at the country club, even if they are merely tribes of the moment. You have to build relationships across tribal lines to move policy. And we need to avoid going to war with the other tribes. In doing so, we prove Henry Adams wrong.

Henry Adams was wrong

Henry Adams was the grandson of President John Quincy Adams and great-grandson of President John Adams, a signer of the Declaration of Independence. Henry Adams' 1907 work, The *Education of Henry Adams,* won a posthumous Pulitzer Prize and is regarded by some observers as the greatest nonfiction book of the 20th century. In this book Adams calls politics "the systematic organization of hatreds."[65]

Adams was born in 1838, and the U.S. Civil War was the defining aspect of his life, so you can understand why he felt as he did about politics.

I reject his premise, but at the same time we should all be afraid that we are heading to a future Adams would recognize well. That, in large measure, is why Phil and I are writing this book.

We reject the idea that politics is how we organize our hatreds. We believe politics is how we organize our existing friendships and relationships—and forge new ones. It is a way to leverage assets to create more assets. We could all stand to relearn how to collaborate, as old divides deepen and new ones open seemingly every day.

In the developed world, some of the middle class and most of the ruling elite have withdrawn to cul-de-sac'd suburbs, gated communities, and other places with exclusionary zoning. The children of the rich interact with the poor in another city while volunteering in a soup kitchen primarily to fluff up their college applications.[66]

Relationships

> There are no ordinary people.
>
> —C. S. Lewis, *The Joyful Christian*

> Be kind, for every man is fighting a hard battle.
>
> —Ian Maclaren, Scottish minister and writer

The poor and working poor find themselves increasingly without adequate resources or relationships with people in the middle class and ruling elite. The loss of low-skilled manufacturing jobs makes it harder than ever for the poor to pull themselves up even to the lower middle class. Their lives of many of them are getting grimmer, and they are looking at bourgeois society with piercing gimlet eyes.

Like most of us, people in poverty need better relationships with the powerful.

Politicians look for gatekeepers. These are people whose position in the community helps them disperse knowledge and makes them good listening posts for what is happening and the general mood of the people. In a city or legislative district of 100,000 people, finding the gatekeepers is a shortcut to productive breakfasts.

Can you fill that role of gatekeeper—now or in the future? Could you evolve so you could do it? If not at the political end of the spectrum, how about at the policy end? Both? If you can position yourself as a gatekeeper in the realms of both politics and policy, you can be a true influencer.

With whom did you go to kindergarten?

 Politics is simply the means we use to make
our nation work, and to make our states
and communities better places to live.

–Larry J. Sabato, "Professor Sabato Welcomes
the Nation's Newest Citizens at Monticello"

What matters in politics is also the length of time the relationship has had a chance to flower. Ideally you went to kindergarten with the politician you want to work with, but that's unlikely. So what to do?

Befriend all politicians when they are starting out.

As elected officials move up the political food chain, they represent more people, and their time becomes dearer. Develop relationships early on when they have plenty of time. Beginning politicians, like plankton on the food chain, face potentially short futures, and they actively seek allies. Be an ally who can give advice; be an influencer.

Influence is something to develop over time; that is why the most influence is often held by people with gray hair. Once you have it, as Lord Varys notes in "Game of Thrones": "Influence grows like a weed." Make them focus on you.

Because of the sheer scope and number of issues faced by elected officials, if they don't have ADHD when first elected, they probably will after a few years in office.

How do you cut through the chatter and get elected officials to focus on your cause?

Whether you have a relationship with the elected official already or not, ask to meet for breakfast or lunch on a weekday. Be sure it's a day on which their official body doesn't meet.

Choose a restaurant that serves breakfast all day and doesn't serve alcohol. This will quell anyone's potential romantic ideas and ensure that no one drives home after drinking. Places that serve breakfast all day also tend to be inexpensive and very public. They are populated by regular folks, not the ruling elite.

Just sitting in a humble place will help remind the official that there are people out there who have modest means. Take two other friends with you, sit at a booth, and have the official sit in an inner seat. That way when someone else stops by to chat with your guest, the official won't jump up and start chatting with the interloper. You are paying for the pancakes; get your money's worth.

In order for your policy efforts to be effective, elected officials need to know you well enough to relax around you and not be on guard. They need to trust you, and that takes time. You are developing influence, which is very different from power.

Power and influence are different

> America, if eligible at all to downfall and ruin,
> is eligible within herself, not without.
>
> —Walt Whitman, *Democratic Vistas*

Power comes from the ability to make things happen. Influence comes from knowing the best ways to help those things happen.

If you win the lottery, you can have power. You can make donations and convince elected officials to take certain actions—until your money runs out. Then everybody will go back to ignoring you, as they should.

Influence is different; it doesn't rise and fall with your investment portfolio. It grows incrementally over time. In policy and politics, influence is attached to you personally. It doesn't matter whom you're working for, in what capacity, or what your title is that week.

The more influence you have, the more you get, as long as you use it wisely and, yes, sparingly. You can squander it by being stupid or increase it by being helpful. What help are politicians seeking? They want to know how to handle tough issues, and few issues are tougher than poverty.

Most elected officials shy away from tough issues. They might put things off by establishing a task force. The task force studies the issue, and then its report is filed away on a dusty shelf. When the next person comes into office, they create a new task force whose new report goes on the same dusty shelf next to the old report. Why? Because of what happens to many of those who actually follow through on changes: Frequently the public turns on them and rends them to pieces.

Mediocre political skills can get you elected on a platform promising change. Strong political skills are needed to follow through with proposed changes and successfully navigate that landscape.

In advocating for Bridges and Getting Ahead, you are proposing change. Elected officials know how often change has derailed their predecessors; they may well have won their position by being against change. They will likely be cautious in supporting your cause, even if you have gained access and built strong relationships.

What can you offer that will bring elected officials on board as Bridges and Getting Ahead advocates too? Data and the science that produces data. As Bertrand Russell said, "Without science, democracy is impossible."

Stories versus data: Is one better than the other?

> Objective, impartial data collection by federal statistical agencies ... make[s] it possible to have a productive discussion about the advantages and disadvantages of particular policies, and about the state of the economy.
>
> –Nicholas Eberstadt et al., "'In Order That They Might Rest Their Argument on Facts'"

While policy geeks love data, most humans respond to stories. We spent many millennia huddled around campfires telling stories in caves. The stories were meant to illustrate lessons needed for survival in the harsh natural environment.

We tell the same stories now. Instead of a glowing campfire, we sit in front of a glowing television or computer screen or tablet or smartphone, but the stories still deliver lessons on interpersonal relationships, how to avoid scary situations, and how to uphold justice. For the most part, the bad get punished, and the good are rewarded.

How do you move voters and elected officials? You move them with stories that scare them.

Some parents have refused to vaccinate their children against measles (and other diseases), contrary to advice given by medical professionals and researchers. Measles is nothing to be trifled with as it can lead to convulsions, brain damage, hearing loss, and death.

A study divided young parents into three groups. One group was shown ghastly photos of the devastation of measles. A second group had participants read about research that proves the vaccine doesn't cause other diseases, and the control group was given unrelated science research to read.

Which was the most effective in convincing parents to vaccinate? The photos. The data might prove the point, but the photos tell a story and therefore have a bigger impact.[67]

The lower officials are on the power food chain, the more they respond to personally gripping stories and will use those stories to guide them. The fact that they make emotionally guided decisions is often the reason they are in lower leadership.

The farther you move up the ladder in politics, the more it's about the data and the less it's about the stories. The pinnacle of this kind of thinking can be found in the staffs of governors and presidents. They will prefer scientific articles over gripping stories, but even then they will home in on the stories that the graphs and charts impart. This is how they got so high up on the food chain in the first place. They will recognize the best initiatives are those that appeal to both logic and emotion.

Power comes from data; huge power comes from data that support a story with emotional appeal. Imagine a study that says states requiring 20 hours of driving instruction experience 87% fewer teen deaths due to car accidents. That short sentence (if it were true, which it's not) would have legislators falling over themselves to introduce a bill requiring 20 hours of driving instruction for teens. How do you manage your data behind policy development?

Informed policy development

Data management is a vital tool for those moving to the policy level. According to Dan Quigg, CEO of Public Insight:

> Few would dispute the value of data reported by government agencies. But if the goal is analysis, the numerous silos of data provide no intrinsic value. The problem is that blending data across government agencies is hopelessly complicated. It requires a database expert to construct complex data models to get to analysis. According to *Harvard Business Review,* 90% of time spent on self-service data analysis is data management.
>
> Public Insight makes every piece of public data available to browse for free using the data browser tool.
>
> Self-service business intelligence is an emerging, growing area which entails pre-curating the data across topical areas and then presenting it visually with dynamic filters or "slicers."[68]

Public Insight Interactives are, in effect, research in a box. They are available on a subscription basis and require no licensing or software downloads. Public Insight also develops custom interactives.[69]

What do political and policy leaders care about? What are their favorite data points?

They want data that can show them how to save money and increase revenue while providing better services for the constituents who vote for them. Remember that poverty scares the bejeebers out of most elected officials. It's costly, it prevents money from being allocated for other causes (such as education), and it puts a crimp in economic development.

All registered voters have a lever and a fulcrum; can you develop yours to move your community, city, county, state, or even nation with data and stories? How can you collaborate with others who are doing similar work?

The next chapter will explain where to set up your lever, how much force to use, and where to find the fulcrums.

Chapter 9

It Don't Mean a Thing if You Ain't Got That Swing (Voter)
Gene Krebs

The cares of politics engross a prominent place in the occupations of a citizen in the United States; and almost the only pleasure which an American knows is to take a part in the government, and to discuss its measures.

–Alexis de Tocqueville, *Democracy in America*

> The focus of this chapter: Who are the swing voters, how do you identify them, and what is important to them? Why do politicians value them so much? How do you reach out to them and get them to value your issues? Might they be the big levers you've been searching for?

There are two groups in America that have longer levers than most, and that is because they "swing." They've done nothing particularly dramatic to earn this greater leverage. They aren't smarter or better-looking than other voters. They're just more unpredictable than most of the populace largely because they're notably resistant to the prevailing groupthink. While nominally called members of one party or another, the swing groups often change their voting patterns. This variability is what gives them power.

Swing voters are not independents, who usually don't vote in primaries because they resist being identified with either major party. Many independents are sick of both parties and the mudslinging up and down the ballot. These individuals, also eschewing groupthink, could therefore be more open than many to what Bridges/Getting Ahead stands for. Since Bridges/Getting Ahead is about getting to what works, these independents seem to care more if the cat can catch mice than what the cat looks like.

Because independents seldom vote in primaries they don't have the same degree of clout as the next two swing groups. If the independents come along, that's great. Swing, however, is different from independent; swing is housed somewhere, while independents are politically homeless by choice. They can get a better home via such reforms as ranked-choice voting, which is discussed in greater detail in Chapter 11.

This chapter is intended to help you understand the two main groups that swing, what motivates them, how Bridges/Getting Ahead could fit into their worldviews, and how to frame your issues in a manner that speaks to their concerns. If you can gain the support of the swing voters in both parties, you will thereby gain the support of the ruling elite of both Republicans and Democrats. Turn your issues into a bidding war, because the parties are fluid over time.

This reality could help propel Bridges/Getting Ahead further into this nation's consciousness as a tool for combating social problems. It could even prove to be a national model for political discourse. Bridges/Getting Ahead can help create the post-partisan universe that many politicians keep claiming they can deliver.

The different tribes inside the parties

In America, the principle of the sovereignty of the people ... is recognized by the customs and proclaimed by the laws; it spreads freely, and arrives without impediment at its most remote consequences.

–Alexis de Tocqueville, *Democracy in America*

In this nation's two-party system both parties are collections of disparate but overlapping groups that come together *temporarily* to promote a candidate and/ or platform that meets their ideals. Each party contains one tribe that is "in play." These groups are therefore the most sought after, and they are inadvertently the most powerful within their parties. They are like free agents in professional sports: Teams will bid very high to land them on their roster. You, the Bridges/Getting Ahead advocate, should know who they are and how to appeal to them in order to get *both* parties on board.

Swing group No. 1: The NPR GOP

The NPR GOPers are Republicans who don't listen to conservative talk radio. When in the car or puttering around the house, they listen to National Public Radio (NPR).

The NPR Republicans see the world as nuanced. It's not black and white or even gray; rather, they see it in pastels that gradually fade into each other, more like a J. M. W. Turner watercolor than a Jackson Pollock abstract. They're usually educated, often female, and live in well-to-do suburbs. They enjoy having calm, thoughtful discussions at dinner parties where they discuss Turner and Pollock.

About a fifth of NPR listeners are conservative, and NPR listeners are the second most affluent group of media consumers, topped only by those who read *The Economist*.[70] Among NPR GOPers are many white, suburban women who normally vote Republican, but change their voting patterns based on attraction or revulsion to candidates, often by significant percentages.[71]

Reflecting a certain degree of Calvinist influence, the NPR GOP takes a calm, dispassionate view of politics and business. That view also contributes to their rejection of the angry tone of conservative talk radio. Since they aren't motivated by emotion to the same degree as most other groups within the Republican Party, they have more staying power and will stick to a cause when others have moved on.

Most NPR GOPers care deeply about the less fortunate in their community. They are belongers engaged with the local Rotary Club and Junior League. You can reach them there and through social media. Later we discuss how a briefing book can help—with candidates, elected officials, and even the NPR GOP. And, of course, you can try to get the local NPR station to cover the growing collaboration between Bridges/Getting Ahead and the NPR GOPers.

Swing group No. 2: The Bourbon Democrats

The other major group of swing voters in the U.S. has a long lever due to population size, but they also have a lower voting rate than the NPR GOP. The Bourbon Democrats are different from the Chardonnay-drinking Democrats you find at Manhattan dinner parties—in more than just their choice of libation.

> As social conditions become more equal, the number of persons increases who ... owe nothing to any man, they expect nothing from any man; they acquire the habit of always considering themselves as standing alone, and they are apt to imagine that their whole destiny is in their own hands.

–Alexis de Tocqueville, *Democracy in America*

On the other side of the aisle from the NPR GOP, and indeed their opposite in education and outlook, are the Bourbon Democrats. To reach Bourbon Democrats requires mass-media celebrities (think Reagan, Schwarzenegger, Ventura, and Trump), AM radio, and social media. They respect local leadership while detesting the national elite, so your efforts might well center on local leaders.

The label "Bourbon Democrat" was first used in the 1800s. I'm reviving it here to distinguish a long-standing group of Democrats from their more progressive, Chardonnay-drinking counterparts. Bourbon Democrats are conservative leaning on many issues, but differ from the readers of *The National Review* and other conservatives in that they sometimes lack a philosophically consistent view, which is partly why they're swing voters.

Sometimes called "Reagan Democrats," Bourbon Democrats are leery of "crony capitalism" and are generally not fans of rapidly changing dynamics in the country. They're suspicious of big business and acquiesce to big labor as a necessary balance, but they aren't very responsive to the urgings of union leadership to vote in a particular manner. In fact, working-class union members flocked to Trump in 2016.[72]

That tension has increased between those who, as noted by Charles Murray, physically hurt at the end of the day and those whose brains hurt. In the 1830s, Alexis de Tocqueville points out that "in the United States, the more opulent citizens take great care not to stand aloof from the people; on the contrary, they listen to them, and speak to them every day."[73] But as we outline in this book, the ruling elite no longer live near or personally know virtually anyone different from themselves. This plays out in practical terms in this manner: Bourbon Democrats loathe the college-educated ruling elites.[74]

And it's safe to say they take offense at being called "deplorable." Their lives are becoming precarious though.

From 1996 to 2014, among white males in the U.S., wage and salary income for high school graduates dropped by 9% overall while the income for college graduates increased by 23%. In 2014, income was $94,601 for college graduates and $36,787 for high school graduates.[75]

Bourbon Democrats often work in a trade, whether skilled or unskilled. They view immigrants with alarm, as immigrants often bring with them new skills, an unfamiliar visage, and a desperate work ethic. Immigrants also increase the pool of people working in various trades. Bourbon Democrats believe that they pulled themselves up "by their bootstraps"—and are frankly and openly baffled why other people can't.

Famously, in 2008, then-presidential candidate Senator Barack Obama suggested that "they get bitter, they cling to guns or religion or antipathy to people who aren't like them or anti-immigrant sentiment or anti-trade sentiment as a way to explain their frustrations."[76]

The areas of the country where they live and/or claim heritage are seeing an increase in various health issues and greater mortality. Middle-aged whites in the U.S. without a college degree have experienced increasing midlife mortality over the past decades, while other groups have experienced improved health outcomes.[77]

Many Bourbon Democrats feel that others have gotten to where they are via special privileges awarded by the largess of the federal treasury. In short, they believe the United States is a meritocracy, but it's "rigged" against them because they are white and therefore don't constitute a group that can get special consideration.

The word *Bourbon* in their title is helpful in understanding the Bourbon Democrats. Bourbon is traditionally a Southern drink, distilled in Kentucky, a somewhat Southern state, and Bourbon Democrats are like many Southerners. Indeed, quite a few of them are Southerners or of that heritage.

Bridges/Getting Ahead appeals to the values of Bourbon Democrats because it's about helping people rise up out of their circumstances, similar to how they view their own story. Because they work with their hands—and their bodies ache after a long day at work—Bourbon Democrats resent people getting anything for free if it's paid for with taxes taken out of their paychecks.

Non-college-educated whites are almost twice as likely as college-educated whites to believe that the poor prefer to stay on welfare rather than seek full-time employment.[78]

Do not presume that only men make up Bourbon Democrats; women also vote in a similar pattern based on cultural heritage, geography and educational level. These women sometimes do break with the men, though, on the need for the government to aid and assist with workforce training. Perhaps they see fewer gender barriers to various new kinds of employment.[79]

Bourbon Democrats seem flummoxed by the world they are now encountering. They would like to step again into Heraclitus' river and find the same water, even though it has moved on downstream.[80] To a certain degree, they may be pining for a world that never was as they remember it.

East Liverpool, Ohio: A case study

> To save both development and democracy, political systems need to leap to a new stage, as the economy itself is doing. Whether that enormous challenge can be met will decide whether the ultimate powershift that approaches will protect or enslave the individual. The primary ideological struggle will no longer be between capitalist democracy and communist totalitarianism, but between 21st century democracy and 11th century darkness.
>
> —Alvin Toffler, *Powershift*

What is happening to much of the U.S.A.? What are the economics behind these changes, what explains the failure of workforce development in America, and are there any possible reforms that can be undertaken? Might there be a community that encapsulates these trends?

East Liverpool, Ohio, lies in Columbiana County next to the west bank of the Ohio River, south of Youngstown and near Pittsburgh, Pennsylvania. It is a small city of 11,000 souls that has lost 60% of the population it had in 1970. Composed of 4,600 households, the median household income is $27,000, and the median house value is $57,000. About 7% of the city's population has a college degree.[81]

East Liverpool was once a major producer of high-end pottery, but competition in labor costs, mechanization, a strengthening dollar, the extinction of local fine-clay resources, and changing consumer tastes ended that industry.[82] Later, residents commuted to Youngstown or immediately across the Ohio River into the Pittsburgh region seeking skilled and unskilled jobs, often in union-staffed steel mills or associated industries.

On September 19, 1977, on what became known to locals as "Black Monday," steel manufacturer Youngstown Sheet and Tube laid off 5,000 workers and shut down. The ripple effect was huge, eventually leading to the loss of 40,000 manufacturing jobs regionally and 400 satellite businesses. The coke and steel plants closed one by one, and the skies became clear. People could breathe easier, but they were uneasy.

As we will discuss later, this job loss was caused mostly by technological change. America today is producing about the same amount of steel as it did in the early 1980s, but not nearly as many workers are operating the steel mills.[83] Indeed, manufacturing as a percentage of all employees is going down at a fairly steady rate.[84]

For years rumors swept through "The Valley" that the steel mills had been purchased and were going to start making steel again. More than anything else, these constant rumors of a return of the good old days of a blue-collar utopia prevented the residents from determining a new future. Why risk what little you have on a new venture when soon the heavens will open up again with steel jobs pouring out like rain? The rumors crippled a response to their economic plight and stifled the entrepreneurial spirit.

Columbiana County is evenly split between the two parties. It makes a good case study and test case for examining attitudes toward workforce development, as well as the changing nature of industry, education, and the expectations of swing-voting Bourbon Democrats.

If you understand Columbiana County and East Liverpool, you might understand Bourbon Democrats and why workforce development is failing in America.

Democratic nations often hate those in whose hands the central power is vested, but they always love the power itself.

–Alexis de Tocqueville, *Democracy in America*

In September 2015 I attended a workforce development hearing in East Liverpool for Representative Tim Derickson's Community and Family Advancement committee; 10 witnesses from Columbiana County presented.

During the question/answer portion, *three* of the witnesses separately volunteered that it was a shame that the old days were gone when you didn't "even need a high school diploma to qualify for a job where you made enough money to afford a house, a car, a boat, and a camper." And always in that order: house, car, boat, camper. Each and every time, this statement was met with wild applause and shouts.

I found this ironic considering this small burg is a short jog down the road from Pittsburgh, where in 2002 Richard Florida wrote his influential *The Rise of the Creative Class* while at Carnegie Mellon University. While in the past a compliant nature and strong back could suffice to provide for a family, Florida predicted a future that belonged to those who worked with their minds, not their muscles. Yet here was the first witness calling for repudiation of that book, which is a major influence on modern workforce and urban revitalization policy.

When the final speaker, a highly respected community leader who owned a small restaurant, made the podium-pounding argument that it was wrong that you "even needed a high school diploma to qualify for a job where you made enough money to afford a house, a car, a boat, and a camper," I began to think more deeply. Obviously we had missed something earlier; this was shocking and real.

The restaurateur was emphatic that even without a high school degree or technical skills, you should be able to get a meaningful job that paid close to five times the minimum wage. His statement was a complete rejection of training and workforce development and was well-received by the audience. Obviously no one there had read Richard Florida's book—or any of the hundreds of white papers it inspired. Nor did they seem to care.

Do not dismiss this concern; their view of the world is just as legitimate as others. Why the massive disconnect between those who study work and those who actually work? Does this explain why we have millions of jobs unfilled in the U.S. as not enough people want to get the training? What do the data actually show?

Don't deny the data

> In God we trust; all others bring data.
>
> —W. Edward Deming, U.S. business writer and consultant

Data show that many assumptions that U.S. residents of all income levels have about the causes of economic decline in the non-college class are simply wrong. (Perhaps soon the college-educated will be facing similar pressures with automation and artificial intelligence.) What is causing the discomfort is not what you think, but how you think.

It is only by dispelling the myths that we can begin to approach Bridges/Getting Ahead as a possible solution in some circumstances. What is prompting this willful denial of the march of history and policy in East Liverpool—and perhaps in your state as well?

Let's establish that manufacturing jobs are disappearing in the U.S., and later in the book we will discuss how this could accelerate even beyond current trends.

In 1980 there were about 19 million manufacturing jobs in the U.S. In 1994, after a 14-year decline, there was actually a spike in the number of manufacturing jobs shortly after NAFTA (North American Free Trade Agreement) was approved, an increase you may not have heard about before. Since 1998's peak of 17.5 million manufacturing jobs, however, the number had declined sharply to about 12 million by 2014.[85]

The problem is not that all these jobs moved overseas. Another way to say it is even if space aliens blow up the world, except the U.S.A., it won't cure this problem (of course space aliens with nukes would be an even bigger problem). The increases in manufacturing efficiency are such that products it formerly took 25 people to make now take just 6.4 people.[86]

If we're so much more efficient, why are so many people anxiety-ridden? One more bit of data: In those communities where jobs are "routine" and easily transferable, there were shifts in the voting patterns. It has been historically true that these "low-skilled" manufacturing jobs are how the lower classes lifted themselves up to the middle class. That option is evaporating like rain on hot asphalt.[87]

Less educated workers have taken it on the chin. In "The Long-Term Decline in Prime-Age Male Labor Force Participation," the Obama White House noted almost no decline in college-educated men's participation in the workforce, but found an 11% drop for those men with only a high school degree.[88]

Justifiably or not, the desperation of white, undereducated, middle-class men is increasing. Will we see modern-day Luddites emerge? Just over 200 years ago British workers (known as Luddites) destroyed machinery, especially in cotton and woolen mills, that they believed was threatening their jobs. The word Luddite has become a metaphor for anyone who resists technological advances.

What can be done to increase the voters' comfort level and faith in our political/ economic systems? Or is it that we all have different visions for our country? Can we tolerate all this intolerance of those different from us? Or can we start fixing it before the next great tech wave washes over us?

Prozac for America?

> We have an inborn tendency to establish types in our minds and to divide mankind according to them. ... [H]owever advantageous and revealing such categories may be, no matter whether they spring from purely personal experience or from attempting a scientific establishment of types, at times it is a good and fruitful exercise to take a cross section of experience in another way and discover that each person bears traces of every type within himself and that diverse characters and temperaments can be found as alternating characteristics within a single individual.
>
> –Hermann Hesse, *My Belief: Essays on Life and Art*

Saying the anxiety level has risen in some regions of the United States in recent years is an understatement. Since the Great Recession of 2008–09, for example, residents of the U.S. have experienced declining longevity in some areas of the country. Mitt Romney in 2012 was outperformed by Trump in 2016 in counties with the highest levels of premature mortality.[89]

In addition, economic mobility in the U.S. has pretty much collapsed over the past 50 years. In 1940, fully 90% of Americans could count on a higher standard of living than their parents; now it's about 50%—and just 41% for men.[90]

The ability of low-skilled manufacturing jobs to pull families out of chaos and into the stable middle class may be a thing of the past. The Bridges/Getting Ahead model may well be one of our last best hopes.

Doors appear to be closing in some parts of the country. Local funds may not have long-term viability, and changes in tax law may decrease charitable donations. Due to recent alterations to the federal tax code, blue areas of the U.S. in particular could find it increasingly difficult to raise taxes to address systemic racism and other issues affecting the poor in this country.

The ability to support and work with those lower on the economic ladder may be closely related to how much extra income, or GDP (gross domestic product), our community generates. Areas of the country that rely on local taxes to support human-services activities could find the cupboard getting bare in the future, as the rich, blue counties are growing both bluer and richer, yet due to the aforementioned tax-code changes may find it more difficult to deal with societal issues.[91] This is creating "prisons of geography" where low-income people in rural counties or inner cities find themselves surrounded by hostile attitudes toward job training, and there is little funding for workforce development.[92]

What's going on here? When you look at economic or labor statistics, you might think of them like warm butter on fresh toast: spread evenly. In reality, economic and labor stats are like cold butter you've tried to spread on Wonder bread: kinda lumpy and covering only certain parts. (This visualization can be applied to many aspects of policy, as well as life itself.)

Look at your state. You'll have spots that are doing fine, usually in cities that have attractive physical assets, such as a river or mountain. They often have at least one well-respected university. Educated millennials, also known as the young and creative class, flock to them. Yet for African Americans unemployment rates, almost regardless of educational attainment, is about twice as high as for whites.[93]

Does immigration depress wages in America? It depends on where you sit. If you're less educated and living in Greater Miami, Florida, then a multitude of undereducated workers, such as the nearly 125,000 Cubans who emigrated during the 1980 Mariel boatlift, will depress wages in your field.[94]

How about China? Can we blame it? Yes, but for only some of the decline. Imported items from China are responsible for about 20% of job losses since that market opened up and blossomed.[95]

Research shows that in those communities that faced stronger economic pressures from China, the politics has become more polarized, with moderates losing offices.[96] This research indicates that as time goes on, the middle gets stretched, and the parties nominate more and more of those from the extreme wings. Divisiveness increases.

Some of the policy solutions being proposed may not work as well as their advocates hope. One short-term solution is to increase the number of jobs in advanced industries. Training and education get you about a one-third premium in the advanced-industry sector. Sometimes the problem is cultural; many don't want the training or education, as we've seen in Columbiana County and elsewhere.[97]

Could Bridges/Getting Ahead *bridge* that cultural chasm so the citizens of Columbiana County can adapt before the next wave, that of artificial intelligence and robots, crashes over them? In what ways might Bridges/Getting Ahead help this country deal with its myriad divides?

Chapter 10

Dealing with the Divides

Philip DeVol

*To restore equilibrium in society, moderates tend to
adopt some of the soundest attitudes and principles
of all parties and facilitate agreements between them
in order to calm passions and heal wounds.*

–Aurelian Craiutu, *Faces of Moderation*

Leaders from Bridges communities describe in this chapter how they work across the divides to support people in poverty and to elevate local discourse. In our experience, political and social narratives seldom get in the way when Bridges communities are working to overcome barriers and smooth the pathways for people climbing out of poverty.

When we began talking with legislators in Ohio about Bridges, we did not imagine that funding would be provided to build Healthier Buckeye Councils. One introduction led to the next; one person after another was attracted to Bridges ideas until the ideas clicked together.

As we listened to people from several Bridges sites testify before the Community and Family Advancement Committee, it became clear that legislators from both sides of the aisle liked the ideas. And it also became clear that people in Bridges communities came from both sides of the aisle.

We were curious about how people in Bridges communities were dealing with the political divide in the United States and the many other divides that separate us. It was obvious to us that the Bridges communities were doing well at working across the political divide. But we needed to actually ask the questions and discover if it was an accurate perception and to discover how the other divides were experienced and navigated.

We started with two questions: Are there people from both the left and the right involved in the poverty work you are doing? And, if so, do the narratives of the left and right ever get in the way when you're addressing barriers that Getting Ahead graduates encounter when they are working their plans to climb out of poverty?

In every case the response to those two questions were "yes" to the first question and "no" to the second. We were surprised that some people seemed slightly baffled by the questions. Apparently political ideologies were not on their radar screens. We concluded from the interviews that the political divide was less important because Bridges people were putting their concerns about poverty first, ahead of political ideology.

> [Moderates] seek to protect and foster the balance between diverse social and political forces and interests on which political pluralism, order, and freedom depend in modern society.
>
> –Aurelian Craiutu, *Faces of Moderation*

To describe how people in Bridges communities deal with the divides, we need to address the following topics:

1. The changes in thinking that occur as people address poverty

2. What people in Bridges communities tell us about working across the divides

3. Thinking tools to help overcome the divides

4. The political divide in academia: What researchers say about the Bridges model and the closely related Getting Ahead model

1. The changes in thinking that occur as people address poverty

The changes in thinking that occur as people deal with poverty: Letting go of what we know (our knowledge) to reach a deeper understanding.

Climbing the ladder is a common metaphor for getting out of poverty.

In Bridges we know that to climb the ladder, you have to let go of the rung you are on so that you can reach up to a higher rung. That act is a metaphor for a change in thinking. In your mind you must let go of what you hold to be true, your knowledge, and what feels more comfortable in order to reach the next rung of understanding.

Changing mindsets is the
highest order of change.

Bridges and Getting Ahead challenge an individual's existing truth or knowledge about poverty. For example, Getting Ahead investigators have a wealth of knowledge about how to stretch a dollar, make the most of what little food they have, keep a car running, work the agency systems, and maintain and use relationships in order to survive.

In Getting Ahead groups those relationship-based, problem-solving skills are honored. But they also are challenged. Investigators explore the idea that when individuals begin to work toward goals or achievement, like going to college, they may have to modify or give up some relationships—at least for a period of time.[98]

A Getting Ahead graduate who was in her first year at Youngstown State University in Ohio explained how she and her friends helped each other through hard times. They were always there for each other. And she explained how they would get together on weekends; it would be all day Saturday and all day Sunday.

When she was introduced to the idea of giving up relationships for achievement, it shed new light on those weekends with her friends. It explained why she was tired when she went to class on Monday and why her coursework wasn't getting done.

College, for an adult student, takes time away from children, friends, and family. But if you give less time to your friends and more time to your studies, you won't be as available to help them with their problems. And they may not be there to look after your children while you're in class or studying.

Relationship-based problem solving is all about reciprocity: I do for you, and you do for me. The Getting Ahead graduate's friends weren't exactly happy with her when she said she could be with them only two or three hours on the weekend.

For middle-class students who are following in their parents' footsteps to college, giving up high school friendships (at least for a while) also comes with the achievement territory. For people in a relationship-based world, though, it's even harder. One college student said, "If I have to choose between relationships and achievement, I'm choosing relationships." On hearing this, other students expressed surprise that the young woman would make that statement, given the fact that she was in college, but she clarified, "My older brother graduated from college, and he never came back. I'm not doing that to my parents."

Another Getting Ahead investigator dealt with the relationships dilemma by putting this message on her answering machine: "I'm making some changes in my life, and if I don't call you back, you are one of them."

That's funny but rather harsh. It does illustrate why it's important in Getting Ahead to give the investigators multiple opportunities to discuss this issue. Difficult topics like this are woven into several of the modules and reinforced so investigators can find ways to manage relationships while working on achievement. There are no easy answers, and no two stories are the same.

These Getting Ahead investigators were climbing the ladder, releasing the rung of the old truth and knowledge so they could reach a new understanding of their situation and decide how to handle it.

Turning to the middle class and wealthy, these individuals might need to let go of some of their truths and knowledge too. For the volunteers and staff of organizations that are involved in Bridges, it might be necessary to examine narratives about how they got where they are in life.

It could be that their financial security, solid education, and social standing were not so much earned by them as by their parents—and that their place in society was "paved" by structures that favored their class, race, gender, and/or nationality. Many people have come to realize the truth of the '86 statement by then University of Oklahoma football coach Barry Switzer: "Some people are born on third base and go through life thinking they hit a triple." Letting go of such assumptions can lead to new understandings and new ways of relating to people from other classes.

With regard to political views, the first thing to release is the political ideology of conservative and liberal approaches to poverty and adopt the both/and approach. Poverty is caused by the choices of the poor and it is caused by systemic issues. In Bridges we address the causes of poverty identified from both right and left, but we also identify the causes of poverty posed by where we live and exploitation as described in Chapter 4. Again, the technique is to release the rung of current understanding to reach higher understanding.

Only the closed mind is certain.

—Sam Neill, in the movie *Dean Spanley*

2. What people in Bridges communities tell us about working across the divides

Mike Saccocio, a leader in the Bridges movement from Schenectady, New York, shares these thoughts:

> Sure, we absolutely work across political lines. We never really did until we came across Bridges. I think the key for us was the information on the four causes of poverty. And when you get a group of people studying that together and realizing that there are multiple causes and not just one, it got us out of our silos.
>
> So people who were saying that the behavior of the individual was the cause started realizing, "Wow, we better make sure our table includes people who are passionate about the lack of human and social capital or exploitation, or economic and political systems." We never set out to diversify the planning table, but just by embracing the four causes, it happened organically.
>
> We had people from across the entire social spectrum. People who were from the far left, very progressive, and people from the religious right, and I thought, *Where else in America is that spectrum coming together under one roof, listening to the same thing, applauding together and then being able to break out and have discussions and be united by this Bridges concept?*
>
> It's not easy … They give you tools to cross political lines, and I think there is always an art to that and a commitment to some internal things like being a good listener. If you bring diverse groups together, then somebody has got to be the chief listener in the community.

Here is Christina Fulsom, founder of East Texas Human Needs Network, in Tyler, Texas:

> If you were to look at politics as two extremes, we are helping the individual, and we are here to make sure they're OK. And at the other extreme, they need to help themselves. The truth is both. I think that probably there are some people who think I am Republican, and there are some who think I am a Democrat. That's because there is truth in all of it.
>
> Politics have not been a part of my life perhaps because in my childhood politics were in the forefront of every conversation. There was always an angry feel at home. I decided that I was going to make up my mind about the world without having someone tell me what I should think and believe.

I think that understanding the perceptions and the beliefs of people from different political viewpoints is beneficial—if it allows me to be inviting and engaging rather than alienating.

Stephen MacDonald, coordinator of the Impact Coalition in Toledo, Ohio, says:

After the conference we went out to dinner with some board members. At dinner Al Rivett, the president, told a story in which he revealed that he is the chairman of his county's Republican Party in Florida. I was shocked, not because he was a Republican, but because it had never come up. I'm a dyed-in-the-wool liberal, and we had worked shoulder to shoulder to alleviate the suffering of people in poverty. Political ideology was not even on the radar, and it was because we had this common language and understanding of what the problems are that we could sit around the same table and roll up our sleeves and get to work.

There are always things that you can find that people can unify around, regardless of political ideology. The employer-sponsored, small-dollar-loan initiative in Toledo is an example of one. I have never found anybody who has said that was a bad idea. People understand that gouging vulnerable people with high-interest loans is just not good.

3. Thinking tools to help overcome the divides

It's not easy for any of us to give up deeply held beliefs about the causes of poverty or what to do about it. Peter Senge, who wrote *The Fifth Discipline,* says that we carry mental models in our minds about how the world works on any number of topics. These develop through personal experience, reading, debate, and education.

Bridges books and workshops present a new mental model of poverty that often challenges old thinking patterns. Those who read or hear things that clang against their belief system often have a "fight or flight" response. They either carry on an internal point/counterpoint battle over each assertion or they take flight on their handheld devices. Senge recommends that people consider a third option: simply suspend their own mental models long enough to learn something new.

We hope you, our reader, will suspend your mental models of poverty. Deeply held, entrenched ideas about poverty have brought our communities to where they are now. According to Albert Einstein, "No problem can be solved from the same level of consciousness that created it."

How 'silos' get in the way

Individuals who change their own thinking will almost certainly run into another barrier to change: the silos in which they exist. There are many types of silos: academic, sector, political, corporate, departmental, religion, race, class, and cultural to name a few.

Before naming the problem with silos we should identify their value. They provide structures for handling a complex world, and they provide a sense of order. Academic silos produce people with expertise in many subjects. We need doctors and nurses, engineers, journalists, social workers, and other specialists in their fields of study. People climb professional ladders within their places of work. Our communities depend on individuals in schools, hospitals, manufacturing, transportation, government, etc., to operate efficiently and effectively.

Silos, however, can get in the way. We first met Gillian Tett in Chapter 3. Her book *The Silo Effect: The Peril of Expertise and the Promise of Breaking Down Barriers* describes how we can break down our silos.[99]

She is an economist and editor of the *Financial Times US*. But, as noted previously, she started her academic career as an anthropologist. From that field she identified some of the problems with thinking in silos, saying they lead to competition, failures to communicate, the stifling of innovation, mental blindness, and tunnel vision. Worse, they keep individuals from meeting people who are different from themselves, and they keep institutions and communities from collaborating.

The anthropologist's look at the world is from the bottom up, seeing micro-level patterns, looking with an open mind to see different groups and interactions, looking at the totality and examining the parts of life that people often don't want to talk about or even think about.

She encourages us to take the insider/outsider perspective. This means learning about "the other" and also looking back on our own lives with fresh eyes. Some people get the insider/outsider perspective because they were "tossed across borders, or moved between different worlds." She says, "Above all, we need to leave ourselves open to collisions with people and ideas outside whatever silo we inhabit."

How the Bridges model helps

In Bridges work our intention is to offer people from poverty, middle class, and wealth an insider/outsider look at the other classes and a way to examine our own lives. As a people we have been separated by years of income inequality, housing segregation, and political animosity. Bridges concepts give us a way to learn about each other in a way that replaces judgments with understanding.

Another intention is to encourage people to come together above the organizational silos. One Bridges group has a rule about "leaving your agendas at the door" allowing them to operate above organizational, academic, departmental, and professional silos. This group operates in the same spirit as the music stars of 1985 when "We Are the World" (an aid effort for Africa) was being recorded. Director Quincy Jones told the stars: "Check your ego at the door."

Disruption leads to new relationships, new paradigms

Mike Saccocio says of the work in Schenectady:

> We speak Bridges. You can't have a Bridges movement without bringing different classes together. I would tell you that diversifying the table and bringing in community leaders is very disruptive. Those who wanted to be comfortable and have things manageable came close to pulling the plug on it. I will tell you that we, those who are most comfortable, are the people who were most disruptive in the early days. And now, people in poverty, passionate advocates and what they give us, their life experiences and perspective, is a priceless gift. We ride their coattails and their credibility when breaking new ground.

I am a problem solver.

I will view the frustrations and struggles in my life as opportunities for growth and motivation for change.

I am a problem solver.

—Mantra created by Getting Ahead
investigators in Oklahoma City

Christina Fulsom reports on changing beliefs:

> The one thing that I have seen, and I guess it may have to do with people's political beliefs, is people who have come to me after many months of working together and said that the work we are doing has really changed the way they look at the world. It is often a very painful experience for individuals to recognize that their beliefs have in the past either prevented them from helping others or even hurt others in the process. They didn't do it [purposely] or knowingly. They were ignorant. They feel like now that they know better, they want to do things differently, but there is also … guilt about what they didn't do or did do when they believed differently.

Jim Ott, a school psychologist and member of the Dubuque (Iowa) Circles® Initiative, puts it this way:

> Bridges gives a person a new mindset, and from that mindset, the skills to cross any boundary. It always starts with the recognition that the way that I think is based off of my experience, and other people's experiences aren't right or wrong. Where they land and the way they think makes sense to them based on their experiences. I may not think like you, but it isn't about right or wrong. It's about why those experiences make sense to you and how we can come to a common understanding, how a barrier could be overcome by that. I feel Bridges has better equipped me to address every divide.

The class divide is not the only divide

What about the other divides that Ott speaks of, such as race, gender, sexual orientation, immigration, educational level, and religion? Following the 2016 presidential campaign, identity politics intensified. The battle over political and social issues only made it harder to address poverty effectively. And it's the people who are struggling the most who will suffer the most.

In Bridges we analyze and act on poverty through the economic lens. That allows us to throw the widest net over the problems created by poverty. There are, however, many other issues that divide us, many forms of diversity.

The value of diversity

When forming Getting Ahead groups, we stress the importance of bringing as much diversity into the group as possible. We know that it enriches the learning experience for everyone. The greater the diversity, the better the conversations.

The investigators dig into their own experiences to process the content of Getting Ahead and to put their lives into a broader context. This means including people who have experienced poverty in different ways, such as those in generational poverty and situational poverty: men and women; people of different ages; abled-bodied and disabled; and people from different cultures, religions, sexual orientations, and races.

Poverty is experienced differently by people who come from diverse backgrounds and locations. Poverty on a Native American reservation is different from poverty in a Rust Belt city, suburbia, or Appalachia. When you consider that each individual brings another set of variables—families, friends, work, education, health, beliefs, experiences, and personalities—you can see diversity as a grid or a tapestry. In Bridges and Getting Ahead, stories are told that help the storyteller and the listeners soften judgmental attitudes and make cross-divide friendships possible.

To use Tett's terminology, Bridges and Getting Ahead make insiders/outsiders of us all when we are "tossed together" to work on poverty issues. Building relationships of mutual respect is one of the core constructs of Bridges. This requires that we each analyze our attitudes toward people who are different from ourselves.

Diversity and rankism

To understand diversity we must first acknowledge that there is a dominant group in society, a group whose experience, point of view, and social status have been normalized. In the U.S. that group is white, male, middle-class, urban, and a user of the formal language register. They are heavily represented in government, academia, entertainment, and business. The dominant group, using its own experience and norms as a guide, designs and implements most poverty programs. This goes a long way in explaining why so many poverty programs and policies fail. After all, what experience have they had of poverty?

Having the power to analyze, plan, and build programs without the input of those who are impacted by the program or policy has a name: rankism. Robert W. Fuller in his book *Somebodies and Nobodies: Understanding Rankism* grants that rank is necessary in organizations, most obviously in the military and police force. It also is seen in many organizations with a CEO at the top of the organizational chart.

In human interactions and society, however, rankism takes the form of racism, sexism, ageism, anti-Semitism, classism, ableism, and colonialism. Yes, the "isms." Rankism is an assumption of superiority when one group can make decisions about another and can determine what they do.

Rank tends to be invisible to those who have it

Rankism is normalized in society and in the experience of those who hold rank. Sometimes middle-class people don't realize they have rank over others because all they can see is the rank of the people higher on the ladder than they. So their own rank is largely invisible. The same could be said of those who hold power or those whose skin is white. It's invisible; it doesn't come to mind or have to be thought about in the course of the day.

On the other hand, people who have little power, low rank, or have brown or black skin are very aware of power, rank, and skin color. For example, white people don't have to teach their children how to deal with the police in the same way that black people do. They don't have to explain why the law may not work in their favor. They don't have to practice with their children how to talk to and respond physically so as not to appear threatening.

When someone "pulls rank," it's a form of disrespect, whether it's intentional or not. Pulling rank makes the setting unsafe, shuts down discussion and learning, and makes it very hard to have authentic relationships.

Well-meaning people who work on poverty issues should know how ingrained rankism can be. It's built into middle-class norms of planning, action steps, making lists (and checking them off), efficiency—in short, all things having to do with achievement, the driving force of the middle class.

Identifying rankism means releasing the "truth" or value of being an efficient planner and a "get the job done" person.

The impulse to control, fix, and get things done is baked into the middle-class achievement model. In Bridges we stop the "doing" by identifying the impulse and then changing directions. We share the doing, the decision making, and the control with others. Once again, it's a matter of letting go, releasing the old way, that allows the middle-class person to gain a greater understanding.

Obvious examples of rankism:

- Talking about, for, and at people in poverty, but seldom really listening

- Planning or running an activity, event, program, or policy without fully involving people in poverty

- Forming committees, advisory boards, and governing boards without a strong representation of people in poverty.

> If you have come to help me, you can go home.
> But if you see my struggles as a part of your own
> survival, then perhaps we can work together.
>
> —Lila Watson, Aboriginal woman from Australia

Jim Ott again:

When we approach people we always emphasize that we are apolitical, we are not a political organization. We are an informational organization. In Getting Ahead we investigate how systems work and, instead of viewing politicians from a party point of view, we develop a way of understanding where people are coming from.

At our weekly meetings we eat dinner together. When they first come, it's like, "What in the world have I landed in?" I think the sharing of meals is one of the greatest equalizers. When you sit down at a table to eat together, you don't talk politics right away, you ask what they're doing with the family and what you're doing this weekend or how the Hawkeyes are doing. Sit around a table and get to know each other's kids. I think that changes everything. Whatever it is that comes up is how relationships are formed.

I heard a preacher talking about politics and saying that the best thing to do when you encounter someone who has a different opinion than you is to ask them how they came to think that way. When you ask that question, people will tell you a story. Once you know the person's story, it's really hard not to have some kind of connection, affection, or compassion. Once we know a person's story, it becomes a relationship. That's a micro solution to a macro problem.

> I see Bridges as a way to bring
> civility back into public discourse
> at the community level.
>
> —Jim Ott, school psychologist,
> Getting Ahead facilitator, and
> national Bridges trainer

Continues Ott:

> So if you come to a Bridges event with a strong political agenda, either you will amend the way you're presenting it or you just wouldn't fit in. You wouldn't be able to get people riled up because we just don't process problems that way. I think people want to be accepted. I think people want to be in relationships. I think we all wish we could be in a place where we are emotionally safe [and] intellectually safe, where we can make friends.

> There is nothing better than the healing of broken relationships. And broken relationships can be between a person and their community, or a culture, or race, or class, or people who represent the many nuances of society. When you can be part of healing relationships, which I think is what Bridges is all about, there is nothing better. Nothing better.

Knowing another person's story leads to the growth of bridging social capital between individuals, as well as social cohesion in the community.

Let's step back and review the Bridges and Getting Ahead definition of poverty. We say instability in daily life and low resources can land a person in poverty. Therefore, the way out is to build stability and resources.

One of the resources is social capital, particularly "bridging social capital," as defined by Robert Putnam in *Bowling Alone*. Upon learning this, Getting Ahead investigators immediately begin looking for people they meet in the course of the day: individuals in schools, clinics, courts, and the workplace who might be open to such a relationship. And middle-class people working in those settings who have been trained in Bridges are often open to new relationships with people whom they had previously seen only in the context of "student, client, patient, offender, or new hire."

The reward for working in Bridges initiatives? New relationships across the divides

Social cohesion is a factor in the definition of poverty in Mexico. Social cohesion is the willingness of members of a community to cooperate with each other in order to survive and prosper. It exists when the bond of working together links members of one class with members of another. In the Bridges context, we mean cohesion with the whole community—beyond the Bridges initiative itself.

This sense of unity includes the concept of giving back to the community. In Getting Ahead, investigators do a self-assessment of the 11 resources using a five-point scale:

1. Urgent/crisis

2. Vulnerable, high-risk

3. Stable

4. Safe/secure

5. Thriving/giving back

The key phrase is "giving back." Another word for it is philanthropy: doing for and giving to others. It is more than giving money; it is also caring, nurturing, and enhancing the lives of others. This need to give back, to help others in poverty is often what motivates people to join Getting Ahead. In fact, it's one of the best recruiting tools.

Prior to the Getting Ahead experience, while living in the tyranny of the moment, people weren't as likely to take part in society in clubs, interest groups, politics, and school activities—or to serve on boards or committees. They weren't as likely to work toward common projects to better the neighborhood. And almost never were they being called on to share their ideas and knowledge.

During Getting Ahead, investigators often form intentions and plans to help their families, neighbors, schools, and the community in order to improve the quality of life for others. First, though, they focus on building the resources they choose to work on, and this can take some time. Getting Ahead graduates might spend considerable time building their own financial resources before they can contribute much money themselves. But some of the other resources can be built more readily, so while they are working on making changes in their own lives, they can be helping their families, friends, neighbors, and the Bridges initiative too.

Here is a story about giving back and social coherence from Oklahoma, as shared by Deborah Price, divisional director of Poverty Initiatives, Salvation Army's Arkansas-Oklahoma Division:

> A person went home after the investigation into economic conditions in the community and apparently gave it a whole lot of thought. She came back the next week and said, "I have something I need to share. I went home and I looked around my neighborhood, and I thought, *This neighborhood looks awful.* Then she said, "I looked at my own yard: my grass, the weeds were overgrown, there is junk all around. I have received multiple notices from the city to cut my yard. It's reached that height where I have to cut it." She went on, "I ignored the notices. Then they fined me, and I just ignored that. I didn't pay them because I just haven't cared."

> Then she said, "I realized for the first time, that if a new employer came to our neighborhood and looked around to see if this was a good place to start a new business, they would look at our yards and think, *If those people can't take care of their yards, what kind of employees would they be?"* She said, "I realized that I was part of the problem, and I better mow my yard." She concluded by saying, "I mowed this week. And then I went to all of my neighbors and told them why they needed to mow theirs if they wanted to get a job, if they wanted new employers to come into the neighborhood. They needed to take responsibility for their yards because they were part of the problem."

Here are some typical ways that Getting Ahead grads have contributed to their communities:

1. Volunteer their time to attend Bridges trainings to share their stories and insights
2. Become certified Getting Ahead facilitators
3. Become certified Bridges trainers
4. Serve on steering committees of Bridges collaboratives
5. Serve on committees and boards in the community
6. Testify at public hearings
7. Speak at conferences
8. Join incarceration reentry programs, PTAs/PTOs, food banks, etc.

9. Co-create post-Getting Ahead programs (often called Staying Ahead programs) on financial literary, transportation, and work readiness

10. Create a college or university Bridges student union

11. Serve in focus groups

12. Volunteer at schools

4. The political divide in academia: What researchers say about the Bridges model and the closely related Getting Ahead model

The divides that this book addresses exist not just in the political realm, but in most aspects of life, including academia. Some academics have criticized Ruby Payne's first book, *A Framework for Understanding Poverty,* but they haven't paid much attention to *Bridges Out of Poverty, Getting Ahead in a Just-Gettin'- By World,* and the many other publications that contain some of Payne's original work.

Michael Jindra and Ines W. Jindra, research scholars at the University of Notre Dame, South Bend, Indiana, are the first to include Bridges and Getting Ahead in an article on the "divide" between relational work of nonprofits and proponents of structural approach: "Poverty and the Controversial Work of Nonprofits."

The abstract reads:

There has been a significant shift among antipoverty nonprofits toward what we call "relational work" which involves working with clients over time on life changes. Some scholars discuss this, often in negative terms, as part of a broader neoliberal trend. We argue that relational work is an important and unavoidable part of ongoing efforts against poverty and homelessness. We also discuss the broader theoretical context that make scholars suspicious of this kind of antipoverty work, and argue for a multifaceted approach to poverty that includes attention to relational work and the agency of clients.[100]

To reduce poverty, change people or social structures— or both?

The Jindras ask the question, "To reduce poverty, should one change people or change social structures?" They use the term "relational" to describe the work that is done with people to make life changes over time, whereas "structural" work is to make policy changes to reduce poverty and inequality.

Relational work is largely done by nonprofits like the Atlanta Housing Authority, Big Brothers/Big Sisters, Bridges Out of Poverty, Catholic Charities, Habitat for Humanity, and others. Their case management work consists largely of one-to-one counseling, mentoring and coaching, and group sessions. They help people meet immediate needs, create action plans, build relationships, address problem areas, and offer skills training.

The Jindras add that relational work is to include motivational and empowerment-oriented strategies, reflexivity, asset building, and helping clients become active agents with a sense of control over their lives. The clients develop interdependent relations with staff and follow participants as they begin navigating the world of work, school, and the middle class.

The researchers have found that critics, largely from academia, fear that the work of nonprofits may "gut the universal governmental safety net and offer a patchwork of services and program." The critics prefer to put more responsibility on low-income people and rely on the markets to lift people out of poverty. The critics also are concerned about "unjustly blaming the poor for their predicaments and not political/economic structures."

The Jindras see a shift in relational work toward reflexive approaches. They mention two providers, Bridges and Grace Ministries, that call for self-reflection or analysis.

Grace Ministries, which serves the homeless, interprets mistakes and conflicts in Christian terms. The goal is to seek restoration and guidance through self-evaluations and devotions. This leads to more stable lives, more responsive family members, and a way out of poverty.

Bridges Out of Poverty, operated in a secular context, "... uses reflexivity based on cognitive theory to help people self-organize and become proactive."

The Jindras recommend a more complete view of poverty to take in factors such as structural, cultural, and individual agency (the capacity to exert power). In their conclusion they note that "... nonprofits serve as perhaps the strongest link between the lives as the poor and the wider society they are often alienated from, and their work is crucial in allowing people to have more options."

Finally, they state:

> Ideally, organizations will include some aspect of all these approaches, such as Bridges Out of Poverty, with its analysis of community barriers, exploitation and other structural forces, its focus on the

tools needed to overcome social and cultural class barriers, and its encouragement of reflexivity that encourages individuals to consider their lives. Undergirding this is often a moral ethos that commands help for those who are struggling.[101]

The Jindras' article is available online at the web address listed in the Bibliography.

In this chapter we have laid out how Bridges and Getting Ahead can work—and help with class and political divisions: the "divides." Looking back at our nation's history, what has been tried that missed the mark or even made things worse? Looking forward, what reforms and policy changes can we consider for the healing of the country?

Ali Plum, a Getting Ahead graduate from Oklahoma City, describes in two poems what the Jindra study "Poverty and the Controversial Work of Nonprofits" describes in scholarly language. The poems are about how the Getting Ahead experience helped Plum "consider her life" and the barriers she and others face. The poems can be found in Appendix D.

Chapter 11

Does History Repeat or Rhyme?
Could We Learn Something?

Gene Krebs

It was never assumed in the United States, that the citizen of a free country has a right to do whatever he pleases; on the contrary, more social obligations were there imposed upon him than anywhere else.

–Alexis de Tocqueville, *Democracy in America*

America is undergoing profound changes—but not for the first time. How are some of these changes undermining our civic capacity? In this chapter we examine structural reforms that have failed, along with some that might work and why. Finally, we look at how elected officials create an ecosystem where their voters can thrive.

The 1896 presidential election was an inflection point in U.S. history, as before that time farmers and associated small-town groups dominated the country's electoral process. Mark Twain is believed to have said that history seldom repeats but often rhymes, with similar themes reappearing in later eras. There may be lessons from 1896 that could help you deduce what the future holds for your community.

The rise of William Jennings Bryan in 1896, along with his call for an inflationary monetary policy, was of benefit to the farmer classes, who often were in debt and could then pay off those debts with devalued coinage. The big-city manufacturing class and their workers, however, were much more comfortable with a stable currency as represented by gold. The battle lines were drawn.

The election of 1896 was the last hurrah of the farmer and rural businessman: Their man Bryan was beaten by the gold bug McKinley. If elected, Bryan would have been a disjunctive president, the last gasp of the previous electoral coalition, as were Pierce, the Adamses, Hoover, and Carter.

What we are seeing now in the country might be the last stirrings of the industrial class, including calls for high-paying, unskilled jobs in Columbiana County as they are confronted with the creative class, where knowledge rules—and where diversity of thought, visage, and cultural attitudes is highly valued.

The industrial portion of the U.S. won't disappear, just as the farming practices haven't disappeared since the founding of the country, but the nation will have to make room for the next wave of change. Now only about 2% of the population actively farms.[102] What if someday only 2% of the population is engaged in manufacturing?

The change will not be pretty. Voters who have traditionally embraced manufacturing as employment and a lifestyle feel disconnected from the ruling elite, who are part of the creative class by education and inclination. This is leading to a decline in our civic capacity, our ability to govern ourselves, by ourselves, and we would be advised not to tempt the elites to step in, armed with white papers.

Why the decline in civic capacity?

> All things considered, and allowance made of the various degrees of morality and enlightenment, we shall generally find in small nations more persons in easy circumstances, more contentment and tranquility, than in large ones.
>
> —Alexis de Tocqueville, *Democracy in America*

The ruling elite want to help the poor, even though most of them know no poor, talk to no poor, were not raised with the poor, and helicopter home after visiting the poor.

This is separating us from understanding our civic capacity and where it is strong or weak—and why.

We have all enjoyed water from a well we did not dig. We have all been educated in a school we did not build. We have sat in a house of worship we did not help create. We have all benefited from the civic capacity of those who went before us, but now our society seems to be living only for the moment and not for the long term. It seems to have lost its future story; it has become decadent.

The roads and bridges are crumbling, and Flint, Michigan, had lead in the water. In some cities gun violence is rampant, with attendant murders. Opioids consume vast swaths. How could this happen? How can we have a government and society that are seemingly so indifferent and incapable of solving big problems? According to Gallup polling, the 14 institutions that tie together our society are now trusted by only 32% of U.S. residents. If we remove the military as an institution from that poll, the numbers plunge to the "friends and relatives" level.[103]

What's going on? Why the big perceived disconnect between voters and their elected leaders? Why do the ruling elite read Richard Florida while everyone else watches "Access Hollywood," but the two groups almost never meet for worship, pizza, coffee, Chardonnay, or bourbon to discuss these issues? Again, as noted in the chapter about levers and fulcrums, it's partly about size.

There are 435 congressional seats in the U.S. House of Representatives. The population that each elected official represents ranges from a half million to a million resident citizens, with 700,000 being a good enough average.[104]

As mentioned earlier, only 2% of the population voted in the early 1800s. Our nation was designed with a much different form of government than the one we have today, a form of government that held power for 40 years until the 1830s: small, wealthy, intimate, and literate, plus very white and male, and in many Southern states restricted to those who attended the "right" church. Ninety-eight percent of the population just lived here and had limited participation. The "old days" were not that good; it's indeed ironic that 98% of the population had taxation but no representation.

What that means is that for the first 40 years of the republic, knocking on doors and attending events and parades could get you exposed to a significant percentage of voters. Just showing up at church could suffice. Now, at 700,000 citizens to a congressional seat, it's almost impossible to reach out to all those people in a personal manner.[105]

This problem of size is devastating to democracy. As Jason Brennan writes about the impact this has on voting:

> After all, the chances that any individual vote will decide the election is vanishingly small. As a result, individual voters tend to vote expressively, to show their commitment to their worldview and team. Voting is more like doing the wave at a sports game than it is like choosing policy.[106]

Because our states and legislative districts are so large, our one vote has little impact. Before we have done the math, our brains do a first-order approximation and come to the conclusion that doing serious research on candidates is a serious waste of time. So most of us vote like we order coffee: on a whim.

Lest we judge our fellow citizens too harshly, remember what astronomer Carl Sagan once said: "Let us temper our criticism with kindness. None of us comes fully equipped."

Can we construct solutions that can overcome this problem? Yes, but with caution, as so many reforms espoused in the popular media either fall short or are in fact counterproductive.

The solution to pollution is dilution

I may here be met by an objection derived from the electioneering intrigues, the meanness of the candidates, and the calumnies of their opponents. These are occasions of enmity which occur the oftener, the more frequent elections become.

–Alexis de Tocqueville, *Democracy in America*

What are the problems that seem to be part and parcel of American politics? What are the reforms being proposed, and why won't so many of them work in the manner devised? Which small number may work? Why are we left with the Bridges model as a core solution?

How do you, as an ordinary citizen, get your candidate to stop dialing for dollars and pay attention to your issues … and to you? We have talked about relationships, but now we need to discuss the fiscal aspect of all this.

You can try to dilute the impact of big money with lots of small donations. "Glamour" races, those for president of the United States, some U.S. Senate races, and maybe some governorships, can attract donations from the ordinary citizen, often online. Bernie Sanders redefined how to fund campaigns, outraising any other candidate in the 2016 primary election cycle, but that is a glamour race. He raised $222 million, of which $132 million came from small donors.[107]

Some readers may posit that *Citizens United v. Federal Election Commission,* which ruled that free speech applies to corporations and unions, is a cause of many problems. That, however, ignores the fact that big money was disruptive long before *Citizens United.* It has been a major factor since 1896, and overturning *Citizens United* won't usher in rainbow-colored unicorns. On the other hand, 80% of Americans don't think corporations are people and therefore don't deserve free-speech protections. They think the U.S. Supreme Court in its *Citizens United* ruling went too far. So changes are needed.[108]

Some critics maintain that direct funding of campaigns from public coffers is the answer. In response, Brian Balfour of the Civitas Institute says "there's a moral argument against compelling people to pay for the speech of others, oftentimes candidates with whom they disagree."[109]

How do we rebalance? Once again, we will look to Ohio. Partly as a response to graft and pay-to-play issues in the 1990s, Ohio adopted a $50-per-person tax credit for a donation going to legislative or statewide candidates ($100 for a married couple filing jointly). You just check a box on your tax return and take the credit if you owe taxes in excess of $50 that year, which in Ohio means just about everyone who has a job.[110] Every year this pumps about $4 million into the political system, diluting the pollution of big money, although in a small manner. It could generate more revenue, but it's simply not promoted.[111] In addition to receiving better promotion, this tax credit should be raised to $500. There are many races that are not "sexy" enough to attract a lot of donations from the general public, and a bigger tax credit would help.

Next we look at term limits.

One good term deserves another

> In aristocratic governments, public men may frequently do harm without intending it, and in democratic states, they bring about good results which they never thought of.
>
> —Alexis de Tocqueville, *Democracy in America*

Bridges/Getting Ahead advocates need to know about term limits and why they need not be distracted into following that path.

In this book we already have discussed the importance of relationships. Voters, however, also have expressed concern about the inability to form those relationships with their elected officials, as they usually don't feel they have an equal chance to develop such a relationship due to the size of the district or city. Their favorite countermove is instituting term limits for legislatures and city councils and mayors across the country.

When people believe that their elected officials are out of touch, one of the ways they punish them—if gerrymandering (this will be addressed momentarily) and economic demographic segregation preclude this action—is to impose term limits. In my view, term limits result in making elected officials weaker, turning them into "lame ducks" before their time. There's a common saying of unknown authorship: "We already have term limits; they're called elections."[112]

Since the 22nd amendment to the U.S. Constitution was passed in 1947, the president of the United States can serve no more than two terms: eight years. A case can be made for other term limits as well. Incumbents in the U.S. Congress are notoriously difficult to unseat—98% in the House and 93% in the Senate[113]— but setting term limits is a superficial solution at best and a major mistake at worst. I've seen terms limits give tremendous power to unelected lobbyists and bureaucrats.

Now to the aforementioned gerrymander. Have you ever eaten one? Downright tasty.

Roasted gerrymanders with onions

> They packed all the Democrats into districts, very Democratic districts. What that's done is made our party urban, more liberal, and so those people are doing what their constituents want. But that's not what *my* constituents want. I don't know how you change that. There's hardly anybody left like me in the Democratic Party in Congress. These districts have been so gerrymandered that, in most of them, a Democrat can't win. Somebody like me trying to start off today, he'd never get endorsed. Because I'm too conservative.
>
> —Collin Peterson, quoted in Ingraham, "Why Rural Voters Don't Vote Democratic Anymore"

Bridges/Getting Ahead advocates need to know about gerrymandering. It's not that the Bridges approach can fix gerrymandering; it's rather that the solutions and processes inherent in Bridges/Getting Ahead can work past gerrymandering and even in spite of it.

Let's pause and consider the word *gerrymander* itself. It's derived from the name of New England politician Elbridge Gerry, who is blamed for designing the first tortuous district boundaries to create an advantage for one party over another. Some thought his "creative districting" resembled the approximate shape of the lowly salamander.

Gerrymandering reform can make seats competitive again. Or it can ensure close to equal numbers of Republicans and Democrats are elected, but it can't do that all at once. The parties do not want all the seats competitive, as it makes their jobs harder. They want as many of the candidates of their party as possible to run in seats that are "safe."

As Democrats now tend to concentrate in larger cities, to a certain extent they gerrymander themselves. Think of it this way: If most of the Democrats in your state move to the big city, but the Republicans stay out in the rural areas, the Republicans will dominate the rural seats comfortably and win a number of suburban districts in your state.[114]

Here is the best idea so far: Some folks in Wisconsin are putting forward something called the "efficiency gap" that devises districts so that the fewest number of voters have their votes "wasted." If the winning margin is too large, then the extra winning votes were not needed (i.e., they were wasted), and that district might be guilty of gerrymandering. The districts designed using efficiency would be competitive in most years.[115]

The big advantage of this approach is that it allows for an algorithm to replace the human, subjective approach. In short, it's about the data.[116]

You need swing seats in order to get officials to focus on issues of interest to the greatest number of citizens and not just narrow interest groups. Your issues are of broad interest.

Where does the blame reside for so many of our districts being lopsided and uncompetitive? The fault lies all around us in our myriad land-use decisions; even sprawl is partly to blame.

Democracy loosens social ties but tightens natural ones; it brings kindred more closely together, whilst it throws citizens more apart.

–Alexis de Tocqueville, *Democracy in America*

Most communities built after the development of the limited-access highway are simply too homogenous to easily provide a mix of races, cultures, and outlooks in a legislative district. Under the efficiency plan, the best you might hope for is a third to a half being competitive, which would be a vast improvement.

Why they call it a horse race

Combating this winner-take-all mentality that permeates
many societies would help to reduce the stakes of
conflictand weaken the intensity and polarization
that afflicts contemporary politics. We need to
figure out ways to de-escalate conflict and widen
the number of winners. When people perceive
conflict as a zero-sum game, it encourages
extremism and immoderation.

–Darrell West, *Megachange*

Political races are often compared to horse races. How do you make sure your jockey, the politician who values Bridges/Getting Ahead, is on a fast horse? Change the primary system.

The nonpartisan Cook Political Report rated just 37 of 435 U.S. House seats as competitive in 2016, less than 9%. As a result, primary elections have become tantamount to general elections in the vast majority of seats. In 2014 only 14.6% of eligible voters participated in congressional primaries. That means a tiny fraction of the most hardened partisan voters essentially elect 91% of the members of Congress. And these low-turnout primaries are often easy prey for ideological interest groups.[117]

When narrow primary bases dominate
elections, everyone loses. And politicians
as a whole get blamed.

–David Wasserman, "The Political Process Isn't
Rigged—It Has Much Bigger Problems"

There's another method of electing public officials called the ranked-choice system. Voters rank all the candidates, first, second, third, etc., on down the ballot. With each tally, the lowest vote gatherer is dropped and the next-place votes are assigned. Sometimes known as instant-runoff voting, it already has been adopted in about a dozen cities, including Minneapolis and San Francisco.[118] Both Ireland and Australia have been using it for decades with few problems.[119]

A two-part question: Is it best to require ranked-choice voting in party primaries— or have one massive ballot in the general election? For the purpose of creating a climate where the top issues in a campaign are of general interest, perhaps general elections are the place to have such a process, and we'd be better off banning the current practice of publicly financed party primaries. Parties could still endorse candidates or conduct conventions, but the population as a whole would now decide.

Because Portland, Maine, has ranked primaries, the state of Maine went to the ballot in 2016 to examine whether or not to adopt them statewide. Voter turnout in Portland is up 40% over previous years, with greater civility overall and more unanimity for the winning candidate.[120] Voters approved the change to ranked choice in both state and federal elections.[121]

The change was then ruled unconstitutional by the Supreme Court of Maine, but since the voters approved it, only a foolish legislator would not try to amend Maine's constitution to allow it to work (even though the ruling political elites are scared of the change).[122] The fact that the ruling political elite of Maine are so opposed to ranked-choice voting may be its best endorsement.

The question for the reader to ponder is if a ranked-choice voting system could work to elect officials at the local and state level, officials who listen to all classes. And could we combine this with a Bridges/Getting Ahead structure? It might work to develop a coalition across many communities and classes. Such a candidate in the ranked-choice voting system would need to have broad appeal. Unfortunately, many politicians have a desire only for people like them to live in their voting districts. If gerrymandering is about choosing voters off the shelf, then the Curley Effect is about creating an ecosystem that encourages only one type of voter to prosper and pushes the others out of town.

Neither Larry, Curly, nor Moe: A different stooge

Larry: *"All for one!"*

Moe: *"One for all!"*

Curly: *"Every man for himself!"*

–The Three Stooges, in the
movie *Restless Knights*

The Curley Effect, named not for the middle Stooge but for a former mayor of Boston, is another way elected officials choose their citizens. Bridges/Getting Ahead advocates need to know about this because some officials, especially mayors and county officials, may subconsciously oppose work on poverty. Such work could change the nature of their communities, which they have carefully nurtured.

Chapter 12

The '85, 50, and 1' Rule:
How to Pass Your Legislation

Gene Krebs

In great centralized nations, the legislator is obligated to give a character of uniformity to laws, which does not always suit the diversity of customs and of districts ... since the legislation cannot adapt itself to the exigencies and the customs of the population, which is a great cause of trouble and misery.

–Alexis de Tocqueville, *Democracy in America*

This chapter describes how to pass the best political solutions—and how they're different from the best policy solutions. We offer specific examples of policies that generated both discord and acquiescence. You'll learn some of the best outreach strategies to officials. We examine pitfalls of working with the government, see where things often fail, and offer modest insights as to why.

The most successful legislation from the *political* standpoint (not the policy standpoint) are those where 85% of the majority party votes yes for the bill; 50% of the minority party votes yes; and one mayor, governor, or president signs it into law. Hence the "85, 50, and 1" rule. Bills that have 85% of the majority party's support, 50% of the minority party's support, and that are signed into law are rarely "undone" by subsequent legislation, at least not for decades.[124]

Four concrete examples at the federal level come to mind, where two obeyed the rule and two didn't: the Civil Rights Act of 1964 and the Personal Responsibility and Work Opportunity Reconciliation Act (welfare reform) of 1996 on the one hand, and the Affordable Care Act of 2010 (better known as Obamacare) and the GOP corporate tax cut of 2017 on the other.

One of the main reasons there was—and continues to be—so little opposition to the 1964 Civil Rights Act is that by negotiating compromises with the Democrats in Congress, GOP Congressman William Moore McCulloch created a piece of legislation that, while perhaps not the *policy ideal* of many, was a political ideal that has withstood the tempests.[125]

Despite numerous potshots taken at it by both right and left since its passage, the welfare reforms of 1996 have survived for more than two decades. All the Republicans in Congress and half the Democrats supported that legislation, and the president signed it into law. It was another example of durable legislation that follows the 85, 50, and 1 rule.[126]

In contrast, the Affordable Care Act (ACA) did not follow the 85, 50, and 1 rule and has been seen as a political disaster by those steeped in the craft. Even getting just a few votes from the Republicans would have solved many problems.[127] Because the Democrats rammed it through with no GOP votes, the ACA became the piñata of 2010–16 American politics, with just about every Republican politician trying to bash it with a stick.

A case could be made that the GOP-led corporate tax cut in December 2017 was Obamacare in reverse. History, however, still needs more time to render its verdict regarding this violation of the 85, 50, and 1 rule.

Policy advocates need always to bring along some members of the minority party. If your majority caucus sponsor tells you that not a single member of the minority caucus will vote for your legislation, panic. Then improvise like crazy, and remember what filmmaker Ingmar Bergman said: "Only someone who is well-prepared has the opportunity to improvise."[128] Find a minority party member with whom you have a good relationship, and find out why they won't support the bill.

Winning over the '1'

So far we have concentrated on the 85 and the 50, but not the 1. How do you convince the mayor or governor to adopt your proposal? This can be the most difficult part.

At the state level, the legislator who is your advocate should keep the governor's staff apprised of the issue. Do not request to meet with the governor; doing so devalues the governor's staff you are working with. Meeting with the director of the state agency or the head of that policy division in the governor's staff is sufficient and helpful, as you can often explain how this proposal will work "on the ground" with a kind of detail the member of the legislature may not have time for. Your legislator advocate is very helpful here in arranging meetings.

You can often figure out who are the key administration people by attending a hearing. After they're done testifying, introduce yourself. Praise their testimony.

Give them a copy of your favorite Bridges/Getting Ahead book. (Maybe this one?) Ask them if you can chat further in two weeks.

What can be difficult is when the governor proposes something that is Kryptonite to your cause. If a top-down solution to poverty is presented, offer the governor's office not an either/or but a both/and scenario. Both of your solutions are implemented and tracked using the best data-collection methods.

Be confident in Bridges/Getting Ahead. Always ask for strong evaluations of your programs. If the state is running out of money due to a downturn and your programs have a good return on investment for the government, then you have more protection.

Also, remember that the higher up you go on the political food chain, the more data are valued—and less so the moving stories. A meeting with a director of a state agency is a good time to pull out a white paper showing the positive aspects of the policy from a state that has already adopted it. Point to the bar chart in the white paper, then walk the agency head through how this proposal will make their job easier.

But if the agency director and governor are of opposite parties than the legislator carrying your legislation, make sure you attend the meeting with a member of your staff (or maybe a member of your board) who is of the same party as the governor and has a known political pedigree. Being politically inclusive is not just high-minded utopianism; it gives you better results than machine politics.

There's a tendency for a governor's or mayor's staff to view any proposal that didn't come from them as suspect, unless the staff believes you to be a true believer who went to kindergarten with the leader. Sometimes, if it's a really good idea, the governor or mayor will steal it from you, rebrand it, and make it their own. Let it happen. In policy advocacy, humility gets you farther than hubris. The upright nail gets hammered down.

To entice legislators, governors, mayors, and city and county officials to endorse your platform, offer a candidate forum early in the campaign. Invite candidates to come in one at a time to speak to your conference. The candidates will need to engage in a crash course on your policy so they can converse intelligently on your issues. So you win.

Don't sponsor a debate. They're really tough to pull off, and the candidates may not appear.

Another strategy is to ask local elected officials to tour your facility. Many local and legislative bodies prepare certificates with lots of cool-looking gold leaf;

ask them to present such a commendation to your Getting Ahead graduates at a Getting Ahead graduation ceremony. I suspect that such external validation also may prove beneficial to word of mouth regarding your program.

Give them data and talking points. Introduce them to the Getting Ahead investigators you have worked with. Be sure to broadcast it on social media. If they run for the state legislature or higher office, they already know you and your good work.

You may find yourself saying, "The 85, 50, and 1 rule is all well and good, but if one party controls my state or city and likely will forever, why should I seek the minority caucus's input or support?"

The answer is that there is extensive groupthink in politics, and you should use it, not be used by it. There are massive wave elections in politics now that can sweep aside long-held majorities and upend conventional wisdom.[129] How do you avoid such groupthink?

You too can be nonpartisan

> It is true that, when the majority of a democratic people change their opinions, they may suddenly and arbitrarily effect strange revolutions in men's minds; but their opinions do not change without much difficulty, and it is almost as difficult to show that they have changed.
>
> –Alexis de Tocqueville, *Democracy in America*

When confronted by groupthink, Phil and I both tend to break out in hives, even though we have very different views of how the world works—and ideally can work in a bipartisan or nonpartisan manner.

Is there a difference between bipartisan and nonpartisan? Increasingly, I like to think in nonpartisan terms—yes, recognizing partisan differences, but also seeing a bigger picture that affects us all.

I'm a Republican, and Phil is a Democrat; even this book is a nonpartisan effort.

So ... what is nonpartisan about it? While everyone comes from different "tribes" with different outlooks, in practical terms for modern life human beings have created institutional processes that allow us to interact in a manner that best serves the whole population. The institutional processes operate by reducing the importance of our "tribalness."

Eating meals and chatting with people who are not like you in politics develops an appreciation of diversity. Working in an office with those who aren't like you helps you understand that these are also real people with strengths and weaknesses, along with hopes and dreams.

> People teach their dogs to sit; it's a trick. I've been sitting my whole life, and a dog has never looked at me as though he thought I was tricky.
>
> —Mitch Hedberg, on the CD
> *Strategic Grill Locations*

Here's a simple (human!) trick you can use to start thinking more like a nonpartisan. Stop referring to the party you personally support as "we," as in "we Republicans" or "we Democrats" (or "we Libertarians" or "we Greens," etc.). Instead refer to your own party as "the Republicans" or "the Democrats." Remove your mental ownership. After a few months you will find this simple brain trick has an effect on how you view and process; it gives you a more objective veneer of remoteness from the party.

On a related note, if an advocate visits an elected official's office and has worked on a campaign against that elected official in a previous election, there could be a problem. The official can smell the guilt. If you enter the advocacy world, you may want to reduce your public activity in campaigns in your own state or community. But watch out for wave elections, and be careful when working with the government on poverty issues. Yes, it can be a bear.

Dancing with a bear

> You can't always get what you want
> But if you try sometimes
> You might find you get what you need!
>
> —The Rolling Stones, on
> the album *Let It Bleed*

These complex interactions with the government can be hard to choreograph—and they're fraught with dangers and unintended consequences. It's like dancing with a bear. These ursine government partners usually are much bigger and stronger than you, and they have sharp teeth and claws. Plus they can do things you can't because they control policy and have funding sources through taxes. In short, they have leverage.

The next few pages will illustrate how well-meaning people have fallen flat on their faces in attempts to move public policy and polity. How difficult is it to get things right? Very. Ideas like micro-lending, which sounded good enough to entice U2's Bono to support it, have little impact on reducing poverty.[130]

And here's what looked like a good public-policy idea gone seriously bad: Marine reefs are good. Used tires are bad. Let's cable used tires together and dump them into the ocean to increase marine life and diversity by creating artificial reefs. What could go wrong?

The cables rusted away. The tires broke free. Now they act like scrubbers, moving across the ocean floor with the action of the waves, destroying any reefs they come in contact with and stubbornly refusing to biodegrade.[131]

Zoning laws, originally intended to help, sometimes become a problem. While initially created to keep a rendering plant from setting up shop in the middle of a city, zoning has morphed over the years into exclusionary boundaries, the end of public transit, and the death of jobs for many low-income workers.[132] A number of our cities as they're now planned contribute to racial and class divisions due to various zoning laws and exclusions.[133]

Zoning is a good example of top-down culture in public policy. Rather than an organic development, like you see in quaint historical districts where originally all the classes lived near each other and rubbed elbows, a master planner sits in an office and dictates where restaurants can be located, where to put houses, how many residences can occupy each acre, and how to keep affordable housing "not in my backyard" but in the next city or town. Many of these planned areas have little charm; top-down designs rarely work in planning or in poverty reduction.

Why does drafting a law follow quantum mechanics?

Laws to encourage good behavior can have unexpected, even weird, consequences. Five examples:

- Laws that require bicycle safety helmets for children seem like a good idea. Except they lead to slightly lower usage of the bike, with attendant higher rates of obesity, which is enough to cancel out the reduction in brain injury in looking at general health indexes.[134]
- If you give teenage girls realistic robotic babies to take care of, you should see fewer teenage pregnancies since the girls now understand the stress and hassle that babies add to your life, right? Wrong. This program actually has increased teen pregnancies. It seems the girls like the attention having a baby brings to a person.[135]

Chapter 13
'Extending Your Ear to Listen': Tips from Staff
Gene Krebs

*Politics is a matter of taking
the long view and enduring.*

– Nicholas Dames,
"The Stubborn Optimist"

Here we offer practical tips on talking to staff of elected officials, as well as giving testimony in hearings. We also provide you with numerical means to gauge the effectiveness of your efforts with government staff and officials.

The coolest "kids" you'll encounter when doing advocacy are the staffers of the elected officials. Why call them kids? Because in many cases this is their first job out of college. They see the world as full of possibilities, and I have shoes older than some of them. If you find yourself wondering how a 12-year-old got this job, just remember: Thirty years ago, someone thought the same thing about you.

The gatekeepers

Staffers are the gatekeepers of the elected officials' time. They arrange their schedules and keep them busy, but not too busy. If you call and act as if you're a big shot when requesting a meeting, don't expect to meet for a while. Be pleasant. Make sure the elected official's staffer knows why you want to meet. Don't say it's private or that it's for the official's ears only. That could sound like a shady deal and, despite what you see in made-for-TV movies, most politicians are trustworthy. Their staff, reflecting the culture at the top, will recoil from you if you present the prospect of shady dealings, even by mistake.

Tell the staffer why you want to meet, and give a timeline of when you need to meet. Explain why the meeting needs to happen before that date, and explain who will be coming to the meeting with you. Your follow-up e-mail should be comprehensive, including the names and titles of the other attendees.

Follow up with occasional phone calls, but don't call every day. Also, don't call on days when you know the elected official has legislative sessions or city council meetings, as the staff will be busy on those days getting ready and juggling schedules.

When you call or leave voicemail, speak slowly and spell your name, and repeat your contact information twice. This increases your chances of getting a call back. In my office we used to say, "Garble in, garbage out."

Avoid scripted calls. They work only if thousands call. And call. But sometimes they just annoy the elected official, who then declares there is no way that bill will pass as no other work could get done in the office. This actually happened to me once in the Ohio Legislature.

Be polite when you call; demanding to speak to the official now or on your terms never goes over well. Don't threaten that in the next election the official will go down in flames if the meeting isn't held on your terms and timeline. Give the staffer as much flexibility as possible in setting the meeting time. If meeting outside the office, meet at a place convenient for the elected official. Doing so will give you more face time, which is what you're after. As mentioned elsewhere, breakfast places are good, easily found, and inexpensive.

When stopping by the elected official's office, do you bring cookies or other forms of food bribery for the staff? No. However, private thank-you notes do work after a meeting. If the elected official publicly pushes your issue, a thank you on social media or a letter to the editor of the local paper is golden. Expressing appreciation to staff helps also.

Be nice to all staffers, no matter how lowly. In and around city buildings, county courthouses, and statehouses all across the country, you will encounter menial staffers who, in a decade or two, will become elected officials in their own right, sometimes at the federal level. This is how Speaker of the House Paul Ryan got his start.

Every now and then you'll be lucky enough to come across a staffer who breaks the mold, who really *gets* Bridges/Getting Ahead, and who proselytizes it all over that level of government. The authors were very fortunate to have Brie Lusheck, an aide to Ohio GOP Representative Tim Derickson, as a supporter of Bridges/Getting Ahead. According to Lusheck, staffers connect the dots for the boss, highlighting the important parts. Think of staff as being in the middle of the spider's web that is their level of government: They feel every tug and small vibration.

If a staff person expresses genuine curiosity, then they're interested in policy, and you are their new best friend. If they start to put your issue in context with other issues, they're policy wonks. As Lusheck noted when we interviewed her for this book: "Everyone can really learn from each other and move people out of poverty by extending a hand, but even more importantly by extending your ear to listen, you can change everything."

We also were fortunate to talk with Dominic Paretti for this book. Paretti is a longtime Democratic legislative staffer and a member of the Columbus City Schools Board of Education, has staff himself, and as such gives this insight: "Staff filters. Being an elected official is somewhat like drinking out of a firehose, and staff is supposed to be like a check valve to moderate the stream."

The emerging issue of Bridges/Getting Ahead getting support from the government is similar to charter schools, which are also public/private partnerships. To avoid the problems and pitfalls charter schools face in many states, Lusheck notes that Bridges/Getting Ahead advocates need to keep the power diffuse and the money flows transparent.

You will need to monitor your initiative constantly, and if it gets a bit out of line (and could cause a headline later), jump in and fix it immediately.

Another aspect of working in a public/private partnership is giving testimony. Not to worry! No one is on trial. But from time to time you may be called upon to testify before elected officials in a committee setting. Here are some thoughts about that …

Testified and justified

When your legislative hero asks you to testify before a legislative committee, take a deep breath, and do it with a smile on your face. In your testimony, tell them who you are and the name of your organization in the first paragraph. Then tell them what you will say. Then say what you have to say. Then tell them what you said.

But, please, no long, shaggy-dog stories. Don't brag about how great your program is; they hear this all the time. Use citations and footnotes. The best-case scenario is that legislators will lift whole paragraphs of your testimony and use them in speeches to local groups and maybe even in a floor speech on the bill in question. If you include citations, legislators will use the data because if they're challenged on a given point, they can use the citation as an affirmative defense.

Use a mix of data and sources, and include one good story. Graphs and charts are good, as is being polite. Do not argue with a legislator or city councilperson. If they're nasty and attack you or your cause, just grin and bear it. It is up to the chair to keep order and chastise unruly actors, not up to you. If the chair is abusive, leadership will reprimand them later. It's not your job to make them behave. In my experience, committee members are usually very polite to ordinary citizens who come in to testify.

Read the bill if there is one, or if this is a program in the state or city budget, just read the section dealing with the issue you're following. Study the various analyses that are supplied for the legislation by the support services of the legislature. You may see fiscal notes, local government impact statements, or even environmental impact statements. In many cases there will be a summary of the bill provided by lawyers who work for the legislature. This summary will likely include the policy aspects.

Your legislative champion may ask you to have several people from around the state testify with you on a bill. Research the committee members and, if possible, get one person from the chair's district to testify, or the vice chair, and/or the ranking minority member's district, but keep your group to five or fewer people testifying. If it's a city/county committee or council meeting, get as broad a cross-section of the city and county as possible. Bring people from a variety of demographics, including race and gender.

Further tips:

- Before you come to the hearing, find out how many committee members there are and print copies of your statement for them using a 16-point typeface. This is what you hand out before you start speaking. Many legislators are of a certain age and dislike using their reading glasses in public. And don't leave your copies in the car!

- To practice beforehand, blow up the typeface of your printed testimony to 28-point font, then read it slowly, out loud. With 28-point typeface, one page takes roughly one minute to read. Keep your testimony to no more than seven minutes.

- In your testimony, refer to other states' successes with Bridges/Getting Ahead reforms and cite any available data or white papers.

- If you are helping to write the legislation in question, leave a small, inconsequential error in the bill so the committee chair can find something to fix. Legislators can and will fiddle with the bill just to put their stamp of ownership on the legislation.

- If your Bridges/Getting Ahead initiative produces a newsletter, be sure to include an article in the newsletter about testifying before the committee. Include contact information for the committee members in the newsletter, and make sure your legislators and local elected officials are on your newsletter distribution list.

- Legislators love concise summaries. Since we haven't done it in this section (the opening synopses for each chapter of this book could be a model), can you boil your issue down to three bullet points?

- While you're testifying, if you don't know the answer to a committee member's question, don't guess or make something up. Tell the committee you'll get back to them on that point.

- Also bring extra copies of your testimony for members of the media, and be prepared to be interviewed.

- Finally, show up early! It may seem like a mundane point to make here, though parking is often a problem near the statehouse when the legislature is in session.

Being invited to help shape legislation is a good sign you're on the right track, but we need a quantitative method of determining the effectiveness of your advocacy. Here's a rubric that just might tell you if you've done enough to get your legislation passed. If you don't score more than 50 points on the following survey, you may need to rethink your effort.

Is Your Advocacy Sufficient?

Your people score:

_____ Number of regions in the state or city helped by your idea

_____ Number of majority legislators carrying the bill (maximum one from each chamber)

_____ Number of agency heads who quietly support your bill

_____ Number of years you've had lunch (at least once a year) with the gatekeeper legislator

_____ Number of years you've had lunch with the governor, multiplied by 5

_____ Dollars (in millions) the state will save by passing your idea (limit: 10)

(continued on next page)

(continued from previous page)

Your impact score:

Funding or policy areas your idea will impact; select all that apply and multiply by 3

_____ Welfare reform

_____ Drug abuse

_____ Workforce development/impact of automation on jobs

_____ Local government

_____ Tax reform

_____ Transportation

_____ Education

Your experience score:

_____ Your experience in public speaking (number of years divided by 5)

_____ Number of times you've testified about your legislation

_____ Number of times the past year you've appeared on TV news shows (limit 5)

_____ Number of social-media accounts allied with your partners who are posting about this issue (limit 5)

_____ Number of statehouse media you know personally (limit 6)

_____ Number of times the past six months your issue has been covered in an area newspaper

_____ Number of newspaper articles the past year about you or your partners on this issue

_____ Number of times the past year you've been in to sit down with the editorial board of an area newspaper

_____ Number of times the past year you've had an opinion piece, including a letter to the editor, published in an area newspaper

_____ Number of times the past year you've appeared on a regional radio talk show or were interviewed by a radio news reporter

_____ Number of times the past five years you've organized on-site meetings with officials

_____ Number of copies of candidate or legislative briefing book handed out (divided by 100; limit 10)

_____ Number of copies of *Bridges Across Every Divide* you've handed out to elected officials (limit 10)

If you scored more than 100, you're ready to author your own book! If you scored between 75 and 100, you almost certainly will win. If you scored between 50 and 75, see where you might be lacking. If you scored less than 50, keep working at it. Some of the points in the rubric take time to accumulate.

Even if you don't use this survey to calculate your precise score, it's worth remembering the rubric's basic formula:

People + Impact + Experience = Effectiveness of Advocacy

I would add that I'm indebted to Daniel Kahneman, who wrote *Thinking Fast and Slow,* for some of the ideas behind this rubric.[140]

The preceding survey includes a reference to one of the best tools for educating legislators: the briefing book. It is your most effective means of getting and keeping the interest of someone, the modern politician, who is notoriously distracted. In the next chapter we offer some tips about assembling the all-important briefing book.

Chapter 14

The Rotary Club: Into the Vortex with *Your* Briefing Book

Gene Krebs

Democracy does not give the people the most skillful government, but it produces ... an energy which is inseparable from it, and which may, however unfavorable circumstances may be, produce wonders.

—Alexis de Tocqueville, *Democracy in America*

> You will learn in this chapter how to create a briefing book—and how it can have a great deal of impact. We examine why many advocates make mistakes—and explain how you can avoid the same mistakes.

Every elected official gives speeches. A lot of speeches. Many of those speeches parrot the prevailing groupthink before a sympathetic audience. The presentations usually are highly partisan, even incendiary, aimed mainly at firing up the base. They basically write themselves, and they're easy sermons to preach to the choir.

Counterintuitively, the speeches that tend to worry candidates and elected officials the most are the ones in front of the local Rotary Club, Kiwanis Club, Lions Club, Junior League, etc. These people are belongers with high social connectivity who can greatly influence local political outcomes.

Rotarians usually include many of the local thought leaders. Each one of them can influence how at least a dozen voters react to candidates, and sometimes their influence is much farther-reaching. Often highly educated, many Rotarians are lawyers, leading businesspeople, and heads of local nonprofit agencies. Some are elected officials themselves. The local school superintendent is usually a member.

When elected officials and legislators speak to this group, they know that groupthink platitudes simply won't cut it. The Rotarians need to hear something real, something that will have a positive impact in their community.

The beauty of the briefing book

This is where you can make the task of the elected official or candidate easier. Prepare a briefing book for candidates and legislators that outlines the basic tenets of Bridges/Getting Ahead, how the effort is playing out in your state or region, and what policies can be suggested. Include all the possible impacts, ranging from better communities to savings on state and local budgets.

Your briefing book needs to live up to its name and be relatively brief, no more than 80 pages. Ideally it should have lots of pictures, charts, and graphs. Mention more than once in the book that your organization is nonpartisan and does not endorse candidates. Let all candidates, legislators, and council members know about the briefing book. If you have the funds, print out copies to send to them. If not, keep it online.

Start with a brief introduction of who you are and what you do. Also list local partners with you in the Bridges/Getting Ahead activity. In the table of contents, the title of each section should sum up the policy problem in eight words or less. The first paragraph for each topic should be a short executive summary. In the next section, outline the key policy analysis; what are the impacts and causes? Then present a series of well-documented facts that frame the issues you care about. Be sure to cite your sources in footnotes or endnotes.

Next illustrate how your issues are intertwined with other issues in your state or region, rejecting silos, once again providing citations. After you pile on the problems, you then let the readers up for air by giving them several policy ideas they can adopt. Feel free to ask your partnering organizations to submit a section on their main issue for the briefing book. For example, if your local drug-intervention group uses Bridges/Getting Ahead as its framework, ask the group to submit a chapter that fits the parameters.

Briefing books are invariably framed in the same manner so the candidates or officials can use them easily in a speech.

Does this work? Absolutely. Many candidates and elected officials will use your briefing book to support their stance on the issues you (and they) care about. Once they do that, you win, as they're now honor-bound to at least try to follow through.

What happens if you get two candidates running for the same office who both use your briefing book as the basis for speeches? Relax; you have now created a bidding war on your issue. Either way, you win big.

Briefing books are used not only by the winners in office, but later the losers might use the book again when seeking another political office.

Can a public agency issue such a guide? If your briefing book remains carefully nonpartisan and includes facts with documentation, and if its title indicates clearly that it's an agency briefing book, you can and should issue such a book. And if you follow the guidelines given here, your briefing book likely will receive high praise from elected officials.

While garnering praise is good, it's also good to own up to mistakes. In the next section we look at some potential pitfalls in politics and policy.

What mistakes might you make?

This rationale, and all the others like it people give, jumbles effect and cause, and puts the cart before the horse.

–Lucretius, *The Nature of Things*

When you're writing new legislation, the task before you may seem simple enough. But public policy is nonlinear, and problems often are hidden from view.

People often assume public policy is like a straightforward shot on a pool table. We identify a problem, call it the 9-ball, and place it somewhere on the far end. We line up our solution, the white cue ball, close to us. We strike the cue ball with the cue stick, sending it directly into the 9-ball, our problem, causing the 9-ball to hurtle into the pocket. We feel like the "Cincinnati Kid"!

We have encountered a policy problem, proposed a solution, and knocked the problem into the pocket with the cue ball. Easy. This is how most elected officials, radio personalities, and TV talking heads view public policy: See the problem, propose a one-shot solution, bask in adulation, and move up the food chain.

In reality, it seldom works out that way. Why?

The model above ignores the other balls on the table that can block your straight shot. Sometimes they block the cue ball's approach to the 9-ball. Sometimes they block the 9-ball's path to the pocket. They can even get between you and the cue ball and inhibit your ability to line up the shot.

These are only the balls you can see; unlike pool, public policy is rife with unwritten (yes, hidden) rules and even hidden balls. You might strike the cue ball cleanly, but it suddenly careens off one of these invisible balls and sinks into a side pocket, causing a "scratch."

Don't be afraid to draft public policy; just remember it's nonlinear and can be unpredictable. Systems theory and chaos theory can explain why so many public polices never actually achieve their intended goals. Each group (each human, even) is a ball on the pool table of your community, country, and world. The complexity this creates, however, is a strength of the Bridges model (see Chapter 2 on welcoming diversity at the table).

In a nutshell, Bridges/Getting Ahead is an organic, locally framed response to poverty. Being adaptive, it can weave its way around the other balls on the pool table of life to impact the 9-ball that is poverty, transportation, workforce development, or whatever policy you're working on—and punch it into the corner pocket.

Sometimes (in service clubs and elsewhere) it's difficult to overcome the common groupthink about how policy is passed, but you also can use groupthink to your advantage.

Chapter 15

How to Use Groupthink—and How Not to Be Used
Gene Krebs

*The individual has always had to struggle to
keep from being overwhelmed by the tribe.
If you try it, you will be lonely often, and
sometimes frightened. But no price is too high
to pay for the privilege of owning yourself.*

–Rudyard Kipling, quoted in Gordon,
"Six Hours with Rudyard Kipling"

Here we describe the nature of groupthink and how to manage it. We also make some recommendations about relating to professional lobbyists.

Despite what Rudyard Kipling said nearly a century ago, we are also social animals; maintaining the tension between these two poles is how we achieve balance in our lives and stay happy (or try to). We can bend to the will or norm of the group, but ideally we don't merely parrot the company line. Birds of a feather flock together, and people often flock to candidates or issues. Caucuses, with a pronounced propensity for groupthink, flock more than most.

The caucuses are governed, and legislation is often introduced, by adherence to availability cascades.[141]

In short, *availability cascade,* a technical term used by sociologists, is a fancy phrase for mild mass hysteria driven by the media. To a large degree it also is driven by legislators reading the "clips," the daily compilation of stories in the various newspapers in the state, and responding only to those that touch the core values. This is one reason you strive to get your issue into those clips.

Your advocacy can be impacted when, for example, video surfaces of someone buying steaks and crab legs with an electronic-benefits card. Soon there are calls for the elimination of food-assistance programs. Conversely, videos of a homeless family just trying to keep it together can tug at the heartstrings and cause an outpouring of support for various social-services programs.

This availability cascade groupthink is toxic and can invade caucuses. Watch for clues about the groupthink of the caucus when meeting with legislators.

Getting beyond the 'really mindless stuff'

Be prepared to chat about a lot of mindless stuff when meeting with legislators. It varies member by member, but sometimes the first 20 minutes of a half-hour meeting are exhausted with the member reminiscing about the awards and plaques on the office wall, or their child's baseball game, or a restaurant now closed. Really. Mindless. Stuff.

Why? Sometimes legislators are bored out of their skulls by groups asking for money, usually with a self-righteous conviction that their issue is the key problem facing the state. Sometimes legislators hate to say no, and if the answer is no, then they would rather say it at the end of the meeting when time is short. Sometimes they know that powerful groups are aligned against a measure, and don't wish to be drawn into a fight they know they can't win.

If the governor's office staff is against your proposal, and the legislator is seeking a job in the administration, the legislator will delay any discussion of your issue until the end of the allotted time. On the other hand, if the legislator plunges directly into a discussion of your topic, that means they value you and the problem. Look for the small clues that determine the status of your proposals.

If the meeting in the legislative office is a first-time "meet and greet," just be cordial and chat to size them up; keep it light. But if you have an "ask," a defined request for money or policy changes, and think the member might be hesitant to engage, plunge ahead as soon as you sit down.

Key follow-up questions

In most cases it's good both to have an ask and to anticipate follow-up questions. Here are some clustered questions:

- If the request is for money, where will it flow? To which state agency and local entities? Who will hold the money? Will it be transparent and/or audited under standards common for your state? How much money? Why that amount and not more or less? Is there a particular funding stream you wish to tap into?

- If it's about changes to a program, why are the changes needed? Do you have sample language or a draft of a potential bill? Who prepared it? Is it a pilot program? How did you determine what counties or cities or wards would be the testing ground? Who will monitor and evaluate the pilot or the program itself?

- Are you suggesting programmatic changes to state law? Who originated the idea? Is it done in other states? Do you have a white paper supporting the policy? Have data been collected? Who evaluates the results?

- Has a cost-benefit analysis been done for the program in other states or communities? Who did it? Can you use TANF (Temporary Assistance for Needy Families) or other dollars for the program that are not from the general revenue fund? Can you use a mix of state, local, and federal dollars? Does this help bridge the gap in rural areas or smaller towns, as well as in the big cities?

- Do you have a coalition? Who else is in it? Are they well-respected groups, or are they enemies of the legislator or caucus you're trying to lobby? Was a cost-benefit study done for your state or community? Who did it? Are they respected? Was it a university or a nonprofit think tank? Was it a think tank that is well-known and respected, or are they considered a front for a particular group or party?

Hand to the legislator a one-page brief on the topic with the three key points bulleted. No more than three. The one-pager should be attached to a white paper or peer-reviewed journal article that supports your case. Also hand to them the candidate/legislator briefing book you have prepared, even if you're sure they already received one. Always carry at least three copies of the briefing book and any studies or white papers you're using. And, of course, be sure you always carry at least three copies of this book to hand out! Finally, hand out media reports on your issue. Watch their eyes, and you can expect to see their pupils linger on the news stories.

If all this sounds challenging to you, you're not alone. Public-policy advocates don't often head into the fray unassisted. Like many of them, you too may want to consider a professional lobbyist.

Paladins: Have PAC, will travel

> I do not think that it is as easy as is supposed to uproot the prejudices of a democratic people, to change its belief, to supersede principles once established by new principles in religion, politics, and morals—in a word, to make great and frequent changes in men's minds.
>
> —Alexis de Tocqueville, *Democracy in America*

Should you hire a lobbyist? It depends. In most cases a legislator who really believes in Bridges and Getting Ahead can act as your guide. But legislators, mayors, and city council members can get distracted, they can decide to seek higher office, they can have changes in staff that cause you to lose your main advocate, and they can even lose their jobs in an election. Especially if one of these hazards befalls your Bridges/Getting Ahead champion legislator, you may want to look into hiring a lobbyist.

Modern lobbyists are a little like medieval paladins. Paladins were the knights-errant of the Middle Ages, the ones who rescued damsels, slew dragons, and led lives of virtue, only occasionally taking on mercenary jobs to do battle against the Austro-Hungarian Empire. At least that's what their PR firm said.

Many modern paladins (lobbyists) still feel as if they have a chivalric code. For a fee they'll right wrongs and, on occasion, will work *pro bono* for groups engaged in enhancing the public good. Modern contract lobbyists view themselves not as the money-grubbing bribers portrayed in TV shows and movies, but rather as the WD-40 of the modern legislature; they keep everything running smoothly and with minimal squeaks.

It is lobbyists' job to know who rooms with whom, what everyone's day job is back home, their religion (if any), and each particular legislator's touchstones. They follow all bills that relate to their clients and give helpful advice on strategy and tactics. Often they are former staffers or agency heads; sometimes they are former elected officials themselves.

Lobbyists don't come cheap. The better ones will want a three-year contract with a monthly retainer that could be $10,000 or more. And if you think you're buying their undivided attention at those rates, keep in mind that lobbyists may have 60 clients or more.

It may seem glamorous on the outside, but lobbying is grueling work because the lobbyists often need to know more about the legislation than the legislators in order to serve, even protect, their clients. Lobbyists normally host a lunch or dinner every single day the legislature is in session. They will sit in night committees away from their families. Much of the money they make in retainers goes toward campaign donations to members, especially chairs and leadership, especially if your state has a "pay to play" mentality.

Lobbyists have to be nice to people they secretly loathe, and some will acknowledge that occasionally they feel as if they themselves are the problem. Even though many lobbyists were attracted to politics in their bright-eyed youth as a way to bring about change, most lobbying efforts work to maintain the status quo. Their divorce rate is high, and many struggle with smoking or drinking. They seem to have short lifespans and too often die young.

Women who are lobbyists sometimes talk about ham-handed male legislators groping them and seeking sexual favors. *Men: We need to stop this yesterday.* Sexual assault and harassment have no place in professional relationships or anywhere else. Psychologists call the root of the problem "toxic masculinity," and it's especially pervasive in politics and policy where power dynamics are at the core of much of the business that gets done.

Until some men stop assaulting and harassing women, you can use countermeasures to mute inappropriate actions by sending two advocates to every meeting. Indeed, it's a sad situation when those professional meetings require a chaperone like a high school prom, but this (and other measures like it) need to be considered.

You also are hereby forewarned that a few lobbyists work slowly on purpose. If they get a client's legislation passed six months after it's introduced, the client will usually stop paying. The job is done, so why honor the rest of the three-year contract? The lobbyist might sue for payment, but such litigious lobbyists tend not to get many further contract opportunities.

So the lobbyist has the bill introduced, and a hearing held, and maybe gets it voted out of committee during that session. During the next session it is passed by the first chamber, but it languishes and dies in the other chamber. Only in the fifth year does the bill pass both chambers and get signed by the governor. Lobbyists call this practice of dragging out the legislative process "milking the cow." One of my sources in the lobbying world, a very successful contract lobbyist, says clients tend to get edgy after five years, so that's about as long as you can expect to milk the cow.

If you're accompanied by your contract lobbyist to a legislator's office, and the lobbyist spends the first 20 minutes of a half-hour appointment talking about baseball, the lobbyist could be milking the cow, or maybe the lobbyist is just being chatty. Taciturn people are rarely successful at lobbying.

To hire or not to hire?

The question remains: Do you hire a contract lobbyist? If you absorb the lessons and guidance of this book, you might not have to hire one. Take the money you would spend in the first month with a contract lobbyist and buy a copy of this book for everyone on your staff, everyone on your board, and everyone in your universe who might interact with legislators, and you may begin to see things working.

> A lot of my lobbyist friends will tell you that they have to be honest. You have to be trustworthy. You have to say what you mean and do what you say you're going to do. There's integrity there.
>
> –Laura Newberry Yokley, United Way of
> Wayne and Holmes counties, Ohio

In sum, volunteers usually can handle the effort, but if anything goes wrong, you can be caught short. (You do get what you pay for.) Make sure you have good relationships with everyone, including association lobbyists like those from the county welfare board who might bail you out if you miss something. This is why you try to be nice to everyone at every opportunity. As Dominic Paretti, a long-time staffer, told us when we interviewed him for this book: "When advocating for an issue, use your inside voice, not your outside voice. It makes a difference."

Sometimes it may seem that everyone in public policy is playing a game, and while many are, quite a few of them are very good people who care deeply.

Another option for advocates is think tanks, which can provide vital data to bolster your case. As the next chapter shows, those think tanks can be indispensable partners for you, so long as you're wary of information put out by "captive" or biased think tanks. Captive think tanks are funded by larger interest groups and are beholden to that group's position no matter what the evidence says. How can you distinguish the good think tanks from the bad ones (the *septic* tanks?!), and how can they help or hurt your advocacy?

The next chapter also deals with the media—and how you can cultivate those contacts.

Chapter 16

Of Think Tanks and Media Types
Gene Krebs

*I am sending you out like sheep among
wolves. Therefore be as shrewd as snakes
and as innocent as doves.*

–Jesus of Nazareth, Matthew 10:16

In this chapter we delve into the mysterious world of think tanks, why you need them, and what to watch for when interacting with the people who inhabit them. We also explore ways to deal effectively with the high priests of the media.

I have a long history working for think tanks. What is a think tank? It's like a freelance research lab at a university, but with no students and a few interns instead. Staffed by smart people, a think tank conducts research. Sometimes the research is original if the think tank is large and well-funded like the Brookings Institution (from the left) or the American Enterprise Institute (from the right). This book relies on excellent research done by both of these think tanks, among others. Many think tanks improve the civic capacity of the city, state, and country.

If the think tank is smaller and perhaps statewide or regional in scope, it will usually conduct literature reviews, with staff summarizing original research. These literature reviews are then published as white papers that indicate certain trends or policies. Smaller think tanks are usually inexpensive to engage in order to study a policy or public problem, as they are usually not affiliated with a high-cost university or college.

Foundations often use think tanks and similar groups to perform studies on public-policy issues. At a very high level, Brookings and AEI sometimes collaborate on various seminars and papers. While nominally nonpartisan, if you look at the affiliations of the staff, you can get a sense of where they fall on the spectrum based on where they worked and for which president or member of Congress.

Don't forget to think about think tanks

In your emerging role as an advocate for Bridges/Getting Ahead, is it a good idea to approach a local think tank seeking a partnership?

Do an Internet search for the think tank in question. How do the media report on it? Do the media cast the think tank as conservative or progressive? If the elected officials see the think tank referred to as "right wing" or "labor backed" in the clips, then they may form an inaccurate preconception of where on the political spectrum the think tank belongs. This isn't fair, but it's the way it is.

Next, look up their IRS Form 990. The 990 is the tabloid of the wonk world. See where their funding comes from. Finding out which groups fund a think tank can give you an idea of what they're espousing.

Labor has captive think tanks that they fund to produce reports about working people. Conservative groups also fund captive think tanks to develop reports and model legislation.

If you work in a state like Utah where the conservative candidate gets the overwhelming percentage of the vote, sit down and have a cup of coffee with someone from the local conservative think tank and talk about Bridges/Getting Ahead. Describe the impact it has and how it's local, organic, and delivers concrete results. Show them the studies.

If you work in a state like Massachusetts where many of the think tanks are blue, buy them a cup of coffee and tell them how Bridges/Getting Ahead treats people with low incomes with respect, gives them a seat at the table, values their input, and produces concrete results. Show them the studies.

As the Bridges/Getting Ahead effort gets under way in your community, get to the think tanks earlier rather than later to help them form a positive opinion of you and your group; get off on the right foot. It's a cliché but true: You don't get a second chance to make a first impression. If they begin with an unfair characterization of your group, it can make your life difficult. Changing people's minds is a daunting endeavor, as any Bridges/Getting Ahead practitioner knows, and they need to understand you, what you do, and why you do it.[142]

In both red and blue states, also reach out to the think tanks that are out of favor with many: those run by labor in Utah or funded by the Koch family in Massachusetts. Don't overlook anyone.

There are certain truths in fables, such as the one concerning "sleeping beauty." In the original story, a fairy was overlooked on the invitation list to the infant's christening—and cast a sleeping curse on the kingdom in revenge. What was the big sin by the king and queen? Just leaving someone off the list.

In other words, make a list and check it twice, then invite some folks from the think tanks to coffee.

Does working with think tanks mean you align yourself with them? Usually not, and be careful about being used by them. Before presenting at local press conferences, encourage both wings of the think-tank world to be there … the more the merrier. Ideally, because the Bridges/Getting Ahead movement is nonpartisan (post-partisan, even), your work will unify folks from across the spectrum—and at the same time acting as a force that expands the civic capacity of your community.

But first we need to discuss the abundance of other opportunities to drink lots of coffee and help shape groupthink.

Raucous caucus

> What is so deceptive about the state of mind of the members of a society is the "consensual validation" of their concepts. It is naively assumed that the fact that the majority of people share certain ideas or feelings proves the validity of these ideas and feelings. Nothing is further from the truth.
>
> –Erich Fromm, *The Sane Society*

A caucus is a group of likeminded people in the legislature or city council who meet to select legislation or policies the caucus will support. As noted in Chapter 15, the caucus is one of the principal places where groupthink is formed and thrives. Caucuses have a "culture" all their own (though without a petri dish). You want to be part of the foundation of the groupthink for caucuses. In any bicameral legislature there are four main caucuses: one for each major party in each chamber. Befriending them all to advance Bridges/Getting Ahead ideas may sound Machiavellian, but it's not. Rather, it's practical.

One of the most effective ways to influence the groupthink is to make a presentation to each caucus during one of their weekly meetings. Your legislative champion can sometimes make that happen. Caucuses often have a retreat, usually in the beginning of the session season, where they discuss the policies facing them. Retreats are great opportunities for advocates to appear. Advocates frequently are given time to present, and members are relaxed and confident, having just won election or re-election to the legislature. For a brief time they focus on policy.

Not every group is so welcoming, however. In fact, some will hate you and everything you're doing, no matter how concrete your results. Understanding why can help you head some of them off at the pass.

Game changer, car charger

> There is nothing more difficult ... than to take the lead in introducing a new order of things, because the innovator has for enemies all those who have done well under the old conditions, and lukewarm defenders in those who may do well under the new. This coolness arises ... partly from the incredulity of men, who do not readily believe in new things until they have had a long experience of them.
>
> –Niccolo Machiavelli, *The Prince*

If you advocate for Bridges Out of Poverty and Getting Ahead as outlined in this book, you're a game changer. And because you're working for change, you also might be barreling headfirst into a brick wall.

By the time you read this book, electric cars may be normal and mundane, but at the time of writing they were still groundbreaking. I test-drove a Tesla, an all-electric car with tremendous power and acceleration; it has the second-fastest acceleration of any production car on the planet.

Since it was my first experience with the car, I wanted to tell everyone about it. I described the thrill of driving the car to a friend who's a true gear head, someone who devours magazines and websites on various engines, fuel injectors, drive trains, and transmissions. His reaction? Disdainful and dismissive. He disputed the results of the speed and handling tests; he demeaned the data. He expressed doubt about the quietude of the car. Rather than being excited with me for the new technology, he was agitated and slung mud at the car's reputation.

I was quite puzzled by this reaction until I realized that Tesla is undermining the "high priesthood" of gear heads by making their sacred cow, the internal-combustion engine, obsolete. People who have spent decades understanding the nuances of particular products or sets of ideas tend to react badly when those products or ideas are supplanted by something new. Their arcane knowledge is suddenly of no more use than books on alchemy are to a quantum physicist. If the old guard is invested fiscally, and they always are, remember what Upton Sinclair said: "It is difficult to get a man to understand something, when his salary depends on not understanding it!"[143]

Change happens, and when it does, there will always be people who would like to turn back the clock.

How do you win them over? Declaring war on them is fruitless; they usually have all the money (tax dollars especially) and plenty of powerful contacts in the ruling elite. Instead, win them over with time and kindness—and by helping them understand that the Bridges/Getting Ahead model is the new wave. Through the law of attraction, invite them to catch it so they can transfer their leadership from a knowledge base into a movement base.

Reach out to them early, and heap praise on their past efforts. It's very important to make sure they understand this new wave will not sweep them into the dustbin of history. Remember that most people crave only the recognition of a very small group. They don't need to see their name in *The New York Times*. Host a conference on how much the Bridges/Getting Ahead efforts are helping, and recognize the status and importance of the movers and shakers in your community, state, or region by inviting them to speak. Make them look good, like heroes. If they feel they're part of your movement, they won't oppose you.

Often the bureaucracy you want to reform will thwart your efforts. A legislative leader in a Midwestern state seized on the idea of passing an amendment in the state budget to require all four-year state universities to reduce their tuition by 5%. After some grumbling, they did so. The higher-ed community then realized that this was a public relations bonanza and proceeded to cut tuition a total of 17%. They did this, however, by increasing fees for just about everything on campus, so they actually upped their net income and are quietly mocking the legislator as he runs around his state touting his legislative accomplishment.

Mainstream media

Moving from the "high priesthood" of gear heads to the "high priests" of the media, let's reflect now on ways your message can be communicated in your community. In many ways the mainstream media constitute the key channels for conveying your message. To achieve your goals and to keep your reforms from fading away, it's far better to work with members of the media than against them.

> The number of newspapers must diminish or increase amongst a democratic people, in proportion as its administration is more or less centralized.
>
> —Alexis de Tocqueville, *Democracy in America*

> Transported to a surreal landscape, a young girl kills the first person she meets and then joins up with three strangers to kill again.
>
> —Rick Polito, TV listing for *The Wizard of Oz*
> quoted in Rivenburg, "Off-Kilter"

How do you avoid the situation where the mainstream media frame your issues like the critic did above for *The Wizard of Oz*?

While perhaps not as powerful as they once were given the advent of social media, the mainstream media still carry a lot of weight. They also love talking to people who care about others, so you should be prepared for your inevitable media appearances.

What do mainstream-media reporters want? To make their editors and producers happy. If you testify on a bill or resolution, you will almost certainly meet a reporter when you're finished. Their superiors want timely stories that are balanced, brief, and to the point. Why should the reader, listener, or viewer care about this story? This is the question producers and editors hammer into their reporters. Your job is to make the reporter's job easier.

After you speak, the media will approach to ask if you can answer a few questions. Always talk to them if you have time. If you have to leave (maybe you have a sick child), ask when their deadline is, then call them back before that deadline.

Also remember to hand them your business card. This ensures they get your name and title right, and they now have your contact information if they have further questions.

Keep your sentences short and to the point. Again, avoid the shaggy-dog stories—unless they're very short (the stories, not the dogs).

Finally, be careful of criticizing the opposition openly in the media. The better policy is to be nice to everyone, even those you suspect wear modified shoes to hide their cloven hooves. According to Goethe, "The way you see people is the way you treat them, and the way you treat them is what they become."

> The characteristics of the American journalist consist in an open and coarse appeal to the passions of his readers; he abandons principles to assail the characters of individuals, to track them into private life, and disclose all their weaknesses and vices.
>
> –Alexis de Tocqueville, *Democracy in America*

Most states have a statehouse news service. You may be tempted to ignore them while looking for the cameras from *60 Minutes,* but don't give them short shrift. The statehouse media outlet sends a reporter to cover every public meeting and every hearing of every committee. Who gets those reports? The ruling elite in your state.

Steve Marks, owner of Hannah News Service, which operates in four state capitals, describes their impact:

> We are the nonpartisan eyes and ears of the most influential lobbyists and political and government leaders who need to be everywhere but can't. Our clients count on our journalists to tell them what is happening in all areas of state government.

Since these publications are usually online, their stories are more complex and deal with public policy nuances that other media, due to space and size restrictions, simply can't. These statehouse media organs can publish long articles that deal in the arcane aspects of public policy, and they often cover conferences where elected officials or key cabinet members are speaking.

The art and science of cultivating media relationships

When speaking to reporters, sum up your issue in fewer than 20 words. For example: *The purpose of this book is to bridge the political divide in order to bridge the economic divide.* Speak slowly and don't rush your words. Stick to your talking points. If you're asked a question you don't know the answer to, find out the deadline and get back to reporters before the story is due. Or give them the name of someone (who's generally accessible) who can provide the answer. Make their job easier.

Shows that cover public affairs, often on a PBS affiliate station, are another avenue for a more complete discussion of your issues in the media. These shows are watched by powerbrokers to gauge the direction of the policy groupthink, and they can really increase the civic capacity of your state or region. Your statewide public affairs show may reach only 90,000 people in your state, but those are the local community leaders, elected and otherwise. These are the people you need to reach. If you ever find yourself on such a show, spread news of your appearance all over social media, and make sure your colleagues and partners do the same. Use it as part of a larger game plan.

National Public Radio (NPR) has tremendous power with the ruling class and the middle class; I've already discussed the NPR GOP. The stories NPR affiliates broadcast are structured for people who want the next level of in-depth reporting. Your local NPR station might have a locally produced show. Call or e-mail the station and ask how you get invited to be on that show.

You also can be your own media outlet and do a YouTube video. While it probably won't get the same exposure as an NPR interview (unless your policy involves kittens playing with puppies), a YouTube video does have some advantages. You control the content, and it makes a readily shareable advertising tool for your effort.

At the time of this writing, commercial radio does still exist, and it does broadcast. Most AM stations now are all-news and talk-radio shows, and most of those are conservative in nature. If you're asked to be on a show on commercial radio, say yes. Also be aware that 91% of the commercial talk radio aligns with conservatives while just 9% skews progressive, so most of the callers will be from the right.[144]

Fortunately the Bridges/Getting Ahead message appeals to both right and left. The main thing to remember is that all media want you to give soundbites that are short and to the point—but not cookie-cutter comments.

If a reporter asks you, "Do you think your workforce-reform ideas will lead to more jobs?" reply with more than a simple "Yes." Instead, fall in step with what the reporter said: "These workforce-reform ideas will lead to more jobs being created, and this will benefit everyone." Indeed, some reporters will be asking leading questions, and you want to be ready to be led, especially if it's a friendly lead. If a reporter says something like "It seems your proposal will help children," be sure to describe *how* it helps children.

For all you know, the reporter was told by the producer or editor to find stories about positive impacts for children to be used in an upcoming series on that topic.

Some people speak to journalists "off the record," but I say don't do it. Ever. There are other ways to make yourself valuable as a news source. Always being on the record is the best policy. It's the same principle as always signing your name to a letter to the editor.

You may be asked for background information; treat this as a verbal white paper. Everything you say needs to have a basis in objective research. This is where you give to the reporter names and contact information for experts. Treat this as though you are on the record. You are training your brain to be careful of your words around the media. Giving reporters unsourced, candid information "off the record" or "not for attribution" is fraught with danger. It might help you build better rapport with some reporters, but the trouble it can get you into is seldom worth it.

The concept of "embargo" is a topic you'll need to be familiar with if your group ever does a report or white paper. On occasion you'll put out a media release Monday for a story that it is *embargoed* until, say, 9 a.m. on Thursday that same week. That way the media have time to read a 60-page report and digest the implications. Reporters often want to cut in line and run a story before anyone else does. A general rule: Don't let them get a scoop they didn't work for. I would add that I've never had a reporter cut in line.

Cultivate relationships with local reporters so they call you. Ask the one who covers poverty issues in your newspaper to enjoy a cup of coffee with you. How do you know who covers poverty? Whenever there's a story on poverty in your local paper, just note who writes it. If a reporter writes three stories in a row on poverty and related issues, you know that's part of their beat. If after several weeks you haven't seen any poverty-related stories in that newspaper, ask around among your friends—or call the city editor or managing editor and ask which reporter you might contact.

Once you reach the reporter, explain who you are and the nature of your interest in poverty. Put the reporter in touch with local graduates of Getting Ahead programs and with a national consultant for Bridges/Getting Ahead. Most reporters like interviewing real people, and editors like it when reporters interview someone with a national perspective, which can give them a competitive edge.

Social media

> The emergence of the Internet has boosted access to information exponentially and made it easy to inflame tensions by disseminating false or misleading claims, as well as valid information.
>
> –Darrell West, *Megachange*

Can you use social media to rally folks to a cause? Yes, but it won't create the cause, nor will it create by itself a force to move policy.

The previous admonitions to be nice—to be civil—are amplified using a bullhorn here. On social media, every moment of bad judgment, no matter how obscure the public figure, has the potential to go viral and attract millions of hateful views. This approach may not be the most "attention grabbing," but it's the best strategy in the long run.

In the years that have passed since the Web 2.0 shift to user-generated digital content (we've come a long way since chatting with each other via America Online), we've learned that platforms change and digital mayflies die. To get started, pick one or two platforms to concentrate on—or line up all your content and launch multiple accounts/channels simultaneously. Do as much as you can, but don't burn yourself out. "Social-media strategist" can be a full-time position these days!

As the next chapter reveals in greater depth, the social-media revolution has been fueled by rapid increases in artificial intelligence and automation. Similar disruptions in technology might mean that what's happening to newspapers and AM radio could soon happen to jobs near you. Maybe even your job.

Chapter 17

All Hail HAL 9000: The Coming of the Next Revolution

Gene Krebs

It would seem as if the rulers of our time sought only to use men in order to make things great; I wish that they would try a little more to make great men; that they would set less value on the work, and more upon the workman.

—Alexis de Tocqueville, *Democracy in America*

This chapter addresses the fact that almost half of current U.S. jobs are at risk due to computerization and automation. What will the impact be on our society? What policies are being discussed to mitigate this problem—and why are most of them destined to fail?

Cutting straight to the chase, here's the punchline for this chapter: Nearly half of current jobs in the United States are at risk of being lost to computerization and automation.[145]

Will the future look like *2001: A Space Odyssey,* the 1968 Stanley Kubrick film that introduced the eerily omniscient computer HAL that almost took over a space voyage?

For the past 100 years, industrialized, free-market countries have used low-skilled manufacturing jobs to move people up the economic ladder. This enabled them to enter the middle class and afforded their children the accompanying opportunities for education. That may be changing. This rising tide of job loss is also coming for the bourgeoisie, and like the 11th-century king, Canute, you can't command that tide to stop.

The data underline the need to move as quickly as our institutions can move to adopt policies based on Bridges and Getting Ahead that help people change their lives and even our political structure. Why change the political structure? Because the gut-wrenching dislocations we're facing could destabilize our country. Facile politicians all too often offer facile solutions that don't work—and indeed could be making things worse.

Are we heading into an era of such rapid change that it would make even Alvin Toffler dizzy? Author of *Future Shock* and *Powershift,* Toffler writes in the former that "future shock" is a condition of distress or disorientation caused by too much social and technological change in too short a period of time.

Rhymes from another century (the 20th)

Perhaps we can learn from an era in the previous century that may have had more social and financial buffers than today, but still resulted in massive disruptions and dislocations.

In 2017 I attended the final service in the Morning Sun United Presbyterian Church, the small rural church of my youth, planted firmly in the Corn Belt in Morning Sun, Ohio. It was a merged church created by some members of the Hopewell Church mentioned earlier in the book and a Covenant Presbyterian church, whose wooden church building had been infested with termites. A fine brick building erected in 1877, Morning Sun United Presbyterian housed a congregation for exactly 140 years, and when it dwindled down to five families, the church hierarchy decided it was time to close this chapter—and the church doors.

At the last service, which was attended by the dispersed heirs of the community, my cousin asked me to say a few words. I reminded the people sitting there that in 1961, when I was a small boy, the pews were so crowded that if someone new moved into the congregation, they would have to find someone who was willing to make room for them in their pew.

Within a decade, when I graduated from high school, the church was half-empty. In effect, with every decade, the population of the church was cut in half. What happened?

Here are some thoughts about that, and most of them relate to the economics and mechanization of agriculture.

The self-propelled combine destroyed both the average 160-acre farm and the landholding small farmer. The modern combine replaced the old-fashioned corn picker. The combine, which got its name by combining several actions, harvested and shelled the corn in the field, placing the grain in a holding tank in the combine itself. Incidentally, it uses an Archimedes screw to unload the grain. Archimedes and his simple machines certainly do get around!

For more than 100 years farmers had had access to threshers used for wheat, oats, rye, and barley. What made this different? Because of what it did to ear corn.

Prior to the mid-1960s, farmers used an ear-corn picker that was powered and pulled by their tractor and harvested one row at a time. On a good day the farmer could harvest one wagon of ear corn in the morning, and one in the afternoon, for a total of 200 bushels a day. He rarely had more than 4,000 bushels' worth of storage on the farm.

Farmers then moved the ear corn out of storage by hand with a large, unwieldly scoop shovel. The shovel also was handy for smacking at rats that had moved into the corn crib—and during the late summer for swatting ineffectually at bumble bees that made nests between the ears of corn. The ears of corn were unhandy and did not shovel easily.

The combine allowed the farmer to shell the corn in the field, and augers would move the grain, with no sweat from him. With a modern combine, a farmer could harvest 10,000 bushels a day.

It used to be that the size of a corn farm was limited by the amount of ear corn the farmer could shovel out of storage. Because the combine converted ear corn to shelled corn and the farmer transported it into and out of storage by mechanical means, farms could grow much larger. In the early 1960s, farms began to consolidate.

It wasn't large corporate interests that bought the land; it was the neighbors who did the consolidating. When an elderly farmer died, either his widow or the heirs would sell the farm to a neighbor.

In 1961 the typical farmer in the Corn Belt where Morning Sun is located operated 160 acres; in 2018 when this book was published it was 1,600 acres. In just two generations this has resulted in a 90% reduction in the number of farmers, farm families, and attendees in the local church.

On the plus side, farm consolidation has led to a tremendous increase in our ability to feed ourselves cheaply. Many ordinary people have benefited. For example, eggs are still eggs. Data indicate that in 1919 an average worker would have to work for 80 minutes to buy a dozen eggs; in 2015 it was six minutes.[146]

Also over the past century, here are more striking, ag-related numbers: In 1900, 41% of the U.S. workforce was employed in agriculture. By 1970, that percentage had shrunk to 4%, and in 2000, just 2% of the labor force was engaged in farming.[147]

For the average U.S. resident, the technological changes in agriculture have been beneficial, as we spend a much smaller percentage of our incomes on food than we used to.[148]

For the farmers and their unique American social structure, however, the changes have been devastating. Does this country's ag community constitute a cautionary tale? Will low-skilled jobs, especially in manufacturing, be the next to disappear?

Is history rhyming?

> The time is drawing near when man will be less and less able to produce, of himself alone, the commonest necessaries of life.
>
> –Alexis de Tocqueville, *Democracy in America*

This easily could be the future of manufacturing in America, and indeed the world. The combine is an early example of humans not racing against the machine, but rather using the machine to help them race against others. Unfortunately, in doing so we are eliminating some 90% of the other participants.

Will the next technological push eliminate 90% of the labor involved in manufacturing, as robots and artificial intelligence come into their own and begin to displace more workers than they already have?[149]

How will the good citizens of East Liverpool in Columbiana County, Ohio, respond to this shifting and sifting? Remember, they're still longing for the days of full employment in the steel industry under sulfurous, sooty skies. How will they adjust when they're still struggling with their most recent dislocations?

According to Microsoft founder Bill Gates, a whole range of jobs that are clustered in vast warehouses of low-paid workers—and the 3 million truck drivers who ferry goods between them—will disappear in a couple of decades.[150]

It's important for the elite who are reading this to remember this quotation from Tocqueville: "Every aristocracy which keeps itself entirely aloof from the people becomes impotent."[151] In the U.S., we seem to be well on our way to this ominous scenario.

The working classes feel that elites aren't hiring them because they don't have bachelor's degrees. How do you get a bachelor degree? In most cases, by being born well-off. Nearly 80% of kids in the top-earning 25% of families get a bachelor's degree by the age of 24. In the bottom-earning quartile, only 9% get a four-year degree.[152]

In effect, the working classes are feeling shut out of the means to compete in our new meritocracy. They don't have to read the white papers; they see it in their own lives.

The danger is that people may not use all their gifts to discern what is happening and why—and will instead fall back into rote political patterns and solutions. Just about everyone resists data, at least at first, especially when the data imply a need for change.

Here's another example of what I'm talking about.

The greatness of great French wines depends on hot summers, plenty of moisture early in the growing season, and wet falls. Back in the 1980s, Princeton economist Orley Ashenfelter created a formula for predicting the price of a bottle of French wine based on those factors.

Rather than embrace this very helpful formula, wine experts protested. Famous wine connoisseur Robert Parker even called the economist's method "an absolute total sham."[153]

The problem for Parker and other experts is that once you take the human factor out of the equation, Ashenfelter's formula seems to be a perfect predictor of the value of the wine in question. But like my gear-head friend, the "high priests" in the wine world are reluctant to embrace something that makes their skill set obsolete.

The Ashenfelter formula had a small impact; there are only 236 master sommeliers in the world.[154] What happens when 500,000 autoworkers are laid off in a year, or 200,000 truck drivers? How will the political class respond?

Where do the benefits of technological enhancements accrue? Do the profits stay in the communities that lose jobs, or are they instead pushed toward another geographic region and/or economic class? The accumulation of wealth in the San Francisco Bay Area provides an easy answer to that question. Eventually, software allows you to treat everything as a commodity.

We are all increasingly making or dealing with commodities: either corn, or cars, or medicine, or law. Education is the means by which we turn our human capital into a commodity. A farmer can purchase a combine to turn ear corn into a commodity, but people can't simply buy a means of commoditizing their human capital. Unless they embrace education and training, people at the lower end of the economic ladder will be at a distinct disadvantage.

Agriculture is an example of sluggish modernity, one that occurred over a longer time period than that of the liquid modernity we are in now. History rhymes, and what we have witnessed in agriculture is being replicated in manufacturing, especially with the overlay of computerization and artificial intelligence. There's about a 50-year gap between the two economic manifestations: Today manufacturing is roughly where farming was in 1971, and the manufacturing "church," which once was packed with people, is now half full. In the next 10 years it's expected to become three-quarters empty, just as the trend indicates.

Technology has enabled real gross domestic production to march steadily upward,[155] just like it helped farms produce more food (thereby lowering prices). At the same time, however, wages simply haven't kept up.[156] Can we supplement wages with government money? If so, what's the best way to do that?

Go away, Watson, I don't need you

> There are decades where nothing happens;
> and there are weeks where decades happen.
>
> –Vladimir Ilyich Lenin, quoted in Gowland,
> *Britain and the European Union*

Unlike Alexander Graham Bell in 1876, can we tell the technological wave to slow down and be more humane? Could we capture a greater portion of the immense wealth being created and use it to smooth the passage to the next story arc of humanity? If you could choose, what would you do with the money the government has collected?

Retraining? A 55-year-old bricklayer whose job has been destroyed by a maker machine that lays bricks 20 times faster may not want to sit and stare at a computer screen all day. Too young to retire, he also would have to leave his rural or exurban small town and support system to get these jobs. Did I mention he lives in Columbiana County?

Let's say though that the bricklayer just goes on welfare; he is then subject to retraining, but if he ever gets a slightly better position, he may fall off the dreaded "benefits cliff."

One of the ways the U.S. retains the permanent underclass is this cliff. Basically, if you're on public assistance and you start making more than a certain amount of money (by going from part-time to full-time work, for instance), you can lose benefits that are worth more than your increase in earnings. You can work hard, get a promotion and a raise, and lose your housing subsidy, which was worth more than the amount you received in your raise.

So why work hard? When you combine this with increasing stress on the system due to job automation, what can we do?

Are we running with scissors?

Imagine it's the future (say, 2032), and you're running for president.

Every week another 1,000 truck drivers lose their jobs due to self-driving trucks. Lawyers who got their degrees from a night school in 2018 are filing lawsuits against anything that moves; they say it's more entertaining than video games and might pay off their student loans. Radiologists have been replaced by artificial intelligence.[157] Former radiologists are now working on organic farms.

Automation has pushed unemployment to 15% nationally, and you now have a 50% increase in opioid deaths due in large part to unemployment and job anxiety.[158]

Remember the cold-butter-on-Wonder-bread analogy? The U.S. is lumpy and clumpy. This means some areas of the country have 30% unemployment and a 100% increase in opioid deaths. Other areas, like Silicon Valley and Austin, Texas, are doing just fine.

What do you campaign on? Might it be: How do you get enough money to these people to keep the economy going and keep body and soul together? Like running with scissors, is this nation on a course that could lead to economic pain?

How about universal basic income (UBI) as a way to work at this problem? Would this get us past the dilemma posed by the late Democratic Senator Daniel Patrick Moynihan that government bureaucracies dispensing social services to the poor, rather than income maintenance, was like "feeding the sparrows by feeding the horses?"[159]

Beloved on the right by Charles Murray and on the left by Frances Fox Piven and Richard A. Cloward,[160] this plan simply gives every adult a check just for being alive, not unlike Social Security throughout one's adult life. The amounts proposed are usually right around the poverty threshold (about $12,000 a year in 2016),[161] and there is no requirement to work or look for work.

Most schemes would pay for this by cutting social services, so there would be no more "agency time" where the poor spend a lot of their time having to shuttle from one agency to another to stitch together the basic necessities of life. There would be no benefits cliff because everyone would receive the basic income check, regardless of income from work.

Research looking at results over the very long term indicate that if you give poor mothers money, their children do noticeably better all through life as measured in education and lifespan.[162] Murray believes that you should be required to spend some of your basic income check on healthcare insurance, and he projects that cost to be about $3,000 per year.

Not surprisingly, UBI has its critics. As Isabel Sawhill of Brookings has noted, "In the end, the biggest problem with a universal basic income may not be its costs or its distributive implications, but the flawed assumption that money cures all ills."[163] Indeed, Bridges/Getting Ahead puts forth the premise that finances comprise just one of 11 resources that all people need to thrive.

Would we see people with $12,000 a year under their belts (minus $3,000 for healthcare) head off to Wyoming or West Virginia, buy mini-houses, grow some vegetables, and get a small flock of chickens? (Along with a "watch robot" to keep coyotes and mink out of the chicken run?)

Would this lead to a repopulation of the rural United States? Or would the young just lose themselves in a dope-fueled haze of video games? Might there be other options that place more emphasis on the value of work?

Picking NIT?

> Sir, your levelers wish to level down as far as themselves; but they cannot bear levelling up to themselves.
>
> —James Boswell, *The Life of Samuel Johnson, LL.D.*

Some think we need a negative income tax (NIT). First proposed in the 1960s by the grandfather of conservative economic thinking, Milton Friedman, NIT in effect regresses the poor's income halfway to the median. If you make less than a certain amount, often something approaching the average income, then rather than owing taxes that year, the feds put enough money in your tax refund to bring you up to the average. It's like a basic income, but you have to do some work.

But what if you're a laid-off 55-year-old bricklayer living in Columbiana County who can't move to Pittsburgh to find work because your 80-year-old father is in failing health and you need to stay close? You have no income to leverage, especially if the work you *do* pick up is paid under the table.

Earned-income tax credit

The earned-income tax credit (EITC) is very popular in Congress, but it also has some problems in how it's enacted. Based on a single tax filing in the spring, low-income recipients can get one allocation based on their work income. To quote from an analysis by a former colleague of mine at The Center for Community Solutions: "For example, a married couple filing jointly with two children and an earned income of $15,000 in 2016 would receive a tax credit of $5,572. Working-poor childless adults are also eligible for an EITC of a maximum of $506."[164]

Between a sixth and a quarter of eligible households don't apply for the EITC.[165] Coming in a lump-sum payment via tax refunds, it could be better used if spread out over the year.[166]

Furthermore, from 2010 to 2013, the Internal Revenue Service estimated the improper payment rate to be an average of 24.2% per year.[167] That means nearly one-fourth of the folks getting the funds actually don't qualify.

On the plus side, the EITC boosts academic scores more than Head Start, probably by giving the poor more security and turning "agency time" into more time with their young children.[168]

Research also shows that the EITC played a major role in female heads of families joining the workforce. Those who were eligible for the most benefits from the EITC also experienced more wage growth in subsequent years.[169]

No matter how much money you throw at people, however, there are other factors in play that tend to keep most of them from making the transition out of poverty—and staying out permanently. After all, 70% of lottery winners go broke in a few years after winning.[170] After two years of retirement, 78% of former National Football League players have gone bankrupt or are under financial stress because of joblessness or divorce. Within five years of retirement, an estimated 60% of former National Basketball Association players are broke.[171]

Why is this so? Most likely because the lottery and professional sports can move people out of low-income communities, but they don't prepare them for life in wealth. Without an investigation of the hidden rules of economic class like one does in Getting Ahead, they often squander their chance for fiscal stability.

Nietzsche declares that "No one can build you the bridge on which you, and only you, must cross the river of life."[172] While the earned income tax credit, a negative income tax, and a universal basic income can be helpful, there are undoubtedly limits. What else can we do?

The tide just keeps rolling

Are the trends we have outlined going to get better? Probably not.

There are several factors to consider. One is that as long as interest rates are low, borrowing the money to purchase robots and artificial intelligence is cheap. In 2016 CB Insights estimated that new investments were up 76% in artificial intelligence companies and would reach $1.2 billion soon.[173]

Spending on capital equipment is up about 25% while payroll spending remains stagnant.[174] In the struggle between capital and labor, what happens when capital no longer needs labor? We may be seeing that future unwind before us right now, like the farmers of Morning Sun, Ohio, did decades ago.

As money pours into automation, it causes jobs to vanish. Researchers at Ball State University have recently noted that almost 88% of job losses came from automation, with a 1.2% increase in jobs due to cheaper goods.[175] The long-term trend is for manufacturing to continue to decline in employment.[176]

Is there any good news?

We find a correlation between social intelligence, creativity, and longevity in the face of technology. Social skills do indeed seem to be a key. As Frey and Osborne note:

> Jobs with high social skill requirements grew by nearly 10 percentage points as a share of the U.S. labor force. In contrast, math-intensive but less social jobs (including many STEM occupations) shrank by about 3 percentage points over the same period. Employment and wage growth was particularly strong for jobs requiring high levels of both cognitive skill and social skill.[177]

New jobs simply aren't being created, especially in any form agreeable to East Liverpool. The companies being formed are big in value, but they're generally small in total employees.

If the degree of class separation, even segregation, continues to increase, how do we handle it in our society so that we stay intact? With all the other divisions and divides we outline in this book, along with the failure of the political system to cope and address the current crop of issues, what do we do? How will this country fare when the next batch of issues emerges, hard to pin down and hard to blame on anything in particular? Can we fix the problem instead of 'fixing the blame?

Many of the divisions now largely adhere to geographical boundaries. Large cities will grow richer while continuing to "revitalize" or "gentrify" formerly ghettoized, low-income neighborhoods, forcing most of the low-income residents out. Rural areas will suffer as more and more residents leave to find opportunity in the cities. Indeed, the U.S. Census Bureau reports: "From 2014 to 2015, the poverty rate decreased in 16 of the 25 most populous metropolitan areas. None of the 25 most populous metropolitan areas saw an increase in the poverty rate."[178]

Metro areas have more entrepreneurs right now, and that gap could grow wider as more businesses implement artificial intelligence.[179]

The growth in real median income in this country has been driven by prosperous cities. Households inside metropolitan statistical areas saw their incomes rise 6% from 2014 to 2015. This growth accrued mostly inside city limits where households saw their real median incomes rise 7.3%; outside principal cities, in the suburbs, the growth was 4%. Making it appear even grimmer, CityLab notes: "Outside metro areas, there was no growth. Real median incomes in rural areas declined by 2%."[180]

When do we hit a tipping point after which these smaller rural communities or depressed urban cities do not survive? We may be there already in some parts of the country. Robert Inman, a University of Pennsylvania professor, states that if 35% of a city's population is elderly, living in poverty, or a combination of the two, it tips that city into a non-recoverable decline, as taxes must increase greatly to pay for basic needs, and the middle class flees both high taxes and the poor.[181]

I have witnessed personally how this pattern plays out in my home rural county, as the middle-class farming community dies out, along with the small-town merchants. The remaining ruling elite become very possessive of their power. They oppose any new persons or institutions of success, undermining attempts at economic development lest it bring in new centers of power.

This erosion of civic capacity evolves over decades, as the remaining elite all too often bully those lower on the ladder, thereby creating a form of autocracy. It becomes a non-virtuous cycle of decadence, a variation of a social Gresham's Law. All is not lost, however; soon we will describe strategies to counteract this trend.

Poverty increasingly is being concentrated geographically, as Inman points out. Low-wage jobs are routinely being replaced by automation, despite efforts by some businesses and corporations to bring greater humanity and prosperity to the workplace.

But storm clouds continue to form on the horizon. How will any of us handle being told by society that we are no longer needed and, in a word, superfluous?

Chapter 18

Bridges as a Model for Business

Gene Krebs

Look at the fraction of American men age 20 and older without paid work. In the past 50 years it rose to 32% from 19%, and not mainly because of population aging. For prime working-age men, the jobless rate jumped to 15% from 6%. Most of the postwar surge involved voluntary departure from the labor force.

–Nicholas Eberstadt et al., "'In Order That They Might Rest Their Argument on Facts'"

As the need for non-skilled labor continues to decline, will that fact lead to more dysfunctional behavior, including addictions? In this chapter we discuss why corporate structure and visionary businesses may be key to a Bridges-style transformation in America.

If poverty affects brain development in children, how will the artificial-intelligence revolution impact them when their parents' lives are considered pointless?[182] Voltaire states that "Work addresses three great ills: boredom, vice, and need." What happens if there is no work?

When children see their dad play video games all day on a virtual-reality headset, with no real work, how does this affect them? When the parents can't get work, yet companies are crying out for workers, what is going on here?

Mark Aguiar et al. have done some interesting research on this problem and conclude that the allure of video games and similar distractions are so seductive that many young men without a four-year degree are no longer seeking jobs. They spend more time playing video games than socializing with friends. Many of these young men seem to feel they don't need to find a job, only play.[183]

Maybe this is why manufacturers have seen a 300% increase in unfilled job postings despite high unemployment in certain demographics.[184]

There's a cruel irony here: There are many spots for workers to fill, but because all too many of the workers don't want to fill them, companies seek out more automation.

Researchers at the Massachusetts Institute of Technology (MIT) have developed a robot that can build structures using locally sourced materials. Currently construction worldwide is an $8.5 trillion industry, and this robot can do it all.[185] Construction is often the means for low-income men to work their way into the middle class. This pathway will perhaps soon evaporate. How will they respond, and who will they respond to? How about employing them in all the new tech startups?

As the Economic Innovation Group notes, "For the first time, the United States experienced a collapse in new-business creation so severe that companies were dying faster than they were being born." No matter how you measure it, dynamism (which involves risk taking, venture capital, and a strong work ethic) is fading from the map. As a result, we now have more inequality in and among our communities, lower wages for our workers, and less competition in our markets.[186]

> Racial minorities face dismal job opportunities even in the best of times. Owing to discrimination, prejudice, and lack of training, minorities and poor people already have high unemployment rates. And without high-skill training, it will be difficult for them to adapt to the new economy where advanced machines take their jobs.
>
> –Darrell West, "What Happens if Robots Take the Jobs?"

The grimmer parts of the future, with glimmers of hope

> Americans are impatient. When we see a problem, we want it fixed yesterday. That helps explain why public leaders are reluctant to tackle the gnarly problems our society faces: It is difficult to show results in time for the next election.
>
> –Elizabeth K. Kellar, "The Fantasy of the Quick Fix"

Along with the work that Bridges communities and individuals are doing, are there examples of professions or companies that can weather the storms in good order and resist the groupthink of the corner offices? It isn't helpful that traditional companies are increasingly in a tenuous situation themselves. In the 1950s a profitable U.S. company had an 80% chance of remaining profitable a decade later; in the 1990s, it was a 50/50 chance.[187]

Is there a different way of looking at corporations?

Two cases come to mind: the employee stock ownership plan (ESOP) and its close cousin, the worker cooperative. Going back to 1844, there are some core tenets that most such organizations tend to share.

In 1844 these were the Rochdale Principles of Cooperation:

1. Open membership

2. Democratic control (one person, one vote)

3. Distribution of surplus in proportion to trade

4. Payment of limited interest on capital

5. Political and religious neutrality

6. Cash trading (no credit extended)

7. Promotion of education[188]

Lincoln Electric, based in Cleveland, makes welders and other equipment and has almost a century of experience offering an ESOP and has a "no layoff" policy. It has been a subject of many business studies, and it's an interesting mix of Darwinian competition and near socialistic paternalism. Employees are given bonuses based on their piecework, yet they're guaranteed employment. The company also has offered a benefits package for more than a century. While the company is not completely impervious to the vagaries of the modern world, it has proven remarkably resilient.[189]

Worker cooperatives are cropping up across the country, and while they have a whiff of utopianism about them, they also seem to have surprising resiliency. Money made there is kept very local rather than being funneled into offshore accounts. Like ESOPs, they are very democratic in nature, with each worker getting one vote. Also like ESOPs, they often have a multiplier limit on the amount senior management can be paid, usually topping out at 9 to 1. The Mondragon Corporation is a good example.[190]

Sometimes there are failures, such as O&O Supermarkets in Philadelphia.[191] But in essence, these models challenge the workers to rise above mere labor.

These opportunities for people to create their own futures, to chart their own paths, requires us to rethink the roles of capital and labor. The United Steel Workers have decided to develop a working relationship with the Mondragon Corporation mentioned above. Mondragon is a corporation and federation of worker cooperatives with 74,000 employees based in the Basque region of Spain.[192]

Mondragon has several viable subsidiary worker cooperatives, although they have had some fail in tough times. As a study from MIT notes:

> During the 1960s the Mondragon complex leaders adopted a policy of creating a new spinoff firm whenever a product line in one firm reached self-sufficiency. Spinoff firms helped deter the emergence of bureaucratic, corporate-like structures. As this policy increased the number of firms, Mondragon's leaders instituted the cooperative group as an organizing mechanism among firms.[193]

In some ways Mondragon resembles a conglomerate, as it has its fingers in many pies, including heavy manufacturing. However, the key to note is that *ESOPs and the like seem to be resistant to the groupthink that permeates the corner offices in many classic corporations.*

One final note from MIT that could cause local economic development specialists to salivate: "Beyond the innovation of the cooperative network, Mondragon uses a growth strategy of import replacement, where firms produce goods and services that were previously imported into the region."[194]

As noted in Chapter 3, Cascade Engineering of Grand Rapids, Michigan, has more than doubled its retention rate for new hires over the past two decades, continuing to build on the original Bridges concepts the company embraced in the late 1990s. Perhaps the most remarkable accomplishment at Cascade has been the transformation of its workplace culture.

For more examples or technical assistance, look to the Evergreen Cooperatives created in Cleveland by local government, The Cleveland Foundation, Kent State University, and other groups. You also might want to explore the concept of holacracy.

Of all the options we have seen, the best ones that might be able to fulfill the aims of the Bridges model and stave off the worst impacts of artificial intelligence on employment are ESOPs and worker cooperatives. The money stays local, the profits stay local, and with training, many of the young people stay local. But these are "slow solutions" that needed to be implemented yesterday, and voters are seldom patient.

The status quo is not an option

What happens if we do nothing? Remember that for every 1% increase in unemployment, says the National Bureau of Economic Research (NBER) in a 2017 study, there is a 3.6% increase in opioid deaths.[195]

Once again, history rhymes; it doesn't precisely repeat. It would be helpful to review a passage by Sam Quinones from his excellent book *Dreamland: The True Tale of America's Opiate Epidemic* about how and where the opioid scourge began—in fertile ground in which to sprout. It began with industrial decline.

States Quinones: "What is true is that by the 1970s, Portsmouth [Ohio] was collapsing, along with the rest of what was becoming the American Rust Belt—a region unprepared for globalization, competition, and the cheaper labor in countries like Mexico."[196]

Picking up where Quinones leaves off is Johann Hari in his book *Chasing the Scream: The First and Last Days of the War on Drugs*. He writes that many of the U.S. soldiers in Vietnam came into contact with heroin, but 95% of those taking the drug gave it up upon returning home. For most of them, their sense of self-worth and a social connection returned.[197]

When a person's sense of value and place in a system or society is damaged, they often self-medicate. Will self-medication increase with the rise of artificial intelligence?

Let's go back to the impact of automation on society in the Corn Belt. Those farmers had a series of social and financial buffers that partially shielded them, which may be lacking for other people. If you don't manage the change, it will manage you. Our society and institutions need to change smoothly and intelligently, as West notes in his book *Megachange*: "In these types of situations, global leaders have to be careful to avoid scenarios in which change takes place so rapidly that it destabilizes people's personal comfort zones."[198]

Here's the real risk: In the coming upheaval, as automation and artificial intelligence rapidly replace manufacturing employment—like mechanization did on the American farm—will there be an Abbeville, South Carolina, of today that will produce another John C. Calhoun? Will there emerge another politician of similar intelligence and craftiness to Calhoun, whom Richard Hofstadter describes as the "The Marx of the Master Class"? Can we as a society adjust our business models and political structures to prevent this? In short, can we stop the next Civil War before it starts?[199]

As Jeff Immelt, the former CEO of General Electric, once said:

> The difficult relationship between business and government [is] the worst I have ever seen. Technology, productivity, and globalization have been the driving forces during my business career. In business, if you don't lead these changes, you get fired; in politics, if you don't fight them, you can't get elected."[200]

How do we create a safe passage and a way forward for our community, state, and country as automation and artificial intelligence roll like a tsunami toward us?

The Bourbon Democrats will be the key voting bloc again, along with NPR GOPers who have law degrees—but 10 years from now they may be working in call centers.

The vital role of the ruling elite and corporations

The ruling elite have failed in their responsibility to look out for, mentor, and nudge those less fortunate. It's not the NPR GOP or the Bourbon Democrats. It's not the Republicans or the Democrats, nor is it the media, nor some of the politicians. The onus is on the elites, with a few corporate exceptions, such as companies that engage employees at all levels in the decision-making process. Because the vast majority of the ruling elite have kept themselves apart from the rest of the nation's life (and indeed consider themselves above it), they find themselves separated from their fellow citizens and grow more remote and out of touch every day.

To be sure, each of us is a work in progress, and each of us fails on countless occasions. But when the ruling elite step up and shoulder their responsibilities, along with the rest of us, synergistic progress is virtually inevitable.

No one's light should be hidden under a bushel or obscured by poverty. America has already won the lottery and made many sound investments; now is the time to invest in human beings. Tocqueville was right: Too many rulers seek only to *use* people in order to make things great in line with their own self-interest. We must use every fulcrum and lever to try harder to make great *people*—to assign value both to the work *and* the workers.

Chapter 19

Building American Communities
Philip DeVol and Gene Krebs

Acting locally [with a quantum view] allows us to work with the movement and flow of simultaneous events within that small system. We are more likely to become synchronized with that system, and thus to have an impact. These changes in small places, however, create large systems change, not because they build one upon the other, but because they share in the unbroken wholeness that has united them all along.

–Margaret Wheatley, *Leadership and the New Science*

Here we cover how to bring the Bridges community together to identify barriers faced by people in poverty, select good sources of data, use a decision tree to determine the level of action needed, test solutions against Bridges concepts, and establish criteria for good policies. And yes, build American communities in the process.

Key points

1. Form an intention to influence poverty policies.

2. Seat people from all classes, races, sectors, and political persuasions at planning and decision-making tables.

3. Put the interests of people in poverty first when forming policies.

4. Focus on policies, not parties.

5. Form policies that are consistent with Bridges concepts.

6. Identify the problems that policies should address; learn from Getting Ahead graduates.

7. Identify sources of solid information.

8. Use Bridges thinking tools to analyze policies.

9. Have Tocqueville meetings (see next chapter), which are based on Bridges principles.

In this book we have covered the basics of advocacy, why reform in in this country and other large democracies is so difficult, and why certain reforms simply don't get the job done.

Now is the time to put into action everything you have learned from the Bridges and Getting Ahead models by creating a process that restores a Tocqueville-style democracy.

How can you get all classes, including the ruling elite, to engage and be attracted to your efforts voluntarily? How can you help America understand and implement the vision of Alexis de Tocqueville—getting this country back to greater class interconnectedness? And how can you overcome the problem of scale and help restore civic capacity in our political and social processes?

We ask you to analyze and reflect on your own republic with a Bridges investigation. Low-income people are investigating their lives and communities via the Getting Ahead process. We ask you to investigate your community, state, and country to explore how and why we got to where we are—and where we might be headed next.

Bridges investigations: Informing the next phase of the republic

In Getting Ahead groups we investigate the impact that poverty has on individuals and communities. In Bridges collaboratives we investigate how we design programs, services, and opportunities available to people in poverty. In Bridges investigations we analyze issues surrounding poverty, as well as ways in which policy formation happens in our republican form of government.

Economic and social policies and regulations typically come down from on high. Governmental policies start at the federal level and then come down to the states where they are tweaked and turned into administrative codes, and finally they arrive at the county level where they are displayed in three-ring binders.

These are massive, structural approaches to poverty; think of Lyndon Johnson's War on Poverty in the 1960s and Bill Clinton's welfare reform of 1996. Policies on healthcare, education, housing, trade, immigration, and employment frame the barriers and opportunities for people struggling to get by and trying to climb the economic ladder.

Of all the players on the field—corporations, big business, think tanks, academics, lobbyists, and legislators—the players least likely to be heard are those who are in poverty.

The intention of Bridges communities is to gain influence at the city, county, state, and federal levels and bring about systemic change. The ensuing proposal in this chapter and the next for conducting Bridges investigations and Tocqueville meetings is a way to work policy development from the ground up. Kate Uhler, a researcher from Kennett Square, Pennsylvania, calls the Bridges approach "trickle up policies."

> If policies can help people at the bottom
> become prosperous, their prosperity
> will trickle up through every class
> that depends on their work.
>
> –Kate Uhler, U.S. researcher

There are thousands of organizations and millions of people who are concerned about and committed to helping people in poverty. They are especially easy to find in nonprofits, faith-based groups, and governmental programs. They work directly with people in poverty, the working poor, and people in the working class as they struggle with unsteady incomes, intermittent work, and the tyranny of the moment that comes with just barely getting by.

Economic development professionals and business executives are coming to appreciate how the approach of Bridges and Getting Ahead can impact workforce retention and training. In turn, this "legitimizes" the Bridges/Getting Ahead approach to the business community and the elite in many communities. With this insight, Bridges is not just about getting people out of poverty, it also helps the bottom line, stock prices, and yearly corporate bonuses. Now the businessperson's job depends on knowing about Bridges/Getting Ahead and using it on the shop floor. "The Man" becomes an advocate for the working poor who increasingly are seen as pivotal parts of the team.

In Bridges and Getting Ahead we see and admire the courage, grit, grace, humor, and skills of the people we've come to know. Upstream from them we see the systemic causes of many of their situations. We challenge ourselves to reduce the barriers that we have created in our own organizations, and we challenge our communities, counties, states, and national government to change policies that contribute to the problem.

In Bridges communities we stand with the working class, the working poor, and people in poverty by putting their needs first. There are three reasons to stand shoulder to shoulder with them.

First, we personally know people from different classes and races. Through Bridges and Getting Ahead workshops, we have crossed the empathy bridge. The relationships we have made will not allow us to abandon the families we know.

Second, Bridges/Getting Ahead has strategies and outcomes that are proven—at the local and, increasingly, state levels—that legislators and other policymakers need to know about. Hundreds of Bridges communities across the United States (and more than a dozen internationally) demonstrate how both poverty and divisiveness can be reversed.

The growth of Getting Ahead

Getting Ahead has been spreading across the U.S. since 2004 and is now being used in 46 states and five other countries: Australia, Canada, Czech Republic, Scotland, and Slovakia. *Getting Ahead in a Just-Gettin'-By World* has been translated into Spanish, Czech, and Slovak. As of early 2018 there were about 70,000 Getting Ahead graduates. Beyond the two peer-reviewed studies of Getting Ahead described in chapters 3 and 7—and later in this chapter—many local Getting Ahead providers have shared their outcomes on the aha! Process website (see Appendix D).

And **third,** when people get out of poverty and contribute to the economy and society, we all prosper. Recall the golden age of the middle class when jobs were secure, wages were fair, and people could save for emergencies. The disposable income of the working class and middle class did indeed trickle up to shareholders and management. Tax revenue came from everyone, not just the elites selling stock.

All this is possible if we commit to working on policies that can bring about changes in the system that has created these forms of poverty. As authors, we hope that what you have learned in these pages will make it possible for you to join others in making systemic changes. We will need to work in a spirit of cooperation with city, county, state, and even federal legislators—individuals often beset by competing interest groups, entrenched thinking, and the barrier of "the way things are done."

How can we work with legislators and the legislative process?

> Useful undertakings which cannot succeed without perpetual attention and rigorous exactitude are frequently abandoned; for in America, as well as in other countries, the people proceed by sudden impulses and momentary exertions.

–Alexis de Tocqueville, *Democracy in America*

- Bridges work should be focused on policies, not parties. Bridges as a state or national movement should not be branded to one political party. But when both parties are pursuing your policies, you can in effect create a "bidding war" to enact your solutions by appealing to the swing voter (see Chapter 9).

- Use the strategies in this book to establish good working relationships with policymakers.

- Engage legislators in co-creating effective policies. Offer Bridges workshops to legislators and work with those who are attracted to the concepts. Ideally, legislators will think of the people doing Bridges as their constituents.

- Legislators need examples of successful programs that inform policy development. Bridges champions have those examples—and such strategies can inform policymakers.

- Policies should benefit people in poverty, the working poor, the working class, the middle class, and even the ruling elite. (If you punish the rich for being rich, they will avoid you, but you do need the Rotarians and the Junior League.)

- It's not just people in poverty who are living in unstable conditions. Remember that 63% of U.S. residents don't have $500 to meet an emergency without taking out a loan.[201]

- Bridges collaboratives are urged to put those who are struggling to get by before other competing interests. Big banks, big businesses, the insurance industry, and other special-interest groups have their own lobbyists, associations, and think tanks to look after them.

The end result of policies that are implemented should be consistent with Bridges concepts and definitions.

Programs and policies should:

1. Stabilize daily life and the environment

2. Build the 11 resources

3. Result in an increase in income and assets—and reduce use of state and local safety nets

4. Result in self-sufficiency and increased social cohesion

What problems might Bridges collaboratives work on? What policies must be changed?

Information about barriers and opportunities comes from many sources: think tanks, universities, government reports, and investigative reporting done by the news media. Bridges communities, however, are unique in that people in poverty inform us about the barriers they face and the opportunities that exist. They have a direct line to policy development.

That line runs from the Getting Ahead investigations to the Bridges collaboratives, then to local and state officials. Getting Ahead investigators are a primary source of information about barriers. During Getting Ahead sessions they create a Mental Model of Poverty in their community, an assessment of community conditions, and a Mental Model of Community Prosperity. Getting Ahead graduates are at the planning and decision making tables in their communities.

The example given in Chapter 4 about the Getting Ahead graduate and the water fees in Muskogee, Oklahoma, illustrates the role that a Getting Ahead graduate can play and the policy changes that can come from the work of the Bridges collaborative. Further details about that story are presented later in this chapter.

Organizations that apply Bridges concepts are another vital source of information regarding policy issues. By conducting the client life cycle analysis, they identify barriers that clients experience as they are herded through the maze of activities established by organizations.

Barriers are created by the community as well, such as transportation, agency scheduling practices, workplace practices, childcare availability and costs, housing conditions and costs, health problems, and fee structures and fines.

A national study of Getting Ahead participants conducted by Elizabeth Wahler of Indiana University identifies 16 barriers. Remember, this is what the poor and working poor themselves perceive. They are arranged according to the frequency with which they were reported, with bad credit as the most frequently mentioned barrier.[202]

1. Bad credit

2. Unemployment

3. Transportation

4. Affordable housing

5. High debt

6. Physical health

7. Mental health

8. Isolation

9. Underemployment

10. No access to computers

11. Chemical dependency

12. Learning problems

13. Felony convictions

14. Unstable working conditions

15. Lack of affordable childcare

16. Domestic violence

The decision tree: What level of action is needed? Individual? Institutional? Community?

Earlier we made the case that poverty is complex and requires a comprehensive approach. We need to address all causes of poverty, and we need to address it at every level. Thus the question: Who should take action on the barriers that people in poverty face?

It's easy to say that each individual is solely responsible for getting out of poverty, but knowing what we know now, we can be more specific and accurate about assigning responsibility. A decision-tree analysis can help us see what lies upstream from the person faced with a barrier and possible policy changes to recommend.

Decision Tree for Comprehensive Policy Solution

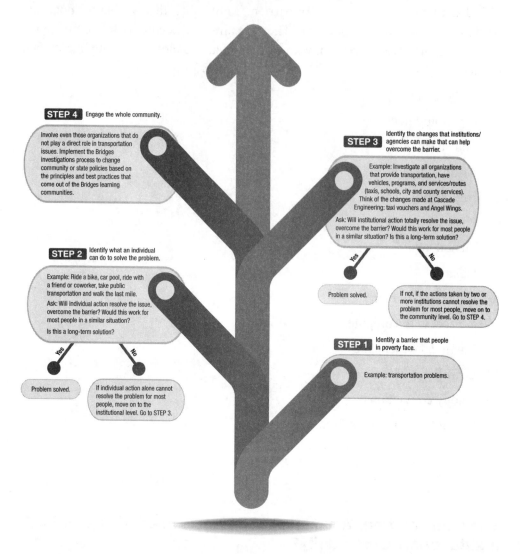

STEP 4 Engage the whole community.

Involve even those organizations that do not play a direct role in transportation issues. Implement the Bridges investigations process to change community or state policies based on the principles and best practices that come out of the Bridges learning communities.

STEP 3 Identify the changes that institutions/agencies can make that can help overcome the barrier.

Example: Investigate all organizations that provide transportation, have vehicles, programs, and services/routes (taxis, schools, city and county services). Think of the changes made at Cascade Engineering: taxi vouchers and Angel Wings.

Ask: Will institutional action totally resolve the issue, overcome the barrier? Would this work for most people in a similar situation? Is this a long-term solution?

Yes — Problem solved.

No — If not, if the actions taken by two or more institutions cannot resolve the problem for most people, move on to the community level. Go to STEP 4.

STEP 2 Identify what an individual can do to solve the problem.

Example: Ride a bike, car pool, ride with a friend or coworker, take public transportation and walk the last mile.

Ask: Will individual action resolve the issue, overcome the barrier? Would this work for most people in a similar situation?

Is this a long-term solution?

Yes — Problem solved.

No — If individual action alone cannot resolve the problem for most people, move on to the institutional level. Go to STEP 3.

STEP 1 Identify a barrier that people in poverty face.

Example: transportation problems.

Basing our work on accurate data and information

Given the ideological divides that run through all strata of society, it's important that individuals in Bridges initiatives know how to identify reliable news, studies, and statistical resources.

In this age when facts and "alternative facts" are disputed, it helps to know where to find reliable sources. Bruce Bartlett, author of *The Truth Matters: A Citizen's Guide to Separating Facts from Lies and Stopping Fake News in Its Tracks,* recommends FactCheck, PolitiFact, and PunditFact for accuracy among opinion writers.[203]

In addition, readers should consider information from the Federal Reserve (especially the St. Louis office). The Brookings Institution, American Enterprise Institute, and Good Jobs First all produce interesting studies. Note: These later sources have a tint of blue or red, and one source must be balanced with another.

Testing policies using Bridges concepts and thinking tools

We have explored the complexities of life at the lower end of the economy and the many barriers faced by those who wish for a more stable life. Now it's time to consider solutions in the patterns that we've discovered.

Some solutions can be found at the individual level. Yes, people in poverty often need to make changes in their choices and behaviors.

Some solutions can be embedded in the procedures and program designs of the organizations that people encounter. Some solutions can be found at the community and state level.

Collectively these solutions can be called policy solutions. There are many policies that need to be changed to make life easier for people at the lower end of the economic ladder.

The following table shows how Bridges concepts can be used to analyze and test existing and proposed policies.

Bridges concepts	Use of Bridges concepts as thinking tools
Mental models of class	• How does the policy affect people in poverty? • Does it reduce or increase the demands on time, money, and cognition (mental bandwidth)? • Does it stabilize or destabilize daily life? • Will it reduce or increase the impact of the tyranny of the moment?
Hidden rules of class	• How does the policy affect interactions and relationships across class lines? • Does it improve or worsen interactions between the classes? • Does it improve or worsen inclusion in the community?
Definition of poverty; 11 resources	• How does the policy help people, institutions, and the community build resources? • Does the policy build or reduce the resources of people at the lower end of the economic ladder? • Does the policy build or reduce the resources of the institutions of the community? • Does the policy build or reduce the resources for the community as a whole?

(continued on next page)

(continued from previous page)

Bridges concepts	Use of Bridges concepts as thinking tools
Getting-by resources vs. getting-ahead resources	• How does the policy impact the balance of getting-by resources and getting-ahead resources? • Is the purpose of the policy to provide a (getting-by) safety net? • If so, is the safety net permanent? Is it temporary? If temporary, is there an end to the resource that isn't a backward step (cliff effect)? • Is the purpose of the policy to support the development of getting-ahead resources? If so, how long will funding remain available? • What is the mix of getting-by resources and getting-ahead resources in the community?
Bridges sustainability grid based on the four causes of poverty	• Does the policy address all causes of poverty? Does it cover individual behavior, community conditions, exploitation, and political/economic structures? • Can action be taken at the individual, community, and policy levels? • What is the impact on the individual? What is expected of the individual? • What is the impact on the community? What is expected of the community? • What is the impact of exploitation? What is expected to be done about exploitation? • What is the impact on the political/economic structures? What is expected to be done by the political/economic structures?
All classes at the planning and decision-making tables	• Does the policy promote/require equity and inclusion at the decision-making table? • Are people who are (or were) living in poverty at the table? What percentage of the group? Are they there as full members? • Are people of different racial and ethnic groups at the table? What percentage of the group? Are they there as full members? • Are people from various sectors at the table? Are they there as full members? • Are people from various political persuasions at the table? Are they there as full members?

Source: Developed by Philip DeVol for *Bridges Across Every Divide*.

Strategies and policies that can build a democracy that serves people in poverty and the working class

The following is a list of actions that are structural in nature. Policies are built on this underlying framework of conditions. If we can influence the structure, we can influence policies.

Reach out to the Bourbon Democrats and NPR GOPers in your community. Convince them, and you convince the political elites. Many people in Bridges communities come from these two groups; in other words, these are the people who are likely to be swing voters.

The country needs gerrymandering reform to create a system where a third to half of the legislative seats are competitive. This encourages legislators to work across the aisle and compromise.

Ranked-choice voting, as described in Chapter 11, will elect officials who have a broad range of support, not narrow support focused on primary voters only.

Tax credits for campaign donations for offices in your state or city. We have had big money since the presidential election of 1896, and it is hard to cage. Dilute the impact of big money with small money.

Keep your local elective districts as small in population as possible. Yes, 9,000 members of Congress would be a nightmare, but having at-large city council seats in a city of a million residents dilutes everyone's vote.

Increase voter participation. Studies of Getting Ahead show that graduates gain a sense of agency, of taking charge of one's own life. While formal studies on the voting rate of Getting Ahead graduates have not been done, there is strong anecdotal evidence from both conservative and progressive communities that Getting Ahead graduates become interested in politics and register to vote. Facilitators of Getting Ahead are instructed to be "agenda free" in all matters, including politics, but many encourage voter participation in general.

Use this book as a guide to advocating for policies specific to your city, county, or state that assist the various groups that need help. They lack a PAC. Be their PAC.

Strategies and policies must build an economy that serves people in poverty and the working class.

Education and well-paying jobs are generally regarded to be the first solutions to poverty. We have learned from Getting Ahead graduates that education and work are interwoven with problems associated with race, discrimination, transportation, housing, childcare, healthcare, and education. These problems of access and cost are not problems that the top-earning 50% of U.S. families have to overcome to get a good education and a good job.

Bridges sites do not experience these barriers and conditions in the same way. As noted before (especially in chapters 3 and 8), where you live matters. Wherever you are, though, these ideas will help prompt elected officials to take action. Right now our system simply does not have a process where policies that impact large numbers of people are discussed. That's where this book comes in.

Have your city, county, or state explore a pilot program based on the *Healthier Buckeye Council model in Ohio*. Many areas of your state are "prisoners of geography" in isolated urban and rural landscapes, and they find it difficult to start and sustain a Bridges initiative. Use small amounts of state money to jumpstart local Bridges initiatives. Funding should last at least three years, preferably five. It takes time to build a comprehensive approach like Bridges and to engage multiple sectors. The Bridges learning communities in cities and counties across the U.S. are ready to share their successes and strategies. Your initiative can collect and use data as part of continuous quality improvement (CQI) activities to build effective programming.

Promote employee stock ownership plans (ESOPs) and worker-owned companies. Try to keep your state and federal governments from putting up unnecessary roadblocks to the creation of ESOPs and worker-owned companies—and also urge any local companies thinking of selling out to a multinational conglomerate to consider forming an ESOP instead. With the proper leadership, ESOP won't be just a fable in your community, but a reality.

Adapt to changes brought about by mechanization, artificial intelligence, and robots. People can adapt, but only if their culture and mental tools allow them to. Help them by sharing Bridges and Getting Ahead concepts and processes.

Make the ballot box your weapon of choice. Encourage elected officials to undertake the reforms we have outlined, or vote the officials out. You do not need vast numbers to move the political needle. Here are two examples of voting blocs made up of a small number of voters who have a great deal of influence in a primary election-based system: One in five voters bases whom they vote for entirely on the issue of abortion.[204] One in four voters says that how a candidate stands on the issue of guns will determine their vote.[205]

Small numbers of people, such as those of us in Bridges communities, who are organized and seeking to unite on an issue can swing elections. Talk to people, and find out their stories. It can move how government works and can stop it from punishing people for being poor.

Aiming high: Policies and whole-system planning, Oklahoma and Brazil style

In Chapter 4 we told the story of the Getting Ahead graduate who brought the issue of water fees to the attention of the local Bridges collaborative and how that resulted in changes to city policy. While this was a significant victory and a great example of Bridges concepts at work, we need to tell the rest of the story.

During the investigation in Muskogee, Oklahoma, investigators looked upstream to see what was happening in the rest of the state. They discovered that most cities in the state were using water fees as a way to generate revenue the same way Muskogee had been.

Looking even farther upstream, the report "Poverty Interrupted" from the nonprofit group *ideas42* identified similar revenue-generating fee structures being used in many sectors and states in the U.S.[206]

The success in Muskogee hints at how policy change can be taken to the state level. To move from hint to action requires an intention to do whole-system policy change.

As described in Chapter 7, Bridges initiatives often start small but grow in influence as they add new sectors that use Bridges ideas. We have urged you to become intentional about having a big impact on poverty. Now we're saying don't be afraid to aim at whole-system planning. An excellent example of that comes from Curitiba, Brazil, a city of nearly 2 million in the southern part of the country.

I [Phil], who learned about Curitiba from Paul Hawken's *Natural Capitalism,* was invited to join a business mission to South America by Ohio Governor Bob Taft and his wife, Hope Taft. She and I met with Curitiba city planners before being taken to see the results of whole-system planning.

People from around the world go to Curitiba to see the bus system alone. It has the capacity to move people from their neighborhoods into the city center and to the factories surrounding the city very quickly and inexpensively. Three buses are linked together, the driver can manage the traffic lights to keep moving quickly, and people move off and on the buses from raised station platforms so they don't waste time climbing down from the bus.

Most people in poverty are moved quickly into home ownership. Mrs. Taft and I visited neighborhoods where people help build their own homes (think Habitat for Humanity), picking from four models. In the center of each neighborhood are daycare centers for young children where meals are served four times a day. These are open for 14 hours, allowing parents time to ride the bus to the factories surrounding the city and back.

In the neighborhoods are "lighthouses of knowledge," small libraries where children can go to do homework and have access to computers. Some of the subject matter in schools is based on conditions in Curitiba. For example, math problems use information from the city budget. At night, a police officer is stationed in the "lighthouse" overlooking the community.

These few examples only scratch the surface of the collaborative approaches in Curitiba.[207]

What's important to us is how they designed and achieved those systems. Mayor Jaime Lerner gets much of the credit for Curitiba's success. He was an architect, engineer, and urban planner. He used interdisciplinary charrettes to do whole-system planning (charrettes are a planning process often used by architects and other planners). Imagine an architect bringing people together from all construction trades necessary to build a high-rise—the drafters, ironworkers, framers, roofers, electricians, plumbers, and so on. Having the input and cooperation of each entity is crucial to success.

That's how Lerner approached city planning for education, health, transportation, safety, business development, and city services, to name a few. Importantly, there was one budget rather than several departmental budgets. By working together, they avoided the demands of self-serving silos and found creative solutions.

Not surprisingly, Lerner's approach to poverty helped inform the philosophy of Getting Ahead. He said, "If people feel respected, they will assume responsibility to help solve other problems."[208]

This example may seem on the "fantastic" side and very difficult to achieve in our society. But perhaps the Brazilians' philosophy and approach can inspire and guide the work of Bridges communities—and others who learn from these communities.

In the next chapter we'll look at a technique, Tocqueville meetings, for addressing such challenges. We've used a lot of ink describing how to build a car; now we'll get into more of the nuts and bolts of how to drive that car.

Chapter 20

Tocqueville Meetings: A Way Forward

Philip DeVol and Gene Krebs

*Amongst the laws which rule human societies, there is
one which seems to be more precise and clear than all the
others. If men are to remain civilized, or to become so, the
art of associating together must grow and improve in the
same ratio in which the equality of conditions is increased.*

–Alexis de Tocqueville, *Democracy in America*

We offer suggestions on how to manage a policy-development meeting consistent with the Bridges philosophy; such a gathering engages people from all classes, races, sectors and political persuasions.

In proposing the concept of the Tocqueville meeting, we contend that such a method for policy development, based on Bridges best practices and informed by all involved, will produce better results than those designed by the few.

To be sure, our process may be initially frustrating for those accustomed to rubber-stamping off-the-shelf policies provided by partisan think tanks. Encourage these individuals to imagine what it will be like when *people from all classes, races, cultures, religions, and political persuasions are at the table, with all voices heard, working in a respectful way with their legislators to bring the best policy ideas forward.*

At this stage we have bridged the divides and can see one another, in all our diversity, as the ancient Mayans did. Upon meeting, one would say, *"I am another you."* The reply would be: *"And you are another me."*[209]

Tocqueville meeting purpose: Identify barriers and solutions; create policies that help people in poverty, near poverty, and the working class.

Length of meeting: 90 minutes, unless in a retreat setting

Who attends

- Bridges collaborative members
- All classes, sectors, races, political persuasions
- Guests: legislators and community or state partners

Prerequisites: Everyone must be familiar with the Bridges language. Ideally they will have attended a Bridges workshop in person or online, will have participated in Getting Ahead, and/or will have read this book.

Preparing elected officials

- Invite them to attend Bridges training.
- Invite elected officials and candidates to Getting Ahead graduations to meet Getting Ahead graduates.
- Send elected officials and candidates such items as Bridges newsletters, updates, results, outcomes, and candidate briefing books.
- List officials on the front of newsletters and other communications.
- Meet them for coffee in public places.
- Develop a candidate or legislator briefing book at the local and state level.

Tocqueville meeting preparation

- Review the 10 Core Constructs of Bridges.
- Review Bridges thinking tools and have them available.
- Review data mailed prior to the meeting.
- Choose one of the four methods offered below for engaging everyone in the discussion: six thinking hats, Socratic circle, mind mapping, and flow charts.

Conducting the meeting

Introductions: When bringing together people from varied backgrounds and organizations, it's important that everyone be heard and acknowledged. A collaborative in Paducah, Kentucky, found it helpful to agree on this rule: *Leave your title and your organization's agenda at the door.*

During introductions, the members are invited to give quick highlights of the Bridges initiative in their organization. This serves three purposes: It celebrates the progress being made, it shares best practices, and it serves as a brief review of Bridges concepts.

Policy work

- Identify policy issues to be addressed.
- Use the meeting methodology outlined below.
- Identify solutions and innovations.
- Test possible solutions utilizing Bridges thinking tools.
- Define the policy solution.
- Develop a plan to move policy solutions forward.

Suggested methods for identifying policy solutions and engaging all participants

We do not prescribe one specific method for exploring and recording ideas during the Tocqueville meetings. We do, however, offer four proven methods for your consideration that make it easy for people from diverse backgrounds and situations to be heard and to think outside the box.

1. Six thinking hats

What it is: This thinking system, designed by Edward de Bono, is a tool for individual thinking and group discussion.[210]

- White hat: facts, information, knowledge needed
- Red: feelings, hunches, intuition
- Yellow: benefits, optimism
- Black: cautions, judgments
- Green: creativity, alternatives
- Blue: overview, process, controls use of thinking hats

How it works: "The premise of the method is that the human brain thinks in a number of distinct ways, which can be deliberately challenged ... None of these directions is a completely natural way of thinking, but rather how some of us already represent the results of our thinking."[211] The sessions are generally short, and the red hat (feelings, hunches, intuition) is used for only 30–60 seconds.

Different patterns for different purposes:

- Initial ideas: blue, white, green, blue
- Choosing among alternatives: blue, white, green, yellow, black, red, blue
- Identifying solutions: blue, white, black, green, blue
- Quick feedback: blue, black, green, blue
- Strategic planning: blue, yellow, black, white, blue, green, blue
- Process improvement: blue, white, white (other people's views), yellow, black, green, red, blue
- Solving problems: blue, white, green, red, yellow, black, green, blue

Notice that the colors are often repeated and that the blue hat (the process hat that controls the use of all the hats) is used at the beginning and end of every discussion.

Thinking hats are best for deliberately focusing the discussion on a particular approach.

The leader needs to understand the principles and process thoroughly. The leader usually keeps the blue hat on all the time to make sure things are progressing efficiently.[212]

2. Socratic circle/seminar method

What it is: A disciplined conversation, the practice of examining opinions or ideas logically through a method of questions and answers to determine their validity. It is not a debate as much as it is a process to gain a deeper understanding of complex ideas.

How it works:

1. Prior to the scheduled meeting, the facilitator sends out a short paragraph containing an open-ended question about the chosen topic.

2. The group members come prepared, having taken notes and organized their thoughts.

3. On the day of the meeting, the participants are seated in two concentric circles: an inner and an outer circle.

4. Those in the inner circle read the short paragraph aloud, then engage in a discussion of the topic for about 10 minutes. The outer circle observes the human behavior and performance of the inner circle.

5. Following the discussion of the topic, the outer circle then assesses the inner circle's performance and offers 10 minutes of feedback for the inner circle.

6. Participants in both inner and outer circles exchange roles and positions.

7. The new inner circle conducts a 10-minute discussion, then receives 10 minutes of feedback from the new outer circle.

8. The opening question posed by the facilitator has no right answer; instead, it reflects the genuine curiosity of the questioner. A good opening question leads participants back to the topic. Responses to the opening question generate new questions from the facilitator and participants, leading to new responses. This in turn leads to new insights and information.

Best for engaging all members in a free-flowing and safe conversation that deepens understanding.

The leader plays the part of both leader and member.[213]

3. Mind mapping

What it is: A diagram that connects information around a central subject, often in the shape of a tree.

How it works: The main idea is in the center, and the branches are subtopics or related ideas. Words, images, and colors are used to show hierarchy and connections. Mind mapping aids memory in the same way that mental models do.

Best for group brainstorming, studying a subject, planning, creating a knowledge bank, and solving problems.

The leader needs to learn the basics of mind mapping and, if need be, have an assistant to draw on the whiteboard (or use a computer) while the leader guides the conversation.[214]

4. Flow charts

What it is: A visual representation of the sequence of steps and decisions needed to perform a process. Several types: data-flow diagrams, influence diagrams, work-flow diagrams, process-flow diagrams.

How it works: Each step is noted within a diagram. Steps are linked by lines and directional arrows.

Best for project planning, system design, process documentation, audit process, documenting work flow.

The leader needs to be familiar with the method and, if need be, have an assistant to draw the diagrams.[215]

More thoughts on the Tocqueville meeting

You may not get this right the first time. Remember what astronomer Carl Sagan once said: "Valid criticism does you a favor."

As noted previously, fix the problem, don't 'fix the blame. Refrain from pointing the finger at those responsible. We live in a democratic republic. All citizens are to a degree responsible, all deserve a grain of blame, and all should receive a bucket of absolution.

Revere the data: You decide which data points to use. Open with those charts and graphs. Let the data inform the discussion in the early stages. Think of CharityTracker, Charity Check, and MPOWR, three web-based data collection and reporting tools used by Bridges sites.

Hear from everyone: Political leaders need to hear from people who have "been there," who have met and conquered serious problems. This includes Getting Ahead graduates and people who have applied Bridges concepts in their organizations.

Make sure legislators and their aides get this book early enough to digest the implications; all this takes some time to sink in thoroughly.

Keep it community-based. As much as possible, try to keep each meeting in an area or region that is a subset of the larger community. If you're in a city of 100,000 people with 10 council districts, start with one district. Then move to the others, but only as readily as you can in a reasonable manner.

Tell elected officials and departmental representatives that you appreciate their leadership on your issue. Tell them you are proud of them for being what you want them to become. This persuasive technique sometimes is referred to as altercasting.[216]

When a decision has been made to promote a particular policy, the group will do what all good groups do: establish who is taking the lead and who is responsible for each task. The convener also will establish due dates, reporting responsibilities, and the next meeting date.

Bridges collaboratives are urged to take full advantage of their strengths as laid out in this book. How many policy advocates can make their case with people from different economic classes, races, and political persuasions all speaking the same "language"?! How many have worked directly with their legislators and their aides to include their insights, experience, and of course a briefing book? How many have laid the groundwork with the media?

Closing the meeting

Rituals matter. Find a means of closing the meeting in a way that acknowledges the work of the group and gives expression to the gratitude that is felt in the room.

Conclusion

Be the Anchor Tree
Gene Krebs and Philip DeVol

*A political association draws a number of individuals ...
out of their own circle; however they may be naturally
kept asunder by age, mind, and fortune, it places them
nearer together and brings them into contact.*

–Alexis de Tocqueville, *Democracy in America*

When you drive across the United States, you often see a lone, large tree out in the middle of a field. Powerful looking, it stands in solitary splendor. It is the last remnant of the primeval forest. It is the anchor tree.

Prior to the advent of diesel-powered bulldozers, farmers cleared forests by hand at the rate of about an acre a year.[217] And they usually did it in August, after the wheat harvest and before the corn crop was ready. Stumps were left about four feet high. One tree in the middle of the acre was left untouched; this was the anchor tree for that acre.

The next year a team of horses was brought in and pulled out the stumps using block and tackle attached to the anchor tree. Then that tree was cut down. When the stump's roots had rotted a little, the farmer would borrow horses, ropes, and pulleys from his neighbors and pull against another anchor tree an acre away. This went on for well over 100 years, one acre a year, until all you were left with was a single anchor tree, often a truly gigantic specimen, in the middle of a vast field. The last tree, puzzled over by children as they whiz by on the interstate, has no other tree near enough to help pull it out, and so it remains.

You, your organization, and your community can be the anchor tree that other groups and individuals connect with to help people get out of poverty and create a renewed Tocqueville America, one "acre" at a time.

A call to action

With the exception of the Healthier Buckeye model and ESOPs, we have avoided proposing specific policies for you to consider. Instead, by and large, we have proposed changes to the process and structure of how we organize politically.

What we are about with this book is an exercise in restoring civic capacity, something that has been eroded by zoning, beltways, sprawl, economic segregation, and social/political polarization.

Bridges communities have been an inspiration to us. If this book helps elevate their work to a higher, even more effective level, we will be grateful.

A nation is built upon an enormous number of smaller communities. Learning from Bridges communities means you can help revitalize your corner of the country. It also means you are not alone. In turn, you can give back by assisting others in starting the local and organic process of reinvigorate their corners too.

Along with others in your community, be the tree that anchors the work.

Endnotes

[1] A. B. Lloyd, "Hillary Clinton and the Fake Tocqueville Quotation"

[2] W. Whitman, *Leaves of Grass*

[3] A. de Tocqueville, *Democracy in America*

[4] J. Cott, *Dinner with Lenny*

[5] Pew Research Center, "Political Polarization in the American Public"

[6] G. A. Huber & N. Malhotra, "Political Homophily in Social Relationships"; R. Nauert, "Political Views Influence Relationship Partner Choice"

[7] M. Gentzkow, J. M. Shapiro, & M. Taddy, "Measuring Polarization in High-Dimensional Data"

[8] B. Bishop, "Caught in a Landslide"

[9] S. Webster, "Partisan Geographic Sorting"

[10] Until the Civil War, slaves counted in the U.S. Census as only three-fifths of a person, so that fact accentuated the relative power of the landholding white males in Southern districts. Congressional apportionment made the white male vote even more sought-after. Suddenly removing 135 voters from the rolls could have unbalanced the political universe of Abbeville.

[11] "United States Congressional Apportionment"; "Voter Turnout by Income, 2008 U.S. Presidential Election"

[12] No longer a functioning church building, it is now a historical site. "Hopewell Church—Israel Township"

[13] Thank you to *The Columbus Dispatch* for graciously giving permission to borrow extensively in this passage from an opinion piece written by Gene Krebs in 2013.

[14] "Shelby Foote Compromise"

[15] E. Dourado, "Maybe America Is Simply Too Big"

[16] W. D. Eggers, "A 'Whole of Government' Approach to Social Problems"

[17] T. Britton, B. Lusheck, & W. Tarter Jr. "Budget Landscape"

[18] C. Cox & B. Archer, "Cox and Archer"; R. Frank, "Where the Rich Make Their Income"

[19] M. Quinn, "The GOP Wants to Give States More Medicaid Power"

[20] J. C. Capretta, "Medicaid"

[21] *Ibid.*

[22] Every Getting Ahead group creates mental models of poverty, middle class, and wealth. Based on the work of Getting Ahead participants, Philip DeVol created the mental models of poverty and middle class. Ruby Payne developed the mental model of wealth for the 2006 edition of *A Framework for Understanding Poverty*.

[23] G. Tett, *The Silo Effect*

[24] R. D. Putnam, *Our Kids;* C. Murray, *Coming Apart*

[25] R. Reeves, *The Dream Hoarders*

[26] S. Mullainathan & E. Shafir, *Scarcity*

[27] I. W. Jindra & M. Jindra, "Connecting Poverty, Culture, and Cognition"

[28] J. Champy, *Reengineering Management;* P. Underhill, *Why We Buy*

[29] J. R. Bradley, "Bridging the Cultures of Business and Poverty"

[30] From 2017 Cascade Engineering promotional materials

[31] *Ibid.*

[32] P. E. DeVol, *Getting Ahead in the Workplace*

[33] The Equality of Opportunity Project, "Homepage"

[34] Minnesota Collaborative Anti-Racism Initiative, "Systemic Racism"

[35] E. A. Wahler, "Getting Ahead in a Just-Gettin'-By World: Program Evaluation Results"

[36] P. F. Campos, "White Economic Privilege Is Alive and Well"

[37] R. Reeves, *The Dream Hoarders*

[38] "America Can't Fix Poverty Until It Stops Hating Poor People"

[39] P. Bourdieu, *Distinction*

[40] P. Fussell, *Class;* E. Currid-Halkett, *The Sum of Small Things.*

[41] R. K. Payne, *A Framework for Understanding Poverty*

[42] R. K. Payne, T. Dreussi-Smith, L. Y. Shaw, & J. Young, *Bridges to Health and Healthcare*

[43] R. W. Fuller, *Somebodies and Nobodies*

[44] Ruby Payne's original list of eight resources was first published in *A Framework for Understanding Poverty* and then in *Bridges Out of Poverty.* As Getting Ahead groups analyzed their own resources, they found it helpful to add language, integrity and trust, and motivation and persistence to the list of resources, and that list of 11 now appears in *Getting Ahead in a Just-Gettin'-By World.*

[45] As noted previously, Ruby Payne developed the initial list of resources and the analysis through the individual lens. Jodi Pfarr and Philip DeVol expanded that analysis and added the institutional and community lenses.

[46] R. D. Putnam, *Bowling Alone;* Putnam also writes in *Bowling Alone:* "Economic sociologist Mark Granovetter has pointed out that when seeking jobs—or political allies—the 'weak' ties that link me to distant acquaintances who move in different circles from mine are actually more valuable than the 'strong' ties that link me to relatives and intimate friends whose sociological niche is very like my own. Bonding social capital is, as Xavier de Souza Briggs puts it, good for 'getting by,' but bridging social capital is crucial for 'getting ahead.'"

[47] Jodi Pfarr began asking funders if they were *bringing* resources or *building* resources, and then the resource chart was adapted to distinguish between "getting-*by*" resources and "getting-*ahead*" resources.

[48] "Movement"

[49] M. Saccocio, "Schenectady Bridges Works Toward Long-Term Communitywide Change"

[50] Collective Impact, "About Us"

[51] K. R. Barber, "A Constellation of Connections"

[52] P. Freire, *Pedagogy of the Oppressed*

[53] K. Stern, "Why the Rich Don't Give to Charity"

[54] F. Dobbin & A. Kalev, "Why Diversity Programs Fail"

[55] "Evaluations, Research, Best Practices, and Results"

[56] E. A. Wahler, "A Group-Based Intervention for Persons Living in Poverty"

[57] I. W. Jindra & M. Jindra, "Connecting Poverty, Culture, and Cognition"

[58] "Evaluations, Research, Best Practices, and Results"

[59] "Free Webinar Series"

[60] "Store"

[61] K. R. Barber et al., *From Vision to Action,* vols. I and II

[62] CharityTracker, "Homepage"; Charity Check, "Homepage"

[63] "Presidential Election Voter Statistics"; "The Brookings Democracy Dashboard"; "Demography of the United States"; Greenblatt, "What Would Happen If America Made Voting Mandatory?"

[64] D. Kahneman, *Thinking Fast and Slow*

[65] H. Adams, *The Education of Henry Adams*

[66] N. Taniparti, "What Happened When I Tried to Teach Harvard Undergrads About Inequality and Poverty"

[67] Z. Horne, D. Powell, J. E. Hummel, & K. J. Holyoak, "Countering Antivaccination Attitudes"

[68] D. Quigg, "Bridges Communities Can Take Their Use of Data up by Three Notches"

[69] Public Insight, "Homepage"

[70] Pew Research Center, "In Changing News Landscape, Even Television Is Vulnerable"

[71] F. Chideya, "Suburban White Women Weigh Their Options in a 'Bizarre' Election"

[72] Working America, "Unique 'Front Porch Focus Group' Explores the Appeal of Trump's Right-Wing Message with White Working-Class Voters"

[73] A. de Tocqueville, *Democracy in America*

[74] R. Craig, "Donald Trump and the Value of College"; M. Tucker, "Donald Trump, Education Policy and the Future of American Politics"

[75] J. Coder & G. Green, "Comparing Earnings of White Males by Education for Selected Age Cohorts"

[76] M. Fowler, "Obama"

[77] A. Case & A. Deaton, "Rising Morbidity and Mortality in Midlife Among White Non-Hispanic Americans in the 21st Century"; A. M. Barry-Jester, "How Americans Die May Depend on Where They Live"

[78] D. Lauter, "How Do Americans View Poverty?"

[79] R. Morin, "Behind Trump's Win in Rural White America"

[80] Greek philosopher Heraclitus asserted that change is the foundational principle of the universe: "No one ever steps into the same river twice."

[81] J. A. Begala, "Big City Problems in Ohio's Small Towns"

[82] G. Knepper, *Ohio and Its People*

[83] "United States Steel Production 1969–2018"

[84] Federal Reserve Bank of St. Louis, "All Employees"

[85] M. Muro & S. Kulkarni, "Voter Anger Explained—in One Chart"

[86] M. Muro & S. Liu, "Why Trump's Factory Job Promises Won't Pan out—in One Chart"

[87] J. Kolko, "Trump Was Stronger Where the Economy Is Weaker"

[88] Executive Office of the President of the United States, "The Long-Term Decline in Prime-Age Male Labor Force Participation"

[89] R. V. Reeves, "Middle America's Malaise Helped Trump to Victory, but He Has No Cure"

[90] R. Chetty, D. Grusky, M. Hell, N. Hendren, R. Manduca, & J. Narang, "The Fading American Dream"; R. V. Reeves & D. Halikias, "On the New Chetty-Bomb That Only Half of Americans Are Better off Than Their Parents"

[91] E. Badger, "What Happens When the Richest U.S. Cities Turn to the World?"

[92] M. Muro & S. Liu, "Another Clinton-Trump Divide"

[93] G. B. White, "Education Gaps Don't Fully Explain Why Black Unemployment Is So High"

[94] G. J. Borjas, "Final Version of Mariel Study"

[95] D. H. Autor, D. Dorn, & G. H. Hanson, "The China Shock"

[96] D. H. Autor, D. Dorn, G. H. Hanson, & K. Majlesi, "Importing Political Polarization?"

[97] M. Muro, "Look to Advanced Industries to Help Drive Productivity Gains"

[98] R. K. Payne, *A Framework for Understanding Poverty*

[99] G. Tett, *The Silo Effect*

[100] M. Jindra & I. W. Jindra, "Poverty and the Controversial Work of Nonprofits"

[101] *Ibid.*

[102] American Farm Bureau Federation, "Fast Facts About Agriculture"

[103] J. Norman, "Americans' Confidence in Institutions Stays Low"

[104] "The Population Size of U.S. House Districts"

[105] "United States Congressional Apportionment"

[106] J. Brennan, "Trump Won Because Voters Are Ignorant, Literally"

[107] "Bernie Sanders"

[108] D. Cole, "How to Reverse *Citizens United*"

[109] A. Greenblatt, "The New Strategy for Limiting Money's Role in Elections"

[110] Ohio Revised Code, "Title [57] LVII Taxation § 5747.29 Credit for Contributions of Money to Candidates for Statewide Office or Member of General Assembly"

[111] J. R. Kasich, "Blueprint for a New Ohio"

[112] Despite all of these problems, term limits could work if applied only to the leadership of each chamber, which is where reforms can get logjammed.

[113] K. Kondik & G. Skelley, "Incumbent Reelection Rates Higher Than Average in 2016"

[114] A. Blake, "Why You Should Stop Blaming Gerrymandering So Much. Really."

[115] E. Petry, "How the Efficiency Gap Works"

[116] N. O. Stephanopoulos & E. M. McGhee, "Partisan Gerrymandering and the Efficiency Gap"

[117] D. Wasserman, "The Political Process Isn't Rigged—It Has Much Bigger Problems"

[118] A. Greenblatt, "Maine Becomes First State to Adopt a Whole New Way of Voting"

[119] J. C. McGinty, "Third-Party Candidates Don't Have to Be Spoilers"

[120] P. Plumb & J. Cohen, "Maine Voices"

[121] "Maine Voters Adopt Ranked Choice Voting"

[122] M. Shepherd, "Maine's New Way of Voting Ruled Unconstitutional"

[123] E. L. Glaeser & A. Shleifer, "The Curley Effect: The Economics of Shaping the Electorate"

[124] Negotiation theory is quite clear that if you are attempting to deal with someone with whom you will need to have a working relationship in the future, and you completely win in a deal, they will constantly pick at your ankles until they bring you down. Justified or not, it is human nature. The losers in such a one-sided deal will work harder to make you suffer than you worked on your deal in the first place.

[125] T. S. Purdum, "The Republican Who Saved Civil Rights"

[126] United States House of Representatives, "Final Vote Results for Roll Call 331"; United States Senate, "Roll Call Vote 104th Congress—2nd Session"

[127] K. Schake, "Trump and the Shibboleths"

[128] L.-L. Marker & F. J. Marker, *Ingmar Bergman*

[129] Wave elections and chaos theory are intertwined in that if you watch the surface of the ocean closely from the deck of a catamaran, you will notice that the surface of the water is covered with small waves. It is when they form together in unison that larger waves are formed. Those

waves then combine with others to form extremely large waves. But remember that each massive wave crashing on the beach is actually a collection of smaller waves that have united under the math of chaos theory. In a democracy, each wave election comes from multitudes of smaller waves combining.

[130] B. Casselman, "Microloans Don't Solve Poverty"

[131] "Osborne Reef Waste Tire Removal Project"

[132] P. E. Salkin, "From Euclid to Growing Smart"

[133] D. Budds, "How Urban Design Perpetuates Racial Inequality—and What We Can Do About It"; M. Maciag, "Gentrification in America Report"

[134] P. Walker, "How Bike Helmet Laws Do More Harm Than Good"

[135] S. A. Brinkman et al., "Efficacy of Infant Simulator Programs to Prevent Teenage Pregnancy"

[136] M. S. Kearney & P. B. Levine, "Media Influences on Social Outcomes"

[137] United States Department of Health and Human Services, "Assessing Child Support Arrears in Nine Large States and the Nation—Executive Summary"

[138] J. L. Doleac & B. Hansen, "Does 'Ban the Box' Help or Hurt Low-Skilled Workers?"

[139] J. B. Wogan, "Studies Discredit State Policies That Punish Poor People for Saving Money"

[140] D. Kahneman, *Thinking Fast and Slow*

[141] T. Kuran, "Availability Cascades and Risk Regulation"

[142] A. Lickerman, "Getting People to Change Their Minds"

[143] U. Sinclair, *I, Candidate for Governor*

[144] J. Halpin, "The Structural Imbalance of Political Talk Radio"

[145] C. B. Frey & M. A. Osborne, "The Future of Employment"

[146] J. D. Gwartney et al., "Macroeconomics"

[147] C. Dimitri et al., "The 20th Century Transformation of U.S. Agriculture and Farm Policy"

[148] E. Barclay, "Your Grandparents Spent More of Their Money on Food Than You Do"

[149] J. Harris, "Man vs. Machine"

[150] Q. Larson, "A Warning from Bill Gates, Elon Musk, and Stephen Hawking"

[151] A. de Tocqueville, *Democracy in America*

[152] R. Craig, "Donald Trump and the Value of College"

[153] "What We Can Learn About Investing from the Business of French Wine"

[154] Court of Master Sommeliers, Americas, "About"

[155] Federal Reserve Bank of St. Louis, "Real Gross Domestic Product Per Capita"

[156] J. Bivens & L. Mishel, "Understanding the Historic Divergence Between Productivity and a Typical Worker's Pay"

[157] M. Henry-Nickie, "AI Should Worry Skilled Knowledge Workers Too"

[158] A. Hollingsworth et al., "Macroeconomic Conditions and Opioid Abuse"

[159] D. T. Carter, *Confederate Goliath*

[160] C. Murray, "The Social Contract Revisited"; F. F. Piven & R. A. Cloward, "The Weight of the Poor"

[161] United States Census Bureau, "Poverty Thresholds"

[162] A. Lleras-Muney, "Healthier Kids?"

[163] I. V. Sawhill, "Money for Nothing"

[164] J. Ahern, "Earned Income Tax Credit Lifts Families out of Poverty"

[165] "Earned Income Tax Credit"

[166] A. Berube, "Want to Help the Working Class?"

[167] R. Marcuss et al., "Internal Revenue Service Publication 6162"

[168] G. J. Whitehurst, "This Policy Would Help Poor Kids More Than Universal Pre-K Does"

[169] C. Marr et al., "EITC and Child Tax Credit Promote Work, Reduce Poverty, and Support Children's Development, Research Finds"

[170] T. D. Murray, "Why Do 70 Percent of Lottery Winners End up Bankrupt?"

[171] P. S. Torre, "How (and Why) Athletes Go Broke"

[172] F. Nietzsche, *Schopenhauer as Educator*

[173] J. Markoff, "Artificial Intelligence Swarms Silicon Valley on Wings and Wheels"

[174] K. Madigan, "It's Man vs. Machine and Man Is Losing"

[175] M. J. Hicks & S. Devaraj, "The Myth and the Reality of Manufacturing in America"

[176] Federal Reserve Bank of St. Louis, "All Employees: Manufacturing (MANEMP)"

[177] C. B. Frey & M. A. Osborne, "The Future of Employment"

[178] United States Census Bureau, "New American Community Survey Statistics for Income, Poverty and Health Insurance Available for States and Local Areas"

[179] M. Maciag, "The Metro Areas with More New Businesses"

[180] K. Capps, "Earnings Are Rising, Along with the Damned Rent"

[181] M. Maciag, "Demographics Can Spell Trouble for a City's Finances"

[182] E. Hayasaki, "How Poverty Affects the Brain"

[183] M. Aguiar et al., "Leisure Luxuries and the Labor Supply of Young Men"

[184] B. Casselman, "Don't Blame a 'Skills Gap' for Lack of Hiring in Manufacturing"

[185] S. J. Keating et al., "Toward Site-Specific and Self-Sufficient Robotic Fabrication on Architectural Scales"

[186] Economic Innovation Group, "Dynamism in Retreat"

[187] "The Problem with Profits"

[188] N. Iuviene et al., "Sustainable Economic Democracy"

[189] W. C. Taylor, *Simply Brilliant*

[190] "Mondragon Corporation"

[191] F. Lindenfeld & P. Wynn, "Why Some Worker Co-Ops Succeed While Others Fail"; N. Iuviene et al., "Sustainable Economic Democracy"

[192] S. Kasmir, "Can Worker Cooperatives Save American Manufacturing?"

[193] N. Iuviene et al., "Sustainable Economic Democracy"

[194] *Ibid.*

[195] A. Hollingsworth et al., "Macroeconomic Conditions and Opioid Abuse"

[196] S. Quinones, *Dreamland*

[197] J. Hari, *Chasing the Scream*

[198] D. West, *Megachange*

[199] The U.S. is the only country to have settled the issue of slavery via a war, although Haiti did so through a rebellion; B. Lewis, "Could Slavery Have Ended Without the Civil War?"

[200] D. Roth, "Jeff Immelt Says the Relationship Between Business and Government Is Absolutely Busted"

[201] M. McGrath, "63% of Americans Don't Have Enough Savings to Cover a $500 Emergency"

[202] E. A. Wahler, "Getting Ahead in a Just-Gettin'-By World: Program Evaluation Results"

[203] B. Bartlett, "The Truth Matters"

[204] R. Riffkin, "Abortion Edges up as Important Voting Issue for Americans"

[205] J. McCarthy, "Quarter of U.S. Voters Say Candidate Must Share View on Guns"

[206] A. Daminger et al., "Poverty Interrupted"

[207] Hawken et al., *Natural Capitalism*

[208] *Ibid.*

[209] P. Reed, "In Lak'ech—I Am Another You"

[210] E. de Bono, *Six Thinking Hats*

[211] "Six Thinking Hats"

[212] *Ibid.*

[213] "The Socratic Circle"

[214] M. Pinola, "How to Use Mind Maps to Unleash Your Brain's Creativity and Potential"

[215] "Flowchart"

[216] "Altercasting"

[217] Though indigenous people then and environmentalists now might take exception to the practice of widespread deforestation, that's what many of the settlers did—for the lumber and to create fields for their farms. They cleared a lot of land. It has been said, with only slight hyperbole, that before the coming of the white pioneers, a squirrel could climb a tree on the coast of Massachusetts and go west from tree to tree, not touching the ground again till it reached the Mississippi River.

Appendix A

Glossary of Bridges Terminology

aha! Process, Inc.: the publishing and training company, which focuses on poverty and economic-class issues, founded and led by Ruby K. Payne

Bridges: The book *Bridges Out of Poverty: Strategies for Professionals and Communities* is generally used to train people who serve, work, and engage people in poverty and near poverty. The word Bridges often is used in a broad sense to refer to all things pertaining to the initiative. Rely on the context.

Bridges communities: Hundreds of settings in the United States and around the world where various organizations/institutions use Bridges concepts to improve their work and come together to learn from each other and advance Bridges initiatives

Bridges model: common content and methodology used by institutions and communities that adapt Bridges concepts; adherence to the underlying concepts and core constructs is balanced with encouragement to take ownership of the ideas *and* to innovate.

Bridges steering committee: generic term for a collaborative that communities develop to use Bridges concepts; leadership groups adopt names like Marion Matters, Impact Coalition, and Stillwater Cares.

Causes of poverty: Research on poverty causation falls into four categories— individual choice/behavior/circumstances, community conditions, exploitation, and political/economic structures.

Certified trainers: aha! Process trains individuals to work in institutions and/or communities regarding a number of sector-specific topics, including Bridges, Getting Ahead, K–12 and postsecondary education, health and healthcare, reentry (from incarceration), the workplace, etc.

Client (employee, citizen returning from incarceration, and so on) Life Cycle: an examination of end users' experience as they move through the process designed by the provider; this focuses on the experience of the person being served, not the design as it is written.

Collaborative: when various organizations/institutions and sectors in a community join forces with regard to the Bridges model

Common language: the core Bridges content found in most books and trainings provided by aha! Process; the content and constructs are shared by people from all classes, races, sectors, and political persuasions.

Core constructs: 10 foundational statements that sum up the commitment of individuals who apply Bridges in their lives, workplace, and community (see Appendix B)

Getting Ahead: a facilitated group learning experience based on the workbook *Getting Ahead in a Just-Gettin'-By World: Building Your Resources for a Better Life,* which is used by people in poverty to examine the impact that poverty has on them and their communities; this experience leads to the participants (called investigators) creating a "future story" supported by detailed plans. *Getting Ahead* also is a series of workbooks, including an edition for first-generation, low-income students; citizens returning from incarceration to the community; and entry-level employees.

Getting Ahead investigators: individuals who participate in the Getting Ahead learning experiences; they aren't seen as clients or students but as active participants in charge of their own learning.

Hidden rules of class: unspoken cues and habits of individuals and groups from poverty, middle class, and wealth

Law of attraction: an invitational stance and style regarding Bridges and Getting Ahead practices; it has been found that Bridges is most successful when people aren't forced to adopt or adhere to a "canned" program and information; this extends to staff and volunteers, community members at large, and Getting Ahead investigators. Given an opportunity to learn the information, people are allowed to apply the ideas they embrace. This doesn't mean that organizations shouldn't make institutional changes based on Bridges concepts that impact the daily lives of staff; it does mean that a cultural change of this sort will usually have some staff members who are outliers. They're to be treated with respect and be given opportunities to express their ideas and make any changes at their own pace.

Learning communities: People who know and use the common Bridges language enjoy sharing best practices at the water cooler in their own organization, at community meetings with people from other sectors, at statewide Bridges collaboratives, and with Bridges sites across the U.S. and internationally.

Mental models: Research confirms that drawings and graphics are easier to remember than lots of text. In Bridges and Getting Ahead, mental models are frequently used to convey concepts. Words tend to go in one ear and out the other, while images stick in the mind.

Methodology: application of Bridges concepts; the Bridges model expands when people take ownership and share their innovations with others.

Models: A number of books and workshops are used to help people in poverty learn and utilize key concepts and take charge of their own lives. Individual action, however, isn't enough in most cases to facilitate the climb out of poverty. There are institutional, community, and policy barriers that must be overcome. For this reason "models" are defined that engage institutions and communities in providing ongoing support for those in poverty. Models include Workplace Stability, Getting Ahead while Getting Out (reentry), and Staying Ahead.

Resources: In Bridges the term refers to 11 sources of personal capability named in the definition of poverty. Only one of the 11 resources involves money. The term resources can be confusing because it has other meanings. For example, "resources" can be used to refer to daily needs like water, food, shelter, cash, and so on. The term also is used to describe community agencies and programs. Community leaders might say, "We have many resources for those in poverty." By that they mean the institutions that provide healthcare, education, transportation, etc.

Sectors: The institutions and organizations that use Bridges concepts, such as prenatal care, K–12 and postsecondary education, workforce development, employers, health and healthcare, etc.

Thinking tools: Bridges introduces new ways to think about poverty. Many of these have a mental model associated with them. For example, the "four causes of poverty" are turned into the "sustainability grid" thinking tool that helps Bridges communities address all causes of poverty. Another thinking tool is the "triple lens" (individual, institutional/organizational, community) that reminds us to analyze poverty issues in a comprehensive way. There are 12 such tools.

Tyranny of the moment: short-term thinking that results from living in unstable, under-resourced conditions; this affects people in poverty most severely, occupying mental bandwidth that could otherwise be used for abstract thinking, developing one's future story, and getting ahead.

Bridges Core Constructs

1. Use the lens of economic class to understand and take responsibility for your own societal experience, while being open to the experiences of others.

2. At the intersection of poverty with other social disparities (racial, gender, physical ability, age, etc.), address inequalities in access to resources.

3. Define poverty as the extent to which a person, institution/organization, or community does without resources.

4. Build relationships of mutual respect.

5. Base plans on the premise that people in all classes, sectors, and political persuasions are problem solvers and need to be at the decision-making table.

6. Base plans on accurate mental models of poverty, middle class, and wealth.

7. At the individual, institutional/organizational, and community/policy levels, stabilize the environment, remove barriers to transition, and build resources.

8. Address all causes of poverty (four areas of research).

9. Build long-term support for individual, institutional/organizational, and community/policy transition.

10. Build economically sustainable communities in which everyone can live well.

BRIDGES MODEL

Bridges® OUT OF POVERTY

ahaprocess.com

Philanthropy, Policy, and Quality of Life

Giving Back

Everyone at the Planning Table
Eliminating Barriers

Leadership Development
Long-Term Funding Sources

Succession Planning
Endowments

Attain Critical Mass of Resourced

Staying Ahead Development and Data

Staying Ahead

Trainer Certification

How Much of Yourself Do You Own?
Financial Literacy

Return on Investment
Partnerships

Case Management
Policy and Procedure Changes

Institution to Institution
Planning for Growth and Scalability

Sector Involvement
Barrier Identification
Community Future Story

Getting Ahead

Bridges Training

Getting Ahead Training

Board Selection and Institutional Training

Steering Committee: Selection, Training, Guidelines

Resourced

Under-Resourced

INDIVIDUAL

INSTITUTION

COMMUNITY

Evaluation and Designated Outcomes

Bridges Out of Poverty Constructs and Language

Data collection at every level

Appendix D

Ali Plum's poems derive from the investigations of the Getting Ahead group into the impact poverty has on the community and the individuals themselves. The early part of Getting Ahead is difficult, often painful work. Plum's first poem, "A Mental Model of My Life Now," comes from the early modules, during which the group creates a Mental Model of Poverty in their community, and individuals create mental models of their own lives. Plum's second poem, "Getting Ahead," derives from the future story she creates at the end of the last session. It reflects the information in the book, but more importantly, it embraces the wisdom and support of the other investigators in the Getting Ahead group.

A Mental Model of My Life Now ...
by Ali Plum

Mental model of my life now
I would have to say is
A quagmire of paradox, perplexions, pain
(and ill-timed, fleeting, occasional pleasures
Not the sustaining kind, but the numbing kind)
Chock-full of paradoxes wrapped up in bulk, and put away,
Their presence only adding to daily confusion
Exhaustion from the tyrannies—the urgent things
Never done or not done well enough
To warrant progress or peace of mind
Between two worlds, between two minds in
This one cursed head
Creates disconnects and regrets ... "Not good enough" it says
The mind meanwhile, key parts compromised
Fight or flight all day all night
In constant battle, internal, sometimes external,
the disconnecting ... a descent
Slower, lower, less and less clear between lucid moments
Detached at best
And worst.
Though this mind through struggle seems cursed
Will not give up or give in to the internal indictments, will not quit.
Amidst the struggle of poverty
Compassion wins. Another day to begin, again.

Getting Ahead
by Ali Plum

Like a dirty word
in our society
Poverty
when someone sees they want to leave
Like a car crash kind of thing
It's been a rough road indeed

Taking hostage hope and movement
lulling creativity to sleep
The worry monster striking dread
the living in the head
Looking around for your voice
finding silence instead

If you're not only hungry
you contend with contempt
from oh so very many
who simply don't understand yet

Here is where I've learned to see
a different kind of future
a different kind of me
whether or not there is plenty
there's a voice to set free
We can bring understanding
wherever we may be

Contempt would surely be replaced
with a smile on each and every face
with a giving free of grace
with a building of a safer place

When we all know what we learned here
How similar we are—the worry, chaos, fear
perhaps not about money
but about something near and dear

The highs, lows, losses, gains
We all feel all these, so much the same
We all want love and laughter
instead of that darned pain

When all is lost and we feel alone
rich and poor alike, we long for a safety and home
(see we are so much in the same boat)
We want to be seen and heard
A bank account can't define self worth

You and me we can unlock hope
No longer at the end of our rope
When
connection replaces fear
Where
we can laugh or shed a tear
When
no longer an island all alone
Why
Look how far we've come, how much we've grown!

Though I've still such a long way to go
I've learned I'm not traveling alone
Finding strength in each other
Finding a new sense of hope

When everyone comes to the table
There's so much possibility
For the haves and the have nots
And all in between.

Thankful to have had this time
you wise investigators by my side
to learn and be
TOGETHER
Finding hope
and newfound peace.

Bibliography

Adams, H. (1919). *The education of Henry Adams.* New York, NY: Dover.

Aguiar, M., Bils, M., Charles, K. K., & Hurst, E. (2017, July 4). Leisure luxuries and the labor supply of young men. Retrieved from https://scholar.princeton.edu/sites/default/files/maguiar/files/leisure-luxuries-labor-june-2017.pdf

Ahern, J. (2017, April 12). Earned income tax credit lifts families out of poverty. Retrieved from http://www.communitysolutions.com/index.php?option=com_lyftenbloggie&view=entry&year=2017&month=04&day=11&id=64:earned-income-tax-credit-lifts-families-out-of-poverty

Akerlof, G. A., & Kranton, R. E. (2010). *Identity economics: How our identities shape our work, wages, and well-being.* Princeton, NJ: Princeton University Press.

Alexander, M. (2010). *The new Jim Crow: Mass incarceration in the age of colorblindness.* New York, NY: The New Press.

Altercasting. (2018). Retrieved from http://changingminds.org/techniques/general/more_methods/altercasting.htm

America can't fix poverty until it stops hating poor people. (2017, October 10). Retrieved from http://arthurbrooks.com/news/america-cant-fix-poverty-until-it-stops-hating-poor-people/

American Farm Bureau Federation. (2018). Fast facts about agriculture. Retrieved from https://www.fb.org/newsroom/fast-facts

Austen, J. (2017). *Pride and prejudice.* Seattle, WA: AmazonClassics.

Autor, D. H., Dorn, D., & Hanson, G. H. (2016, January). The China shock: Learning from labor market adjustment to large changes in trade. Retrieved from http://www.nber.org/papers/w21906

Autor, D. H., Dorn, D., Hanson, G. H., & Majlesi, K. (2016, January). Importing political polarization? The electoral consequences of rising trade exposure. Retrieved from http://economics.mit.edu/files/11499

Badger, E. (2017, December 22). What happens when the richest U.S. cities turn to the world? *The New York Times.* Retrieved from https://www.nytimes.com/2017/12/22/upshot/the-great-disconnect-megacities-go-global-but-lose-local-links.html

Barber, K. R. (2015). A constellation of connections: Santa Rosa County's Bridges to prosperity. In K. R. Barber et al., *From vision to action: Best practices to reduce the impact of poverty in communities, education, healthcare, and more* (vol. II). Highlands, TX: aha! Process (pages 61–69).

Barber, K. R. et al. (2015). *From vision to action: Best practices to reduce the impact of poverty in communities, education, healthcare, and more* (vol. II). Highlands, TX: aha! Process.

Barclay, E. (2015, March 2). Your grandparents spent more of their money on food than you do. Retrieved from https://www.npr.org/sections/thesalt/2015/03/02/389578089/your-grandparents-spent-more-of-their-money-on-food-than-you-do

Barry-Jester, A. M. (2016, December 13). How Americans die may depend on where they live. Retrieved from https://fivethirtyeight.com/features/how-americans-die-may-depend-on-where-they-live/

Bartlett, B. (2017). *The truth matters: A citizen's guide to separating facts from lies and stopping fake news in its tracks.* New York, NY: Penguin Random House.

Bazata, B. et al. (2013). *From vision to action: Best practices to reduce the impact of poverty in communities, education, healthcare, and more* (vol. II). Highlands, TX: aha! Process.

Begala, J. A. (2016, November). Big city problems in Ohio's small towns. Retrieved from http://www.communitysolutions.com/assets/docs/Major_Reports/Other_Publications/hubcitiesfinal10.10.16_jb02032017.pdf

Bernie Sanders. (n.d.). Retrieved from https://www.opensecrets.org/pres16/candidate.php?id=N00000528

Berube, A. (2017, June 28). Want to help the working class? Pay the EITC differently. Retrieved from https://www.brookings.edu/blog/the-avenue/2017/06/28/want-to-help-the-working-class-pay-the-eitc-differently/

Bishop, B. (2016, November 21). Caught in a landslide—County-level voting shows increased 'sorting.' Retrieved from http://www.dailyyonder.com/caught-in-a-landslide-county-level-voting-shows-increased-sorting/2016/11/21/16361/

Bivens, J., & Mishel, L. (2015, September 2). Understanding the historic divergence between productivity and a typical worker's pay: Why it matters and why it's real. Retrieved from http://www.epi.org/publication/understanding-the-historic-divergence-between-productivity-and-a-typical-workers-pay-why-it-matters-and-why-its-real/

Blake, A. (2017, April 8). Why you should stop blaming gerrymandering so much. Really. Retrieved from https://www.washingtonpost.com/news/the-fix/wp/2017/04/08/why-you-should-stop-blaming-gerrymandering-so-much-really/

Borjas, G. J. (2016, July 13). Final version of Mariel study. Retrieved from https://gborjas.org/2016/07/13/final-version-of-mariel-study/

Boswell, J. (2013). *The Life of Samuel Johnson, LL.D.* [abridged]. Project Gutenberg. Retrieved from https://www.gutenberg.org/files/1564/1564-h/1564-h.htm

Bourdieu, P. (1986). *Distinction: A social critique of the judgement of taste.* London, United Kingdom: Routledge Classics.

Bradley, J. R. (2003, Spring). Bridging the cultures of business and poverty: Welfare to career at Cascade Engineering. Stanford Social Innovation Review. Retrieved from https://ssir.org/articles/entry/bridging_the_cultures_of_business_and_poverty

Brennan, J. (2016, November 10). Trump won because voters are ignorant, literally. Retrieved from http://foreignpolicy.com/2016/11/10/the-dance-of-the-dunces-trump-clinton-election-republican-democrat/

Brinkman, S. A., Johnson, S. E., Codde, J. P., Hart, M. B., Straton, J. A., Mittinty, M. N., & Silburn, S. R. (2016). Efficacy of infant simulator programs to prevent teenage pregnancy: A school-based cluster randomized controlled trial in Western Australia. doi:https://doi.org/10.1016/S0140-6736(16)30384-1

Britton, T., Lusheck, B., & Tarter Jr., W. (2016, December). Budget landscape: Ohio's health and human services agencies 2018–2019. Retrieved from http://www.communitysolutions.com/assets/docs/State_Budgeting_Matters/2016/sbmv12n06-%202018-19%20budget%20landscape-%20hhs%20agencies%2012012016.pdf

The Brookings democracy dashboard. (2017). The Brookings Institution. Retrieved from https://www.brookings.edu/interactives/the-brookings-democracy-dashboard

Budds, D. (2016, July 18). How urban design perpetuates racial inequality—and what we can do about it. Retrieved from https://www.fastcodesign.com/3061873/how-urban-design-perpetuates-racial-inequality-and-what-we-can-do-about-it

Campos, P. F. (2017, July 29). White economic privilege is alive and well. *The New York Times*. Retrieved from https://www.nytimes.com/2017/07/29/opinion/sunday/black-income-white-privilege.html

Capps, K. (2016, September 13). Earnings are rising, along with the damned rent. Retrieved from https://www.citylab.com/life/2016/09/new-census-data-show-increased-incomes-and-lower-poverty/499820/

Capretta, J. C. (n.d.). Medicaid. Retrieved from http://www.aei.org/spotlight/a-new-safety-net-medicaid/

Carter, D. T. (2000). *Confederate Goliath: The Battle of Fort Fisher.* Baton Rouge, LA: LSU Press.

Cascade Engineering. (2017). Marketing materials. Available upon request from Cascade Engineering.

Case, A., & Deaton, A. (2015). Rising morbidity and mortality in midlife among white non-Hispanic Americans in the 21st century. *PNAS, 112*(49), 15078–15083. Retrieved from http://www.pnas.org/content/112/49/15078

Casselman, B. (2015, December 8). Microloans don't solve poverty. Retrieved from http://fivethirtyeight.com/features/microloans-dont-solve-poverty/

Casselman, B. (2016, September 8). Don't blame a 'skills gap' for lack of hiring in manufacturing. Retrieved from https://fivethirtyeight.com/features/dont-blame-a-skills-gap-for-lack-of-hiring-in-manufacturing/

Champy, J. (1995). *Reengineering management.* New York, NY: HarperCollins.

Charity Check. (2018). Homepage. Retrieved from https://charityck.com/

CharityTracker. (2018). Homepage. Retrieved from http://www.charitytracker.net/

Cherry, R., with Lerman, R. (2011). *Moving working families forward: Third way policies that can work.* New York, NY: New York University Press.

Chetty, R., Grusky, D., Hell, M., Hendren, N., Manduca, R., & Narang, J. The fading American dream: Trends in absolute income mobility since 1940. Working Paper 22910. Retrieved from http://www.nber.org/papers/w22910

Chideya, F. (2016, October 4). Suburban white women weigh their options in a 'bizarre' election. Retrieved from https://fivethirtyeight.com/features/suburban-white-women-weigh-their-options-in-a-bizarre-election/

Coder, J., & Green, G. (2016, October). Comparing earnings of white males by education for selected age cohorts. Retrieved from http://www.sentierresearch.com/StatBriefs/Sentier_Income_Trends_WorkingClassWages_1996to2014_Brief_10_05_16.pdf

Cole, D. (2016, April). How to reverse *Citizens United.* Retrieved from https://www.theatlantic.com/magazine/archive/2016/04/how-to-reverse-citizens-united/471504/

Collective Impact. (2018). About us. Retrieved from http://www.collectiveimpact.com/about.php

Cott, J. (2013). *Dinner with Lenny: The last long interview with Leonard Bernstein.* Oxford, United Kingdom: Oxford University Press.

Court of Master Sommeliers Americas. (2018). About. Retrieved from https://www.mastersommeliers.org/about

Cox, C., & Archer, B. (2012, November 28). Cox and Archer: Why $16 trillion only hints at the true U.S. debt. *The Wall Street Journal.* Retrieved from https://www.wsj.com/articles/SB10001424127887323353204578127374039087636

Craig, R. (2016, March 7). Donald Trump and the value of college. Retrieved from https://www.insidehighered.com/views/2016/03/07/what-donald-trumps-ascendance-says-about-future-higher-education-essay

Craiutu, A. (2017). *Faces of moderation: The art of balance in an age of extremes.* Philadelphia, PA: University of Pennsylvania Press.

Currid-Halkett, E. (2017). *The sum of small things: A theory of the aspirational class.* Princeton, NJ: Princeton University Press.

Dames, N. (2017, April). The stubborn optimist: Following the persevering example of the writer and activist Grace Paley. Retrieved from https://www.theatlantic.com/magazine/archive/2017/04/the-stubborn-optimist/517776/

Daminger, A., Hayes, J., Barrows, A., & Wright, J. (2015, May). Poverty interrupted: Applying behavioral science to the context of chronic scarcity. Retrieved from http://www.ideas42.org/wp-content/uploads/2015/05/I42_PovertyWhitePaper_Digital_FINAL-1.pdf

Daniel Patrick Moynihan quotes. (2018). Retrieved from https://www.brainyquote.com/authors/daniel_patrick_moynihan

de Bono, E. (1999). *Six thinking hats.* London, United Kingdom: Little, Brown.

Demography of the United States. (2018). Retrieved from https://en.wikipedia.org/wiki/Demography_of_the_United_States

Desmond, M. (2017). *Evicted: Poverty and profit in the American city.* New York, NY: Penguin Random House.

DeVol, P. E. (2015). *Getting ahead in the workplace: Building stability and resources for a better life at work and home.* Highlands, TX: aha! Process.

Dimitri, C., Effland, A., & Conklin, N. (2005, June). The 20th century transformation of U.S. agriculture and farm policy. Retrieved from https://permanent.access.gpo.gov/LPS65988/eib3_1_.pdf

Dobbin, F., & Kalev, A. (2016, July-August). Why diversity programs fail. *Harvard Business Review.* Retrieved from https://hbr.org/2016/07/why-diversity-programs-fail

Doleac, J. L., & Hansen, B. (2016, July). Does 'Ban the Box' help or hurt low-skilled workers? Statistical discrimination and employment outcomes when criminal histories are hidden. Retrieved from http://www.nber.org/papers/w22469

Dourado, E. (2016, November 14). Maybe America is simply too big. Retrieved from https://blog.elidourado.com/maybe-america-is-simply-too-big-c3a4f414691b

Earned income tax credit. (2018). Retrieved from https://en.wikipedia.org/wiki/Earned_income_tax_credit

Eberstadt, N., Nunn, R., Schanzenbach, D. W., & Strain, M. R. (2017). 'In order that they might rest their arguments on facts': The vital role of government-collected data. The Hamilton Project and American Enterprise Institute. Retrieved from https://www.aei.org/wp-content/uploads/2017/03/THP_GovDataFacts_0317_Fixed.pdf

Economic Innovation Group. (2017, February). Dynamism in retreat: Consequences for regions, markets, and workers. Retrieved from http://eig.org/wp-content/uploads/2017/07/Dynamism-in-Retreat-A.pdf

Eggers, W. D. (2017, January 17). A 'whole of government' approach to social problems. Retrieved from http://www.governing.com/columns/smart-mgmt/col-whole-of-government-approach-social-problems-veterans-homelessness.html

The Equality of Opportunity Project. (2018). Homepage. Retrieved from http://www.equality-of-opportunity.org/

Evaluations, research, best practices, and results. (2018). aha! Process. Retrieved from https://www.ahaprocess.com/evaluations-research-best-practices-results/

Executive Office of the President of the United States. (2016, June). The long-term decline in prime-age male labor force participation. Retrieved from https://obamawhitehouse.archives.gov/sites/default/files/page/files/20160620_cea_primeage_male_lfp.pdf

Federal Reserve Bank of St. Louis. (n.d.). All employees: Manufacturing/all employees: total nonfarm payrolls. Retrieved from https://fred.stlouisfed.org/graph/?g=cAYh

Federal Reserve Bank of St. Louis. (2018, January 26). Real gross domestic product per capita. Retrieved from https://fred.stlouisfed.org/series/A939RX0Q048SBEA

Federal Reserve Bank of St. Louis. (2018, February 2). All employees: Manufacturing (MANEMP). Retrieved from https://fred.stlouisfed.org/series/MANEMP

Flowchart. (2018). Retrieved from https://www.smartdraw.com/flowchart/

Fowler, M. (2008, November 17). Obama: No surprise that hard-pressed Pennsylvanians turn bitter. Retrieved from https://www.huffingtonpost.com/mayhill-fowler/obama-no-surprise-that-ha_b_96188.html

Frank, R. (2015, April 9). Where the rich make their income. CNBC. Retrieved from https://www.cnbc.com/2015/04/09/where-the-rich-make-their-income.html

Free webinar series. (2018). aha! Process. Retrieved from https://www.ahaprocess.com/free-webinar-series/

Freire, P. (1999). *Pedagogy of the oppressed.* New York, NY: Continuum.

Frey, C. B., & Osborne, M. A. (2013, September 17). The future of employment: How susceptible are jobs to computerization? Retrieved from https://www.oxfordmartin.ox.ac.uk/downloads/academic/The_Future_of_Employment.pdf

Fromm, E. (2013). *The sane society.* New York, NY: Open Road Media.

Fuller, R. W. (2004). *Somebodies and nobodies: Overcoming the abuse of rank.* Gabriela Island, British Columbia, Canada: New Society.

Gentzkow, M., Shapiro, J. M., & Taddy, M. (2017, May). Measuring polarization in high-dimensional data: Method and application to congressional speech. Retrieved from https://www.brown.edu/Research/Shapiro/pdfs/politext.pdf

Glaeser, E. L., & Shleifer, A. (2005). *The Journal of Law, Economics, and Organization, 21*(1). doi:10.1093/jleo/ewi001

Glassman, M. E., & Wilhelm, A. H. (2017, January 3). Congressional careers: Service tenure and patterns of member service, 1789–2017. Retrieved from https://fas.org/sgp/crs/misc/R41545.pdf

Gleick, J. (2008). *Chaos: Making of a new science.* New York, NY: Penguin.

Gordon, A. (1967, June). Six hours with Rudyard Kipling [1935 interview]. *Kipling Journal, 34*, 5–8. Retrieved from http://www.kiplingjournal.com/textfiles/KJ162.txt

Gowland, D. (2017). *Britain and the European Union*. New York, NY: Routledge.

Greenblatt, A. (2016, February). What would happen if America made voting mandatory? Governing. Retrieved from http://www.governing.com/topics/elections/gov-compulsory-voting-switzerland.html

Greenblatt, A. (2016, November 9). Maine becomes first state to adopt a whole new way of voting. Retrieved from http://www.governing.com/topics/elections/gov-maine-ranked-choice-voting-2016-ballot-measure.html

Greenblatt, A. (2017, August 31). The new strategy for limiting money's role in elections. Retrieved from http://www.governing.com/topics/politics/gov-public-finance-campaigns-elections.html

Gwartney, J. D., Stroup, R. L., Sobel, R. S., & Macpherson, D. A. (2016). Macroeconomics: Private and public choice. Boston, MA: Cengage Learning.

Haidt, J. (2012). *Can't we all disagree more constructively? From the righteous mind* [Kindle edition]. New York, NY: Vintage Books.

Hall, R. A. (2014). *Seldom as they seem*. Traverse City, MI: Author.

Halpin, J. (2007, June 20). The structural imbalance of political talk radio. Retrieved from https://www.americanprogress.org/issues/general/reports/2007/06/20/3087/the-structural-imbalance-of-political-talk-radio/

Hamilton, A. J. (2016). *Lead with your heart*. North Adams, MA: Storey.

Hari, J. (2015). *Chasing the scream: The first and last days of the war on drugs*. New York, NY: Bloomsbury.

Harris, J. (2017, November 30). Man vs machine: 9 human jobs that have been taken over by robots. Retrieved from http://home.bt.com/tech-gadgets/future-tech/9-jobs-overtaken-by-robots-11364003046052

Hatcher, D. L. (2016). *The poverty industry: The exploitation of America's most vulnerable citizens*. New York, NY: New York University Press.

Hawken, P., Lovins, A., & Lovins, L. H. (2000). *Natural capitalism: Creating the next industrial revolution*. Washington, DC: U.S. Green Building Council.

Hayasaki, E. (2016, August 25). How poverty affects the brain. Retrieved from http://www.newsweek.com/2016/09/02/how-poverty-affects-brains-493239.html

Hazelton, C. (2010, December 18). 'Getting Ahead' offers big step in right direction. *Cornwall Standard-Freeholder*. Retrieved from http://www.standard-freeholder.com/2010/12/18/getting-ahead-offers-big-step-in-right-direction

Hedberg, M. (1999). *Strategic grill locations* [CD]. New York, NY: Comedy Central.

Henry-Nickie, M. (2017, November 8). AI should worry skilled knowledge workers too. Retrieved from https://www.brookings.edu/blog/techtank/2017/11/08/ai-should-worry-skilled-knowledge-workers-too/

Hesse, H. (1974). *My belief: Essays on life and art.* New York, NY: Farrar, Straus and Giroux.

Hicks, M. J., & Devaraj, S. (2017, April). The myth and the reality of manufacturing in America. Retrieved from https://conexus.cberdata.org/files/MfgReality.pdf

Hildreth, J. A. D., & Anderson, C. (2014). Failure at the top: How power undermines collaborative performance. Retrieved from https://escholarship.org/uc/item/7px2c22n

Hollingsworth, A., Ruhm, C. J., & Simon, K. (2017, February). Macroeconomic conditions and opioid abuse. Retrieved from http://www.nber.org/papers/w23192

Hopewell Church—Israel Township. (2018). Retrieved from http://www.destinationpreble.com/historic-churches/hopewell-church-israel-township/

Horne, Z., Powell, D., Hummel, J. E., & Holyoak, K. J. (2015). Countering antivaccination attitudes. *Proceedings of the National Academy of Sciences of the United States of America, 112*(33), 10321–10324. doi:10.1073/pnas.1504019112

Huber, G. A., & Malhotra, N. (n.d.). Political homophily in social relationships: Evidence from online dating behavior. Retrieved from https://huber.research.yale.edu/materials/38_paper.pdf

Ingraham, C. (2016, November 23). Why rural voters don't vote Democratic anymore. *The Washington Post.* Retrieved from https://www.washingtonpost.com/news/wonk/wp/2016/11/23/how-republican-gerrymanders-forced-democrats-to-abandon-rural-america/

Isenberg, N. (2016). *White trash: The 400-year untold history of class in America.* New York, NY: Penguin.

Iuviene, N., Stitely, A., & Hoyt, L. (2010, October). Sustainable economic democracy: Worker cooperatives for the 21st century. Retrieved from https://colab.mit.edu/sites/default/files/Sustainable_Economic_Democracy%20%281%29.pdf

Jindra, I. W., & Jindra, M. (2016). Connecting poverty, culture, and cognition: The Bridges Out of Poverty process. *Journal of Poverty.* doi:10.1080/10875549.2016.1204644

Jindra, M., & Jindra, I. W. (2016, October 26). Poverty and the controversial work of nonprofits. *Social Science and Public Policy.* doi:10.1007/s12115-016-0077-6. Retrieved from https://www.academia.edu/29592004/Poverty_and_the_Controversial_Work_of_Nonprofits

Kahneman, D. (2011). *Thinking fast and slow.* New York, NY: Farrar, Straus and Giroux.

Kasich, J. R. (2015, January 27). Blueprint for a new Ohio: Gov. John R. Kasich's fiscal years 2016–2017 budget. Retrieved from http://obm.ohio.gov/Budget/operating/doc/fy-16-17/State_of_Ohio_Budget_Tax_Expenditure_Report_FY-16-17.pdf

Kasmir, S. (2010). Can worker cooperatives save American manufacturing? Retrieved from https://www.hofstra.edu/pdf/academics/colleges/hclas/cld/cld-rlr-fall10-workercoops-kasmir.pdf

Kearney, M. S., & Levine, P. B. (2014, January). Media influences on social outcomes: The impact of MTV's *16 and Pregnant* on teen childbearing. Retrieved from https://www.wellesley.edu/sites/default/files/assets/kearney-levine-16p-nber_submit.pdf

Keating, S. J., Leland, J. C., Cai, L., & Oxman, N. (2017, April 26). Toward site-specific and self-sufficient robotic fabrication on architectural scales. *Science Robotics 2*(5). doi:10.1126/scirobotics.aam8986

Kellar, E. K. (2016, September 28). The fantasy of the quick fix. Retrieved from http://www.governing.com/columns/smart-mgmt/col-government-problems-fantasy-quick-fix.html

Keys, E. (2014, August 14). Getting Ahead helps people to a more fulfilling life. *Stillwater News Press.* Retrieved from http://www.stwnewspress.com/news/local_news/getting-ahead-helps-people-to-a-more-fulfilling-life/article_fc36d708-2366-11e4-b709-001a4bcf887a.html

Kneebone, E., & Berube, A. (2013). *Confronting suburban poverty in America.* Washington, DC: Brookings Institution Press.

Knepper, G. (1989). *Ohio and its people.* Kent, OH: Kent State University Press.

Kolko, J. (2016, November 10). Trump was stronger where the economy is weaker. Retrieved from https://fivethirtyeight.com/features/trump-was-stronger-where-the-economy-is-weaker/

Kondik, K. (2016). *The bellwether: Why Ohio picks the president.* Athens, OH: Ohio University Press.

Kondik, K., & Skelley, G. (2016, December 15). Incumbent reelection rates higher than average in 2016. Retrieved from http://www.centerforpolitics.org/crystalball/articles/incumbent-reelection-rates-higher-than-average-in-2016/

Kuran, T. (2007). Availability cascades and risk regulation. Retrieved from https://chicagounbound.uchicago.edu/cgi/viewcontent.cgi?referer=&httpsredir=1&article=1036&context=public_law_and_legal_theory

Larson, Q. (2017, February 18). A warning from Bill Gates, Elon Musk, and Stephen Hawking. Retrieved from https://medium.freecodecamp.org/bill-gates-and-elon-musk-just-warned-us-about-the-one-thing-politicians-are-too-scared-to-talk-8db9815fd398

Lauter, D. (2016, August 14). How do Americans view poverty? Many blue-collar whites, key to Trump, criticize poor people as lazy and content to stay on welfare. *The Los Angeles Times*. Retrieved from http://www.latimes.com/projects/la-na-pol-poverty-poll/

Lewis, B. (2015, January 17). Could slavery have ended without the Civil War? Retrieved from http://www.thegreatfiction.com/2015/01/17/could-slavery-have-ended-without-the-civil-war/

Lewis, C. S. (1996). *The joyful Christian.* New York, NY: Scribner.

Lickerman, A. (2010, March 25). Getting people to change their minds. Retrieved from https://www.psychologytoday.com/blog/happiness-in-world/201003/getting-people-change-their-minds

Lindenfeld, F., & Wynn, P. (1995, September). Why some worker co-ops succeed while others fail: The role of internal and external social factors. Retrieved from http://www.geo.coop/story/why-some-worker-co-ops-succeed-while-others-fail

Lleras-Muney, A. (2018, January 10). Healthier kids? Just hand their families cash. Retrieved from https://www.politico.com/agenda/story/2018/01/10/fighting-health-effects-of-poverty-welfare-000608

Lloyd, A. B. (2016, July 29). Hillary Clinton and the fake Tocqueville quotation. *The Weekly Standard.* Retrieved from http://www.weeklystandard.com/hillary-clinton-and-the-fake-tocqueville-quotation/article/2003585

Lucretius. (2007). *The nature of things.* London, United Kingdom: Penguin UK.

Machiavelli, N. (2016). *The prince.* Project Gutenberg. Retrieved from https://www.gutenberg.org/files/1232/1232-h/1232-h.htm

Maciag, M. (2015, February). Gentrification in America report. Retrieved from http://www.governing.com/gov-data/census/gentrification-in-cities-governing-report.html

Maciag, M. (2016, September 1). The metro areas with more new businesses. Retrieved from http://www.governing.com/topics/mgmt/gov-younger-businesses-startups-metro-areas-data.html

Maciag, M. (2016, September 15). Demographics can spell trouble for a city's finances. Retrieved from http://www.governing.com/topics/finance/gov-census-demographics-cities-fiscal.html

Madigan, K. (2011, September 28). It's man vs. machine and man is losing. Retrieved from https://blogs.wsj.com/economics/2011/09/28/its-man-vs-machine-and-man-is-losing/

Maine voters adopt ranked choice voting. (2016, November 9). Retrieved from http://www.fairvote.org/maine_voters_adopt_ranked_choice_voting

Marcuss, R., Dubois, A., Hedemann, J., Risler, M.-H., & Leibel, K. (2014, August). Internal Revenue Service publication 6162. https://www.irs.gov/pub/irs-soi/EITCComplianceStudyTY2006-2008.pdf

Marker, L.-L., & Marker, F. J. (1992). *Ingmar Bergman: A life in the theater.* Cambridge, United Kingdom: Cambridge University Press.

Markoff, J. (2016, July 17). Artificial intelligence swarms Silicon Valley on wings and wheels. Retrieved from https://www.nytimes.com/2016/07/18/technology/on-wheels-and-wings-artificial-intelligence-swarms-silicon-valley.html

Marr, C., Huang, C.-C., Sherman, A., & Debot, B. (2015, October 1). EITC and child tax credit promote work, reduce poverty, and support children's development, research finds. Retrieved from https://www.cbpp.org/research/federal-tax/eitc-and-child-tax-credit-promote-work-reduce-poverty-and-support-childrens

McCarthy, J. (2015, October 19). Quarter of U.S. voters say candidate must share view on guns. Retrieved from http://news.gallup.com/poll/186248/quarter-voters-say-candidate-share-view-guns.aspx

McGinty, J. C. (2016, September 9). Third-party candidates don't have to be spoilers. *The Wall Street Journal.* Retrieved from https://www.wsj.com/articles/third-party-candidates-dont-have-to-be-spoilers-1473436855

McGrath, M. (2016, January 6). 63% of Americans don't have enough savings to cover a $500 emergency. Retrieved from https://www.forbes.com/sites/maggiemcgrath/2016/01/06/63-of-americans-dont-have-enough-savings-to-cover-a-500-emergency/#1a280d114e0d

Minnesota Collaborative Anti-Racism Initiative. (2006, November). Systemic racism: Daily strategies for survival and beyond. Retrieved from http://www.ahaprocess.com/wp-content/uploads/2013/11/GA-Systemic-Racism.pdf

Mondragon Corporation. (2018). Retrieved from https://en.wikipedia.org/wiki/Mondragon_Corporation

Morin, R. (2016, November 17). Behind Trump's win in rural white America: Women joined men in backing him. Retrieved from http://www.pewresearch.org/fact-tank/2016/11/17/behind-trumps-win-in-rural-white-america-women-joined-men-in-backing-him/

Movement. (2018). Dictionary.com. Retrieved from http://www.dictionary.com/browse/movement?s=t

Mullainathan, S., & Shafir, E. (2013). *Scarcity: Why having too little means so much.* London, United Kingdom: Penguin UK.

Muro, M. (2016, July 21). Look to advanced industries to help drive productivity gains. Retrieved from https://www.brookings.edu/blog/the-avenue/2016/07/21/look-to-advanced-industries-to-help-drive-productivity-gains/

Muro, M., & Kulkarni, S. (2016, March 15). Voter anger explained—in one chart. Retrieved from https://www.brookings.edu/blog/the-avenue/2016/03/15/voter-anger-explained-in-one-chart/

Muro, M., & Liu, S. (2016, November 21). Why Trump's factory job promises won't pan out—in one chart. Retrieved from https://www.brookings.edu/blog/the-avenue/2016/11/21/why-trumps-factory-job-promises-wont-pan-out-in-one-chart/

Muro, M., & Liu, S. (2016, November 29). Another Clinton-Trump divide: High-output America vs. low-output America. Retrieved from https://www.brookings.edu/blog/the-avenue/2016/11/29/another-clinton-trump-divide-high-output-america-vs-low-output-america/

Murray, C. (n.d.). The social contract revisited: Guaranteed income as a replacement for the welfare state. Retrieved from http://www.fljs.org/files/publications/Murray.pdf

Murray, C. (2012). *Coming apart: The state of white America 1960–2010.* New York, NY: Crown Forum.

Murray, L. (2010). *Breaking night: A memoir of forgiveness, survival, and my journey from homeless to Harvard* [Kindle edition]. New York, NY: Hachette.

Murray, T. D. (2016, January 14). Why do 70 percent of lottery winners end up bankrupt? Retrieved from http://www.cleveland.com/business/index.ssf/2016/01/why_do_70_percent_of_lottery_w.html

Nauert, R. (2015). Political views influence relationship partner choice. Psych Central. Retrieved from https://psychcentral.com/news/2011/05/11/political-views-influence-relationship-partner-choice/26073.html

Nietzsche, F. (2018). *Schopenhauer as educator.* Retrieved from https://en.wikisource.org/wiki/Schopenhauer_as_Educator

Norman, J. (2016, June 13). Americans' confidence in institutions stays low. Retrieved from http://news.gallup.com/poll/192581/americans-confidence-institutions-stays-low.aspx

Ohio Revised Code. Title [57] LVII taxation § 5747.29. Credit for contributions of money to candidates for statewide office or member of general assembly. Retrieved from http://codes.ohio.gov/orc/5747.29

Osborne reef waste tire removal project. (2016, August 8). Retrieved from https://floridadep.gov/sites/default/files/OsborneReefProject_09Aug16_0.pdf

Payne, K. (2017). *The broken ladder: How inequality affects the way we think, live, and die.* New York, NY: Viking.

Payne, R. K. (2013). *A framework for understanding poverty* (5th rev. ed.). Highlands, TX: aha! Process.

Payne, R. K., Dreussi-Smith, T., Shaw, L. Y., & Young, J. (2014). *Bridges to health and healthcare.* Highlands, TX: aha! Process.

Petry, E. (n.d.). How the efficiency gap works. Retrieved from https://www.brennancenter.org/sites/default/files/legal-work/How_the_Efficiency_Gap_Standard_Works.pdf

Pew Research Center. (2012, September 27). In changing news landscape, even television is vulnerable: Trends in news consumption: 1991–2012. Retrieved from http://www.people-press.org/2012/09/27/in-changing-news-landscape-even-television-is-vulnerable/

Pew Research Center. (2014, June 12). Political polarization in the American public. Retrieved from http://www.people-press.org/2014/06/12/political-polarization-in-the-american-public/

Pinola, M. (2013, September 19). How to use mind maps to unleash your brain's creativity and potential. Retrieved from https://lifehacker.com/how-to-use-mind-maps-to-unleash-your-brains-creativity-1348869811

Piven, F. F., & Cloward, R. A. (2010, March 24). The weight of the poor: A strategy to end poverty. Retrieved from https://www.commondreams.org/news/2010/03/24/weight-poor-strategy-end-poverty

Plumb, P., & Cohen, J. (2016, September 20). Maine voices: Ranked-choice voting worked in Portland and will work in Maine. Retrieved from https://www.pressherald.com/2016/09/20/maine-voices-ranked-choice-voting-worked-in-portland-and-will-work-in-maine/

The population size of U.S. House districts: By year and by Congress. (2005, June 19). Retrieved from http://www.thirty-thousand.org/documents/QHA-03.pdf

Presidential election voter statistics. (2017). Statistic Brain. Retrieved from https://www.statisticbrain.com/presidential-election-voter-statistics

The problem with profits. (2016, March 26). Retrieved from https://www.economist.com/news/leaders/21695392-big-firms-united-states-have-never-had-it-so-good-time-more-competition-problem

Public Insight. (2018). Homepage. Retrieved from http://www.publicinsightdata.com/

Purdum, T. S. (2014, March 31). The Republican who saved civil rights: How a little-known conservative Ohio congressman changed American history. Retrieved from https://www.politico.com/magazine/story/2014/03/the-movers-behind-the-civil-rights-act-105216

Putnam, R. D. (2000). *Bowling alone: The collapse and revival of American community.* New York, NY: Simon & Schuster.

Putnam, R. D. (2015). *Our kids: The American dream in crisis.* New York, NY: Simon & Schuster.

Quigg, D. (2017, October 19). Bridges communities can take their use of data up by three notches [recording of live webinar]. aha! Process. Retrieved from http://ahaprocess.adobeconnect.com/pbmiwvhetqlx/

Quinn, M. (2017, March 6). The GOP wants to give states more Medicaid power. This is what they may do with it. Retrieved from http://www.governing.com/topics/health-human-services/gov-states-block-grants-medicaid-obamacare.html

Quinones, Sam. (2015). *Dreamland: The true tale of America's opiate epidemic.* New York, NY: Bloomsbury.

Raworth, K. (2017). *Doughnut economics: Seven ways to think like a 21st-century economist.* White River Junction, VT: Chelsea Green.

Reed, P. (2018). In lak'ech—I am another you. Retrieved from http://energetic-mastery.com/lakech-another/

Reeves, R. V. (2016, November 28). Middle America's malaise helped Trump to victory, but he has no cure. Retrieved from https://www.brookings.edu/blog/fixgov/2016/11/28/middle-americas-malaise/

Reeves, R. V. (2017). *The dream hoarders: How the American upper middle class is leaving everyone else in the dust, why that is a problem, and what to do about it.* Washington, DC: The Brookings Institution.

Reeves, R. V., & Halikias, D. (2016, December 8). On the new Chetty-bomb that only half of Americans are better off than their parents. Retrieved from https://www.brookings.edu/blog/social-mobility-memos/2016/12/08/on-the-new-chetty-bomb-that-only-half-of-americans-are-better-off-than-their-parents/

Ridley, M. (2015). *The evolution of everything: How new ideas emerge.* New York, NY: HarperCollins.

Riffkin, R. (2015, May 29). Abortion edges up as important voting issue for Americans. Retrieved from http://news.gallup.com/poll/183449/abortion-edges-important-voting-issue-americans.aspx

Rivenburg, R. (1998, June 23). Off-kilter. *The Los Angeles Times.* Retrieved from http://articles.latimes.com/1998/jun/23/news/ls-62558

Rodrigue, E., & Reeves, R. V. (2016, October 28). As many states look to expand pre-K programs, a study gives reason for pause. Retrieved from https://www.brookings.edu/blog/social-mobility-memos/2016/10/28/as-many-states-look-to-expand-pre-k-programs-a-study-gives-reason-for-pause/

The Rolling Stones. (1969). You can't always get what you want. On *Let It Bleed* [LP]. United Kingdom: Decca.

Roth, D. (2016, July 28). Jeff Immelt says the relationship between business and government is absolutely busted. And no one has a fix. Retrieved from https://www.linkedin.com/pulse/jeff-immelt-says-relationship-between-business-government-daniel-roth

Rothstein, R. (2017). *The color of law: A forgotten history of how our government segregated America.* New York, NY: Liveright.

Rove, K. (2015). *The triumph of William McKinley: Why the election of 1896 still matters.* New York, NY: Simon & Schuster.

Sabato, L. J. (2016, July 4). Professor Sabato welcomes the nation's newest citizens at Monticello. Retrieved from http://www.centerforpolitics.org/crystalball/articles/sabato-welcomes-the-nations-newest-citizens-at-monticello/

Saccocio, M. (2015). Schenectady Bridges works toward long-term communitywide change. In K. R. Barber et al., *From vision to action: Best practices to reduce the impact of poverty in communities, education, healthcare, and more* (vol. II). Highlands, TX: aha! Process (pages 108–126).

Salkin, P. E. (2003, January). From Euclid to growing smart: The transformation of the American local land use ethic into local land use and environmental controls. *Pace Environmental Law Review, 20*(1). Retrieved from http://digitalcommons. pace.edu/cgi/viewcontent.cgi?article=1163&context=pelr

Sapolsky, R. M. (2017). *Behave: The biology of humans at our best and worst.* New York, NY: Penguin.

Sawhill, I. V. (2016, June 15). Money for nothing: Why a universal basic income is a step too far. Retrieved from https://www.brookings.edu/blog/social-mobility-memos/2016/06/15/money-for-nothing-why-a-universal-basic-income-is-a-step-too-far/

Schake, K. (2016, November 10). Trump and the shibboleths: On losing, gloating, and the future of the GOP. Retrieved from http://foreignpolicy.com/2016/11/10/trump-and-the-shibboleths/

Schwartz, P. (1996). *The art of the long view: Planning for the future in an uncertain world.* New York, NY: Currency Doubleday.

Shapiro, T. M. (2017). *Toxic inequality: How America's wealth gap destroys mobility, deepens the racial divide, and threatens our future.* New York, NY: Basic Books.

Sharp, A., Bunton, L., Crown, S., Dwyer, F., Fawcett, S., Harris, A., … Zohrab, K. (Producers) & Fraser, T. (Director). (2008). *Dean Spanley* [Motion picture]. New Zealand: New Zealand Film Commission.

Shelby Foote compromise [video]. (2015, September 21). Retrieved from https://www.youtube.com/watch?v=He4eTjVPuvE

Shepherd, M. (2017, May 24). Maine's new way of voting ruled unconstitutional. Retrieved from http://www.governing.com/topics/politics/tns-maine-court-ranked-choice-voting.html

Sinclair, U. (1994). *I, candidate for governor: And how I got licked.* Berkeley, CA: University of California Press.

Six Thinking Hats. (2018). Retrieved from https://en.wikipedia.org/wiki/Six_Thinking_Hats

The Socratic circle. (n.d.). Retrieved from http://www.corndancer.com/tunes/tunes_print/soccirc.pdf

Standing, G. (2011). *The precariat: The new dangerous class.* New York, NY: Bloomsbury.

Stephanopoulos, N. O., & McGhee, E. M. (2014). Partisan gerrymandering and the efficiency gap. *The University of Chicago Law Review, 82*(2), 831. Retrieved from https://chicagounbound.uchicago.edu/uclrev/vol82/iss2/4

Stern, K. (2013, April). Why the rich don't give to charity. *The Atlantic.* Retrieved from https://www.theatlantic.com/magazine/archive/2013/04/why-the-rich-dont-give/309254/

Store. (2018). aha! Process. Retrieved from https://www.ahaprocess.com/store/

Taniparti, N. (2018, January 5). What happened when I tried to teach Harvard undergrads about inequality and poverty. Retrieved from https://qz.com/1173057/what-happened-when-i-tried-to-teach-harvard-undergrads-about-inequality-and-poverty/

Taylor, W. C. (2016). *Simply brilliant: How great organizations do ordinary things in extraordinary ways.* London, United Kingdom: Penguin UK.

Tett, G. (2015). *The silo effect: The peril of experience and the promise of breaking down barriers.* New York, NY: Simon & Schuster.

Thaler, R. H., with Sussstein, C. R. (2009). *Nudge: Improving decisions about health, wealth, and happiness.* New York, NY: Penguin.

The Three Stooges. (1935). *Restless knights* [Motion picture]. Culver City, CA: Columbia Pictures.

Tocqueville, A. D. (2010). *Democracy in America.* New York, NY: Signet Classics.

Toffler, A. (1970). *Future Shock.* New York, NY: Random House.

Toffler, A. (1990). *Powershift: Knowledge, wealth, and violence at the edge of the 21st century.* New York, NY: Bantam Books.

Torre, P. S. (2009, March 23). How (and why) athletes go broke. *Sports Illustrated.* Retrieved from https://www.si.com/vault/2009/03/23/105789480/how-and-why-athletes-go-broke

Toxic masculinity. (2018). Retrieved from https://en.wikipedia.org/wiki/Toxic_masculinity

Tucker, M. (2015, December 22). Donald Trump, education policy and the future of American politics. Retrieved from https://www.huffingtonpost.com/marc-tucker/donald-trump-education-po_b_8861758.html

Uhler, K. M. (2017). Bridges Out of Poverty as an anti-poverty strategy in Kennett Square, Pennsylvania. Retrieved from http://digitalcollections.sit.edu/capstones/2975

Underhill, P. (1999). *Why we buy: The science of shopping.* New York, NY: Simon & Schuster.

United States Census Bureau. (2016, September 15). New American Community Survey statistics for income, poverty and health insurance available for states and local areas. Retrieved from https://www.census.gov/newsroom/press-releases/2016/cb16-159.html

United States Census Bureau. (2018, January 19). Poverty thresholds. Retrieved from https://www.census.gov/data/tables/time-series/demo/income-poverty/historical-poverty-thresholds.html

United States congressional apportionment. (2018). Retrieved from https://en.wikipedia.org/wiki/United_States_congressional_apportionment

United States Department of Health and Human Services. (2007, July 11). Assessing child support arrears in nine large states and the nation—executive summary. Retrieved from https://aspe.hhs.gov/pdf-document/assessing-child-support-arrears-nine-large-states-and-nation-executive-summary

United States House of Representatives. (1996, July 18). Final vote results for roll call 331. Retrieved from http://clerk.house.gov/evs/1996/roll331.xml

United States Senate. (1996, August 1). Roll call vote 104th Congress—2nd session. Retrieved from https://www.senate.gov/legislative/LIS/roll_call_lists/roll_call_vote_cfm.cfm?congress=104&session=2&vote=00262

United States steel production 1969–2018. (2018). Retrieved from https://tradingeconomics.com/united-states/steel-production

Vance, J. D. (2016). *Hillbilly elegy: A memoir of a family and culture in crisis.* New York, NY: HarperCollins.

Voter turnout by income, 2008 U.S. presidential election. (2009, November 11). Retrieved from https://en.wikipedia.org/wiki/Voter_turnout_in_the_United_States_presidential_elections#/media/File:Voter_Turnout_by_Income,_2008_US_Presidential_Election.png

Wahler, E. A. (2015). Getting Ahead in a Just-Gettin'-By World: Program evaluation results. Retrieved from https://www.ahaprocess.com/wp-content/uploads/2015/10/GA-Program-Evaluation-Results.pdf

Wahler, E. A. (2016). A group-based intervention for persons living in poverty: Psychosocial improvements noted among participants of Getting Ahead in a Just-Gettin'-By World. *Social Work with Groups.* doi:10.1080/01609513.2016.118875

Walker, P. (2017, April 5). How bike helmet laws do more harm than good. Retrieved from https://www.citylab.com/transportation/2017/04/how-effective-are-bike-helmet-laws/521997/

Wasserman, D. (2016, August 4). The political process isn't rigged—it has much bigger problems. Retrieved from https://fivethirtyeight.com/features/the-political-process-isnt-rigged-it-has-much-bigger-problems/

Webster, S. (2016, December 15). Partisan geographic sorting: Where you live can change your partisan preferences. Retrieved from http://www.centerforpolitics.org/crystalball/articles/partisan-geographic-sorting/

Weil, D. (2014). *The fissured workplace: Why work became so bad for so many and what can be done to improve it.* Cambridge, MA: Harvard University Press.

West, D. M. (2014). *Billionaires: Reflections on the upper crust.* Washington, DC: Brookings Institution Press.

West, D. M. (2015, October). What happens if robots take the jobs? Retrieved from https://www.brookings.edu/wp-content/uploads/2016/06/robotwork.pdf

West, D. M. (2016). *Megachange: Economic disruption, political upheaval, and social strife in the 21st century.* Washington, DC: Brookings Institution Press.

What we can learn about investing from the business of French wine [editorial]. (2013, November 20). Retrieved from https://www.betterment.com/resources/investment-strategy/behavioral-finance-investing-strategy/human-vs-algorithm-investing-a-lesson-from-wine-country/

Wheatley, M. J. (1994) *Leadership and the new science: Learning about organization from an orderly universe.* San Francisco, CA: Berrett-Koehler.

White, G. B. (2015, December 21). Education gaps don't fully explain why black unemployment is so high. Retrieved from https://www.theatlantic.com/business/archive/2015/12/black-white-unemployment-gap/421497/

Whitehurst, G. J. (2016, July 30). This policy would help poor kids more than universal pre-K does. Retrieved from https://www.brookings.edu/opinions/this-policy-would-help-poor-kids-more-than-universal-pre-k-does/

Whitman, W. (2000). *Democratic vistas.* Retrieved from http://www.bartleby.com/229/20023.html

Whitman, W. (2012). *Leaves of grass.* Project Gutenberg. Retrieved from https://www.gutenberg.org/files/1322/1322-h/1322-h.htm

Wogan, J. B. (2016, September 13). Studies discredit state policies that punish poor people for saving money. Retrieved from http://www.governing.com/topics/health-human-services/gov-states-welfare-assets-cfed-pew-sage-open.html

Wolff, T. (2010). *The power of collaborative solutions: Six principles and effective tools for building healthy communities.* San Francisco, CA: Jossey-Bass.

Working America. (2016, January). Unique 'front porch focus group' explores the appeal of Trump's right-wing message with white working-class voters. Retrieved from https://actionnetwork.org/user_files/user_files/000/005/179/original/WA_FrontDoorFocusGroup_Pv1.pdf

Index

[Page numbers in *italics* refer to figures or illustrations.]

About the Authors

Philip E. DeVol, president and CEO of DeVol & Associates, LLC, has been training and consulting on poverty issues since 1997. He is the author of a number of books on poverty that, taken together, form a common language for people from different economic classes, a language that encourages them to address poverty in a comprehensive way.

Bridges Out of Poverty: Strategies for Professionals and Communities (1999), coauthored with Ruby K. Payne and Terie Dreussi Smith, is used by people who work with and serve people in poverty. In 2004 he wrote *Getting Ahead in a Just-Gettin'-By World: Building Your Resources for a Better Life* that is used by people who are struggling to get by, as well as by those seeking to get ahead.

That book led to a series of books for different populations and sectors:

- *Investigations into Economic Class in America* (2010), coauthored with Karla M. Krodel, helps first-generation, low-income students navigate the postsecondary experience while living in unstable, under-resourced conditions.

- *Getting Ahead while Getting Out* (2015), coauthored with Michelle Wood and Mitchell Libster, is a pre-release book for people returning to their communities from incarceration.

- *Getting Ahead in the Workplace* (2015) is for those entering the workplace, including entry-level employees.

All the books in the preceding series promote complete models designed to support Getting Ahead graduates during their journey toward stable and increasingly resourced lives.

In addition, *Bridges to Sustainable Communities* (2010) is used by community leaders and legislators to encourage their participation in building collaboratives in their communities among organizations that use Bridges concepts to improve their procedures, practices, and programs serving those in poverty.

DeVol works in North America and internationally with communities to apply Bridges constructs—including sites in Canada, Australia, Slovakia, Scotland, and the Czech Republic. *Getting Ahead* has been translated into Spanish, Slovak, and Czech.

Working with and learning from Bridges/Getting Ahead sites, DeVol has seen the work used to make changes at all levels: individual, institutional, community, and now policy with *Bridges Across Every Divide.*

Investigations into Economic Class in America was honored in 2011 by the Association of Educational Publishers, winning its Distinguished Achievement Award for Adult Curriculum (Life Skills); the book was also a 2011 Innovation Award finalist.

In his current work with his company and as a consultant/trainer with aha! Process, DeVol builds on his 19 years as director of an Ohio outpatient substance-abuse treatment facility in which he designed treatment programs and collaborative systems for school-based prevention, intervention, and Ohio's first alternative school for recovering young people. During this time he also coauthored The *Complete Guide to Elementary Student Assistance Programs* (1993) with Linda Christensen.

DeVol and his wife, Susan, live in the country near Marengo, Ohio, just a few miles from his two children and grandchildren.

Eugene K. "Gene" Krebs spent eight years in the Ohio House of Representatives, three years on a local school board, and four years as a county commissioner.

Krebs has been a research executive in an organization that studies economic development, urban revitalization, and farmland preservation. Later he was an executive in a research group that studies healthcare and human-services issues. He served on Ohio's Joint Committee on High Technology Start-up Business, Sales Tax Holiday Study Committee (chair), and the Eminent Domain Task Force.

He was appointed by Governor Ted Strickland to Ohio's 21st Century Transportation Task Force and by Governor John Kasich to the Local Government Innovation Council. Krebs is a three-time winner of the Watchdog of the Treasury award for supporting fiscally frugal policies.

He also has appeared on a regular basis on the PBS television show *Columbus on the Record* and has been featured on CNN, BBC, *The State of Ohio, The Spectrum,* and *All Sides with Ann Fisher* as a Republican voice on many political and policy issues.

Further, Krebs has been published in *The Wall Street Journal* on economic policy and several times in *The Columbus Dispatch* and *The Plain Dealer* (Cleveland) on state policy issues and is frequently sought by the media for insights on various issues. His scientific research in quantum biology and ethology appeared in the *Journal of Biological Psychology,* and his ag research was featured in *The Ohio Farmer* magazine for his innovations involving the use of zinc as an enzyme inhibitor to reduce nitrogen loss in no-till settings.

Krebs was awarded the Preservation Hero Award from Heritage Ohio for his efforts in drafting, passing, and defending the state tax credit for historical rehabilitation, which is now a national model due in large part to its requirement of cost-benefit analysis of all prospective projects.

He recently resigned as the chair of the Ohio Consumers' Counsel Governing Board. While he was chair of the board, the Consumers' Counsel saved consumers $800 million in utility costs, with another $5 billion projected over the next nine years. Originally appointed by then Attorney General Jim Petro, Krebs has been consistently reappointed to the board by both Republican and Democrat attorneys general due to his expertise in utility law and economics.

A former intercollegiate fencing coach, Krebs is a seventh-generation farmer of 400 acres where he was a pioneer in no-till methodology and still lives on the family farm near Morning Sun, Ohio.

He is married to Jan, an award-winning professional artist who works in many different styles and materials. They have two grown daughters who have blessed them with five grandchildren. His principal hobby is a small flock of mostly Dominique chickens, the breed brought to America by the Pilgrims.